CNN's TAILWIND TALE

CNN's TAILWIND TALE
Inside Vietnam's Last Great Myth
JERRY LEMBCKE

ROWMAN & LITTLEFIELD PUBLISHERS, INC.

Lanham • Boulder • New York • Oxford

ROWMAN & LITTLEFIELD PUBLISHERS, INC.

Published in the United States of America
by Rowman & Littlefield Publishers, Inc.
A Member of the Rowman & Littlefield Publishing Group
4501 Forbes Boulevard, Suite 200, Lanham, Maryland 20706
www.rowmanlittlefield.com

PO Box 317
Oxford
OX2 9RU, UK

British Library Cataloguing in Publication Information Available

Library of Congress Cataloging-in-Publication Data

Lembcke, Jerry, 1943–
   CNN's Tailwind tale : inside Vietnam's last great myth / Jerry
Lembcke.
      p. cm.
Includes bibliographical references and index.
   ISBN 0-7425-2328-4 (hardcover : alk. paper)
   1. Operation Tailwind, 1970. 2. Vietnamese Conflict,
1961–1975—Chemical warfare—United States. 3. Cable News Network. I.
Title.
   DS557.8.O66L46 2003
   959.704'34—dc21

2003000221

Printed in the United States of America

♾™ The paper used in this publication meets the minimum requirements of American National Standard for Information Sciences—Permanence of Paper for Printed Library Materials, ANSI/NISO Z39.48-1992.

CONTENTS

Preface   ix

Acknowledgments   xvii

1 *Valley of Death:* From Blockbuster to Just Busted   1
       Investigative Journalism   6
       Journalism Investigated   7
       The "Sources" Defense   11

2 Tailwind (Take 1): Courage and Covert Operations   17
       America's Secret War in Vietnam   18
       The War on the North: Blind Drops and the Double Cross   20
       Psywar: The Sacred Sword of the Patriot League   21
       Maritime Operations and Paradise Island   24
       On "the Trail": SOG Operations in Laos and Cambodia   25
       Toward the Second Tale of Tailwind   28

3 Tailwind (Take 2): A Government Betrays Its People   31
       It's All about the POWs   32
           Michael Ruppert: Defectors or POWs?   32
           Chris Matthews: The Government Gases Its Own   34
           April Oliver: Did She "Read" the Subtext?   38
       The Seductive Subtext of *Valley of Death*   41

4 Lies and Legends, Men and Remembered Mettle   45
    A Litany of Lies   46
    Gas for Grist   49
    Deserters—But Not Defectors   51
    The Legend of the Lost Command   53
        No-Man's-Land   55
    Laos: This Legend's No-Man's-Land   56
        Go West, Young Man—to Laos   58
    The Defectors: Some Liminal Figures for a Liminal Land   59
    The Making of Military Memories   61
        Male Fantasies   63

5 Two Parts *Apocalypse Now* and a Pinch of Sarin:
Popular Culture's Recipe for *Valley of Death*   69
    Nick and Kurtz: Over the Cultural Fence   70
    Sarin Says It All   75
    Tales Out of (Charm) School   79
    Spite House: Vietnam's Last Secret or Last Fairy Tale?   82
    The Road to Revelation   87

6 Beyond Reason: Revelation in the *Valley of Death*   91
    From Beaches to Babylon   93
        Prophecy in Ezekiel and Daniel   94
        The Book of Revelation   94
        Politics and Prophecy   95
        Enter the Identity   97
    Setting the Table for Tailwind   99
        The Rise of the Religious Right   100
        The Persian Gulf War   101
        Waco: With a Segue through Ruby Ridge   103
    Religion's Imprint on *Valley of Death*   107

7 Consider the Source(s): Thomas Moorer and John Singlaub   111
    Thomas Moorer   112
        Moorer: A "Plumber" Before His Time   113
        Yeoman Radford's Spy Ring   114
        Moorer: The John Birch Society and More   116
    John Singlaub   119
        General Singlaub vs. President Carter over Korea   119
        Out of the Service and Into the Shadows   120
        Singlaub and the World Anti-Communist League   122

8 What Was She Thinking? April Oliver's Willing Suspension
of Disbelief   127
    How the Emperor Got Dressed   128
    Sightings   129
    Paranoia American Style   133
    April Oliver's Landscape   134
        Where's April Oliver?   134
        Not Far from the Tree   138
    Don't Know Much about History   139
        The Perils of Oral History   141
    Fitting the Profile   142

9 The CNN-Tailwind Affair: Journalism in a Fearful America   145
    From Orwell to Huxley   147
    "One Leg at a Time . . ."   151
    The Middle Crumbles, Journalism Stumbles   154
    Fusion Paranoia   155
    September 11 and That "Paranoid Style"   156
    Catnip with Nine Lives   158
    The Problem with Conspiracism   160

Afterword   163

Filmography   171

Notes   173

Bibliography   201

Index   209

About the Author   217

PREFACE

On June 28, 1998, the *New York Times* ran an op-ed piece entitled "Memories of Wars Never Fought." Written by Joe Sharkey, the article caught my eye because I had just finished a book on war and public memory. My research had taken me into the study of how groups of people remember major events like wars, and how easily the boundary between memory and fantasy can be crossed. Sharkey's article told about a story recently aired on the Cable News Network (CNN) and published in *Time* magazine claiming that the U.S. Army had secretly used nerve gas in 1970 to attack a group of its own soldiers who had defected to the North Vietnamese. As the title of Sharkey's piece implied, the *New York Times* was skeptical of the CNN story.

I was more than skeptical. Indeed, my first thought was that the story was a hoax, something like the article that Alan Sokal published in the cultural studies journal *Social Text* in 1996. Sokal, a physicist, had written a parody of the academic field known as literary criticism, a manuscript loaded with postmodern jargon in order to demonstrate that some of America's leading intellectuals would publish nonsense if it flattered their ideological preconceptions. I thought some clever individuals had managed to "put one over" on the CNN reporters in the same manner. Perhaps the reporters themselves were implicated in the prank. In a few days, I was sure, someone, maybe even one of the tricksters, would step forward to reveal their mischief.

But the CNN broadcast was not a hoax. Entitled "Valley of Death," the story was about Operation Tailwind, which had actually been carried out in September of 1970. It was a secret mission into Laos conducted by U.S. Special Forces, popularly known as Green Berets. The troops were under the command of the Army's Studies and Observations Group (SOG), which was responsible for covert operations in Southeast Asia. This much of the story was true. But critics said that the parts about nerve gas and defectors were not true. Investigations, including one by CNN itself, found the story to be "insufficiently supported by the facts." About a month after its broadcast, CNN retracted the story, apologized to its viewers, and fired its producers, April Oliver and Jack Smith.[1]

After the firings, "the story" became Oliver and Smith and how the CNN version of Tailwind had been produced. We learned that Oliver, then thirty-six, had been primarily responsible for the show, the older Smith having been added to the project late to enhance its credibility. The bedrock of Oliver's research was her sources, the veterans of Operation Tailwind. Investigators now zeroed in on their testimony, the methods Oliver had used to obtain it, and the way she had assembled the pieces for the story that aired.

But my interest in *Valley of Death* was different. At the time, my book *The Spitting Image: Myth, Memory, and the Legacy of Vietnam* was just being released by New York University Press. Research for the book had given me a new appreciation for how unreliable personal memories are and what a powerful effect myths and legends have on memories about war. Stories of soldiers being spat on when they returned from Vietnam now seemed to have been the products of imagination. I argued in my book that these stories were mythical, in the sense that they appeared to help people deal with a difficult period of history in which the United States lost its first war. The spat-upon-veteran stories helped construct an alibi for why we lost, namely, that we had been defeated on the home front by liberals in government and radicals in the streets, not by the Vietnamese.

The failure of *Valley of Death* to self-destruct as a hoax made me more interested in it. I doubted that careless use of sources or her violation of ethical standards, both charged by Oliver's detractors, was the whole story. It was perfectly possible, I thought, that Oliver had reported what she had been told, taking only such license with her material as is usual for her profession. My hunch was that the problem lay not with how she used her sources but with the sources themselves. From my own research I knew that men's thirty-year-old memories of any war are problematic and that memories of the Vietnam War are especially questionable because of the heavy distortion of its history in film and literature. This particular story, moreover, was loaded with Rambo-like heroics and the political and technological exotica of defectors and nerve gas that I thought more likely to have converged in someone's imagination than in an obscure base camp in Laos.

Never having heard even rumors of U.S. defectors holed up in Laos, I wondered if that part of the story was a new version of the "Legend of the Lost Command," stories told about troops who went out on a mission and were never heard from again. Were they lost? Had they been killed? Captured? Did they defect? Should we go look for them? The legend, most often set in World War I, was revived as a Vietnam war story in the 1987 movie *Eye of The Eagle*, in which the lost unit defects and is then hunted down by a journalist and the Eagle Team of "good" soldiers.

The nerve gas part of the story also seemed inventive. Again, it seemed odd that twenty-five years after the war I was hearing about the use of nerve gas for the first time. I wondered if it was just coincidence that a report about nerve gas use in Vietnam would surface seven years after the nation had become obsessed over the possibility it would be unleashed by Saddam Hussein against U.S. troops during the Persian Gulf War. And was it just coincidence that the gas allegedly used on the operation was sarin, a name that had been practically unheard of before a mysterious Japanese cult used it to attack a Tokyo subway in 1995? I also knew that the popular film *Jacob's Ladder*, released in the fall of 1990, was a story about U.S. soldiers in Vietnam who were victims of a mysterious chemical agent used by their own forces. How much of the public's willingness to believe the CNN story was due to its having heard "something like it" before, that "something" being the story line of the film? For that matter, did these elements of political and popular culture predispose the CNN journalists themselves to believe elements of a story of which they might otherwise have been more skeptical?

As fascinating as these questions were, my initial interest in them stemmed from their relevance to my work on the myth of spat-upon veterans. How, I wondered, might an examination of *Valley of Death* shed some additional light on the relationship between popular culture and memories of war? I thought an article-length piece extending my analysis to this new case might be warranted, but I did not see it as a whole new terrain to be explored. That changed in August 1998, when I was being interviewed about *The Spitting Image* by Kathy Forest, a reporter at KGNU radio in Boulder, Colorado.

Ms. Forest asked me what I thought of the CNN Tailwind story. I told her that the parts about gas and defectors had initially struck me as the stuff of myth and legend, and that I was not surprised that the story had fallen apart. "Well, I think it's true," she said. When I asked why, she answered that the story had been based on a book called *Spite House*. I had not heard of the book, but I took some notes and told her I would look for it. A few days later, at Midnight Special Bookstore in Santa Monica, California, I saw *Spite House* stacked on the front counter and bought it.

Spite House is a page-turner written by Monika Jensen-Stevenson, a journalist who, with her husband William Stevenson, had previously written *Kiss the Boys Goodbye: How the United States Betrayed Its Own POWs in Vietnam,* a book that had helped foster the idea that there might still be POWs languishing in jungle prisons and that the U.S. government had abandoned all efforts to retrieve them. *Spite House* went a step farther and alleged that the U.S. military actually had "hunter-killer teams" assigned to track down and assassinate American soldiers who had disappeared from their units during the war. The book used the case of Robert Garwood, a former Marine who had returned from Vietnam years after the end of the war, as an example. Claiming he was a defector, the military had hunted Garwood for years when, according to Jensen-Stevenson, the authorities knew all along he was a POW. If *Spite House* was true, some of the POWs the U.S. claimed were still being held by Vietnamese communists had actually been hunted down and killed by their own government. Why would the government fear its own POWs so much that it would rather have them dead than home alive? And was it possible, then, that Tailwind's targets were not defectors at all but, like Garwood, actually POWs that the government did not want the American public to know about?

Now I was hooked—but hooked by the implications, not the substance, of the *Spite House*–Tailwind connection. One implication arose from what it said about the political and cultural origins of the Tailwind story. *Spite House* is a political fantasy—built on a certain amount of historical fact, for sure, but a fantasy nonetheless. It's a kind of "campfire story" that expresses something deeply meaningful to the people who tell and believe it. Its elements of conspiracy and a government's betrayal of its own people, common to both *Spite House* and Tailwind, point toward right-wing political culture as the taproot of both stories.

The fact that journalists would find either of these stories credible also captured my interest. What did it imply about the fired CNN producers that they had bought into something as culturally marginal as a far-fetched conspiracy like this? Perhaps, I thought, they simply did not see this subtler dimension of the story. Or, if they did see it, maybe they were too naïve to grasp its implications. But April Oliver was an experienced professional with an established reputation in the news business, not a cub reporter. Jack Smith, her backup, was even better credentialed. More likely, I thought, they saw everything there was to see in Tailwind, subplot and all, and they believed it—because, well, they believed it. The possibility that the right-wing, antigovernment message embedded in this story might have appealed to the journalists themselves became for me one of the most enticing aspects of the CNN/Tailwind affair.

In the ensuing months, Oliver mounted a spectacular defense of the story and a formidable legal response to her firing by CNN. But as additional documentation came out and we learned more about how Oliver had done her research, the strength of her position seemed to erode. The question that was soon on everyone's mind and not a few pundit's lips was, how could this have happened? How could a story so laden with the makings of myth and legend have been produced by seasoned journalists and aired by CNN, the nation's leader in television news? The situation seemed paradoxical—journalists, whose profession is steeped in a culture of rationality, enraptured by the irrational. How could it be?

My own answer to the question entailed a challenge to its premise, namely, that the rational and the irrational are separable understandings of how humankind knows its world. Classical philosophers demarcated those ways of knowing, or epistemologies, in their effort to distinguish modernism from premodernism. But more recent scholarship, sometimes referred to as postmodernism, questioned whether real-life approaches to the world are that firmly bounded. The interpenetration of the rational and irrational may be more of a constant, even in the later stages of modernism, than we commonly wish to admit.

With that in mind, I approached the "how could it be?" question not as a paradox but as a question to which the answer was self-evident once modernist epistemological assumptions were qualified. It was, I suspected, *precisely* the elements of myth and legend in the story that had made it irresistible to April Oliver and her colleagues. The task, then, would be to set those elements in relief, reveal their deep-seated roots in Western culture, identify the organizations and individuals that linked them to Oliver's sources, describe the events of the post–Vietnam War period that provided a context for the resonance of Tailwind's themes, and reconstruct the biographical trajectory that predisposed her to believe the story. That is the book I set out to write.

This book does what other interpretations of *Valley of Death* have not done—pursue alternative explanations for where the story came from and critically explore *why* April Oliver and her colleagues believed it. Four streams feed into the creation of *Valley of Death*. One, of course, is the *actual* history of Operation Tailwind—it really happened at the time and in the place reported by CNN—and other documentable wartime events that constituted a formidable amount of grist for the story. A second stream is formed by the flow of memories of the men who were in Operation Tailwind or missions like it. That stream, however, merges with a third stream coming out of popular culture. Veteran memories, we know from other studies, are problematic and especially susceptible to the influence of film, literature, and oral history. The nature of the story told by CNN, moreover, makes thirty-year-old memories particularly suspect; the defectors and nerve gas in *Valley of Death*, the two "blockbuster" elements in the story, are almost certainly products of screenwriter and novelist imaginations. The fourth stream feeding into the story is the confluence of political and religious culture. One of this study's most important findings is that stories of this type— hunter-killer teams in search of defector/POWs—were popular among a conspiricist-minded community of ultra-right-wing activists and that many of the story's most active raconteurs were fundamentalist Christian preachers. Among those preachers were several Vietnam veterans, one of whom, Robert Van Buskirk, was a major source for *Valley of Death's* producer, April Oliver.

Why CNN's producers believed this story is more difficult to answer. Why does anyone believe what they do? A subfield of sociology known as phenomenology makes that question its raison d'être. Essential to the method is the idea that truth is as much in the eye of the beholder as in the situation or event itself. In the case of Operation Tailwind, the phenomenological approach would suppose that April Oliver believed what she did because of the background assumptions and values that she brought into her research, as much as because of what the "facts" themselves suggested to her. Not surprisingly, the phenomenological approach is near heresy among professional journalists who want to believe—and want the *rest* of us to believe—that they simply "let the facts speak for themselves." As it turns out, Oliver is strong evidence for the case that objectivity in journalism is ideology as much as anything else.

In pursuit of an answer to why this story was believed, I was led full circle in a sense—back to the question of *what* was believed. The shocking and disturbing conclusion in this book is that it wasn't the empirically accessible issues of nerve gas and defectors per se that attracted and held April Oliver and others to the Tailwind story. Rather, it was the story's myth-laden *subtext* about the U.S. government knowingly assassinating its own POWs that snatched *Valley of Death*'s producers from the realm of reason and held their careers at ransom. Equally shocking is the realization that CNN, at many levels of program management, thought the conspiratorial implications of the story it broadcast would resonate as true with a large number of viewers. That they may have been right is a frightening commentary on America's political culture at the turn of the twenty-first century.

ACKNOWLEDGMENTS

I knew from the outset that this book was going to incur a lot of debts, and, having learned the hard way that important contributors can be forgotten at the last minute, I kept a log as I went along. Then a hard-disk crash two weeks before the manuscript was due wiped out all my good intentions (but not the manuscript, which was well backed up). Doing it by memory, the way it's usually done, I wish to settle my accounts as best I can.

The greatest debts are owed to those who encouraged me to do the book and were generous with their insights and sources. Among them were Scott Anderson, John Baky, Paul Boyer, Chip Berlet, Bruce Franklin, Bill Gibson, Jennifer Morrison, Fred Turner, Richard Shultz, and Susan Weinstein. Writers Arthur Allen and Dennis McDougal had covered the CNN-Tailwind fiasco before me and were willing to talk about what they knew. John Schmaltzbauer's sense that there was a phenomenological point to be made in this book gave it the conceptual focus it needed. April Oliver and Jack Smith (through Marilyn Smith) responded to my inquiries, if not always as helpfully as I would have liked. Michael Ruppert was very generous with his time. Eugene McCarley, a veteran of the real Operation Tailwind, was very helpful, as was Jay Graves whose puzzling relationship to CNN's *Valley of Death* broadcast is made clearer in this book. Monika Jensen-Stevenson was helpful. Keith Freeman, an aide to Gen. John

Singlaub, took time to talk to me, as did Col. Tom McKenney, whose own story as a hunter-killer inspired the Tailwind Tale.

I'm grateful to Tim O'Coin and Patrick O'Connor for talking about war films with me; Julia Crowley and Lauren McCullough for their help in editing; and Marlisa Grogan, Laura Hogan, Craig Jensen, Regina King, Laura Peynado, and Colleen Quigley for the research tasks they helped with. Many others who shared information they had or helpfully pointed in the right direction are remembered in the text or footnotes.

I thank librarians Gudrun Krueger (for her can-do attitude), Irene Mizula (for her patience), and Molly Del Howe-Lembcke, who helped with the final preparation of the manuscript—just enough to get her name mentioned.

During the time this book was written I managed to hang on to old friends Sara Cooper, Marv and Ardy Dunn, Michael Gordon, Martin Hart-Landsberg, Harvey Kaye, Bob Ross, Jim Russell, Dale Treleven, Tim Troy, Richard Schmidt, Michele Sumara, and Roger Walke, while building new friendships with Tim Black, Corey Dolgen, Mary Erdmans, Mary Hershberger, and Don Unger. I appreciate the support I've gotten from John Buckingham, Gary DeAngelis, Daniel Goldstein, Tom Gottschang, Mary Hobgood, Karen Turner, and Steve Vineberg, all colleagues at Holy Cross College.

Thanks to Jennifer Berkshire, I'm working with Gail Leondar-Wright, and thanks to Carolyn Howe, the final printing was glitchless enough to get a manuscript to Mary Carpenter, my trusting editor at Rowman & Littlefield.

1

VALLEY OF DEATH: FROM BLOCKBUSTER TO JUST BUSTED

NewsStand: CNN and Time, June 7, 1998

JEFF GREENFIELD
Earlier this year, the United States nearly went to war with Iraq over chemical and biological weapons. Now, CNN and *Time,* after an eight month investigation, report that the U.S. military used lethal nerve gas during the Vietnam War.

BERNARD SHAW
It was 1970. President Nixon had pledged a no-first-use policy on nerve gas, part of his commitment to the Geneva protocol limiting chemical weapons use. The U.S. had signed the treaty restricting chemical weapons use but the Senate had not yet ratified it. Now, Peter Arnett has the story of Operation Tailwind, a raid into Laos which, according to military officials with knowledge of the mission, held two top secrets: dropping nerve gas on a mission to kill U.S. defectors.

Thus began CNN's broadcast of *Valley of Death,* the inaugural edition of its program *NewsStand: CNN and Time.* For the next eighteen minutes, Peter Arnett, America's best-known war correspondent, narrated the story of Operation Tailwind, a secret incursion into Laos in September 1970 conducted by an elite unit of Green Berets known as the Studies and Observations Group (SOG).[1]

Against the background music of Buffalo Springfield's "For What It's Worth," Arnett began by introducing Robert Van Buskirk, a platoon leader on Tailwind.

VAN BUSKIRK
Death. This was [pause] the Valley of Death.

On camera, we see Van Buskirk circulating among some prison inmates asking, "How many of you realize that God is a spirit? He's gonna set you free, son. You know that, don't ya?" Arnett continued his introduction saying, "Today, Rev. Van Buskirk is a born-again Christian taking his ministry into prisons, while back in 1970, he was Lt. Van Buskirk, with orders to kill everything in sight, including American defectors." Speaking to the camera, Van Buskirk says, "It was pretty well understood that if you came across a defector, kill 'em. It wasn't about bringing them back, it was to kill 'em."

Arnett then switched to the nerve gas story, reporting that SOG had access to *any* weapons. "The arsenal included," he said, "a special weapon known as sleeping gas." Van Buskirk provided confirmation: "Sleeping gas was a slang for nerve gas. In other words, when you got hit with sleeping gas you were going to sleep forever."

Providing an overview of what was to follow, Arnett said:

Tailwind held two of the U.S. military's top secrets. The first: that sleeping gas was indeed nerve gas, deadly sarin, what the U.S. military calls GB. . . . The second secret: hunting and killing American defectors was a high priority on SOG missions, including Tailwind.

Other Tailwind veterans and former military officials provided supportive testimony for the defector and nerve gas elements of the CNN report. Jay Graves, a SOG photographer who had led an advance reconnaissance team into the area, reported seeing "round eyes" in the targeted camp, while Jim Cathey, who was responsible for air force resupply for Tailwind, reported seeing ten to fifteen "longshadows" in the village. On camera, Cathey said, "I believe there were American defectors in that group. In retrospect, I believe that mission was to wipe out those longshadows."[2]

Arnett then introduced Adm. Thomas Moorer who had been chairman of the Joint Chiefs of Staff in 1970 when Tailwind was conducted.

Moorer is shown being interviewed by April Oliver, a CNN staff reporter and producer of the program. The two exchanged comments about the likelihood of nerve gas having been used on the mission; Moorer's responses to her questions seemed to confirm that it had been. Moments later, Moorer declared, "I'm sure there were some defectors, there are always defectors."

ARNETT
    Moorer acknowledged in an off-camera interview that Tailwind's target was indeed defectors. While he would give no firm estimate, Moorer indicated scores of U.S. military had defected during the war. Other senior military officials also confirmed that Tailwind's objective was a group of defectors collaborating with the enemy. These officials said the Tailwind mission was not unique; to SOG, defectors were always considered a target of opportunity—to be eliminated.

ARNETT (against a backdrop of still photos of John Singlaub)
    Former SOG commander John Singlaub told CNN, "It may be more important to your survival to kill the defector than to kill the Vietnamese or Russian. American defectors' knowledge of communications and tactics can be damaging." Singlaub argued it may be better to kill defectors than to risk lives trying to capture them.

Following a break for advertising, Arnett described the raid. With photos and footage of Vietnam-era military scenes for visuals, he told viewers that the SOG team of sixteen Americans and about 140 Montagnard mercenaries had launched its helicopter-borne raid from Dak To, in South Vietnam. Landing near a site where defectors were believed to be camped, the team encountered resistance and called in air power to disperse its opponents. On the third night, planes "gassed the camp with deadly sarin nerve gas." The next morning, Van Buskirk led the assault.

VAN BUSKIRK
    I was on the offensive. I had already been wounded. I was not in a good mood.

ARNETT
    Firing automatic weapons and tossing grenades into the hootches, the commandos met little resistance. Suddenly, Van Buskirk spotted two Caucasians. One went down a spider hole, the second ran toward him.

VAN BUSKIRK

Early twenties, blond hair, looks like he's running off a beach in California, needs a haircut. This is a GI, boots on, not a prisoner, no shackles, no chains, nothing.

ARNETT

Van Buskirk held his fire and raced the man to the spider hole, tried to grab him but missed. The man slid into the hole. Van Buskirk shouted . . .

VAN BUSKIRK

"I'm Lt. Van Buskirk, Fifth Special Forces. I'll take you home. C'mon out." In perfect English, with no accent, he said, "F—— you," only he said the word. And I said, "No, F—— you."

ARNETT

Convinced they were defectors, Van Buskirk threw a white phosphorus grenade down the hole. He believed both men were killed instantly.

When the fighting stopped, Van Buskirk tells us, "Montagnard fighters reported, 'Beaucoup roundeye, many, in the hootches.'"

ARNETT

Bodies that look like Americans.

VAN BUSKIRK

Fifteen. Maybe twenty. . . . When I looked in the hootches, it was a mess. Just pieces of human beings.

ARNETT

According to several commandos, the bodies, thought to be American defectors, were not identified. And no bodies were ever brought out. Later, Van Buskirk says, a SOG colonel, in keeping with SOG's code of deniability, ordered him to delete his description of killing two American defectors from his after-action report.

VAN BUSKIRK

I was told the best thing was to take that out of the after-action report, it wasn't germane. And I did.

ARNETT

With the camp overrun, it was time to get out quickly. More enemy troops were gathering on a nearby ridge. . . . Desperate, the commandos called for gas.

VAN BUSKIRK
I said, "I want the bad of the bad."

Tailwind veteran Michael Hagan described how the gas affected the enemy troops: "They were throwing up, in convulsions on the ground. I don't think too many of them got up and walked away." Arnett recounted how the gas filtered across the elephant grass into the landing zone where the SOG party was to be picked up by helicopters. According to Hagan, the gas was "tasteless, odorless, you could barely see it." Speaking on camera, Hagan said the chemical agent used was "nerve gas," although, he said, "the government don't want it called that. They want it called 'an incapacitating agent' but it was nerve gas." Van Buskirk recalled throwing up as he ran and returned enemy fire. Then there was this exchange between Arnett and Jay Graves, the leader of the advance reconnaissance team:

ARNETT
What was the call sign used for the sleeping gas used on Tailwind?

GRAVES
GB, then they changed it to something else. I can understand why they was doing it.

ARNETT
Why was they doing it?

GRAVES
Because they was using nerve gas in that shit and not telling anybody about it.

After reporting that some veterans of Tailwind remembered the gas as a nonlethal tear gas, Arnett said "chemical experts" had told CNN that the symptoms reported were inconsistent with tear gas. On camera, Amy Smithson of the Henry L. Stimson Center informed viewers that vomiting and convulsions were associated with a nerve agent, not tear gas. "With tear gas, an individual cries," she says, "where the individual with nerve gas exposure is likely to die."

Arnett quoted Admiral Moorer saying that GB—sarin nerve gas—was "by and large available for many other rescue attempts," and then moved into his wrap-up.

ARNETT

Questions remain. Exactly how many times has the U.S. military secretly used nerve gas? On Tailwind, just *who were* the defectors killed? Are military officers sure no *POWs* were killed? Just how many defectors were there in Laos? And, ultimately, who authorized the operation?

INVESTIGATIVE JOURNALISM

At the end of the broadcast, CNN's Special Assignment Unit, responsible for the production of *Valley of Death,* celebrated—and for good reason. The program had been the kickoff episode of a new collaboration between CNN and *Time* that promised to boost CNN's ratings. The two news organizations had proudly announced their partnership eleven days earlier, on May 27, at a Rockefeller Center press breakfast attended by top corporate executives from both organizations: Time, Inc., editor-in-chief Norman Pearlstine; *Time*'s managing editor, Walter Isaacson; CNN president Tom Johnson; and Richard Kaplan, the head of CNN/USA. The premier edition of *NewsStand,* as the new program was called, would be an exposé of the military's use of nerve gas against American defectors in Southeast Asia. *Valley of Death* would be a blockbuster news event, containing clear evidence that nerve gas, banned under international law, had been used by the United States in Vietnam and publicly acknowledging that defectors from the U.S. military had gone to Laos, a shocking new chapter in the saga of American personnel missing in action since the Vietnam War.

The foundation for the CNN/*Time* joint effort had been laid when CNN owner Ted Turner merged his television news company with the Time Warner corporation, owner of *Time* magazine, in 1996. In 1997, CNN hired Kaplan and gave him orders to develop an "appointment viewing" program that would hold viewers between its coverage of crisis events upon which CNN had built its reputation. Turner wanted something that would rival NBC's *Must See TV*. Kaplan was a thirty-year veteran of the business, having produced for the legendary newscaster Walter Cronkite at CBS and the hit news shows *Primetime Live* and *Nightline* at ABC. He had come to CNN from ABC, pushing out Ed Turner (no relation to Ted Turner) as head of CNN/USA. Ed Turner would later criticize Kaplan for bringing to CNN a show-business approach that eroded the organization's journalistic integrity.[3]

Kaplan took an existing program, *Impact: CNN & Time on Special Assignment*, and made it his personal project. Headed by Pam Hill, who had come to CNN in 1989 from ABC, *Impact* was a low-budget operation with a thirty-five-member team assigned to develop news specials. Kaplan immediately pushed for a new format with expanded resources and greater standing within the CNN organization. The result was *NewsStand: CNN and Time*, launched by the exposé of Operation Tailwind.

On the evening of June 7, Kaplan looked like a genius, and the producers of *Valley of Death* looked like shoo-ins for a Pulitzer Prize. The postbroadcast celebration feted producer April Oliver as the driving force behind the story. Oliver had joined CNN in 1994 after ten years at PBS, where she had worked on the *MacNeil-Lehrer NewsHour*. A thirty-six-year-old graduate of Princeton University, she had worked on the story for a year, traveling thousands of miles to interview dozens of veterans, weapons experts, and military officials. For Oliver, the successful production of *Valley of Death* was the culmination of her rapid assent to stardom in television journalism. In recognition, Oliver was given an M-17 gas mask by one of her sources.

JOURNALISM INVESTIGATED

The next day, Monday, the *Time* magazine version of *Valley of Death* appeared on newsstands. Coauthored by Oliver and Arnett and entitled "Did the U.S. Drop Nerve Gas?" the story repeated the basic points conveyed by CNN the night before. The *Washington Times* carried on page 6 an account of the CNN broadcast and also repeated the story. On the surface, it appeared that CNN's Tailwind revelations were playing out as planned. Beneath the calm, however, a controversy was already roiling that would destroy the careers of April Oliver and her coproducer Jack Smith, and threaten to bring down CNN itself. Within hours of the CNN Sunday broadcast, the Reuters news service had tracked down Admiral Moorer for a follow-up interview. Moorer backed away from the claim that sarin gas had been used during the war, telling the Reuters reporter that he had no personal knowledge of the nerve agent's use. Moorer said he had only "heard rumors that it'd been used."[4] Reuters also reported that Defense Secretary William S. Cohen was ordering an investigation into whether or not the military had used nerve gas in Vietnam. On June 9, the *Washington Times* gave editorial endorsement to Cohen's investigation and suggested that the CNN-*Time* report should also be investigated. "We surely ought to know if CNN and *Time* reporters and producers heard what they wanted to hear when Adm. Moorer was talking," opined the editors.

Cohen's investigation wasn't the only one under way by June 9. Working for the Special Forces Association, an organization for retired Green Beret and covert operations specialists like the men who had conducted the Tailwind raid into Laos, retired lieutenant colonel Rudi Gresham, who had been Gen. William Westmoreland's public relations officer after the war, produced a copy of the battle report filed by Robert Van Buskirk just a few days after Operation Tailwind. In the report Van Buskirk identified the gas used as tear gas, not the lethal agent sarin. Gresham also came up with copies of confidential military personnel records for James Cathey and Jay Graves, two other sources used for the *Valley of Death* story. According to the records, neither man had been in Laos or associated with Tailwind.[5]

Retired major general Perry Smith, CNN's in-house military analyst, had also been looking into the report. Smith had been, as he would later reveal, bypassed during the production of the story, but in the week following its broadcast he talked to two pilots who had flown support missions for Tailwind; both remembered dropping nonlethal tear gas. His research found no evidence to support the program's claim that sarin had been used in Southeast Asia or that the U.S. military had targeted defectors for killing. On June 17 he resigned from CNN, telling the *Washington Post*, "I can't work for an organization that would do something like this." On June 18, the *New York Times* ran an op-ed piece by John Plaster, a SOG veteran and author of a book about covert operations in Southeast Asia. Plaster blasted the CNN account of Tailwind.

On about June 19, CNN began its own investigation into the production of *Valley of Death* and hired the highly respected First Amendment attorney Floyd Abrams to conduct the research. CNN also hired Kroll Associates, a private-investigation firm, which used former Central Intelligence Agency (CIA) employees to retrace Oliver and Smith's steps.

In his findings, which were made public on July 2, Abrams wrote that CNN's conclusion that U.S. troops had used nerve gas to kill American defectors in Laos was "insupportable." "CNN," he advised, "should retract the story and apologize." While Abrams had found no evidence of intentional falsification on the part of Oliver and the other producers, his report attacked what he called the "five pillars" of testimony on which *Valley of Death* had stood: that of Admiral Moorer, three highly placed confidential sources, the veterans of Tailwind, other SOG veterans and pilots who flew for SOG, and weapons experts.[6]

Abrams raised questions about the eighty-five-year-old Moorer's memory but focused on how the producers had used what he had told them. According to Abrams, "Admiral Moorer simply does not come close to offering the sort of support for the conclusions offered by CNN that the program asserts that he does." Abrams's report reproduced large segments of interview material that had been edited out of the broadcast and then reiterated that what Moorer had told Oliver and Smith did "not confirm 'that nerve gas was used in Tailwind' or that the Tailwind 'target was indeed defectors.'"

Of the three confidential sources investigated, one seemed to check out but had been an indirect source who had relayed information to Oliver through a third party; thus it was impossible for Abrams to be certain about the use made of the information. Another of the confidential sources seemed to Abrams to have been *led* to support the claim of sarin use after being given the impression that Admiral Moorer thought it was true.[7] Confidential source number three, wrote Abrams, "provided a level of support for the truth of the broadcast but with some of the same problems we have seen elsewhere, a producer overstating her case to the source and a source responding positively but with ambiguity to the producer."

The third pillar of the story comprised the veterans of Operation Tailwind. Capt. Eugene McCarley, who had led the SOG raid into Laos, had been filmed saying he never considered the use of lethal gas on any of his operations, while in the broadcast report Arnett declares that McCarley had told the producers off camera that the use of nerve gas was "very possible." In his interview with Abrams, McCarley denounced his treatment by CNN and said he had told the reporters that his troops had never used nerve gas. He also insisted that the mission had had nothing to do with American defectors.[8]

Then there was the testimony of Jay Graves, the leader of the advance reconnaissance team. As for defectors, the broadcast had quoted Graves as saying, "We saw some round-eyed people," clearly conveying that Graves was an eyewitness to the presence of Americans in the attacked camp. According to Abrams, however, Graves had also told the interviewers, "I didn't ever see any of them," apparently implying that someone else on his team had sighted Caucasians. This omission, said the Abrams report, made Graves's recollections seem more certain than they actually had been.[9]

Abrams was most concerned about Robert Van Buskirk's role in the story. In its June 22 edition, *Newsweek* had reported Van Buskirk as saying he had "repressed" the details of Tailwind since 1974, when he was in a German prison on charges (later dropped) of selling weapons to a terrorist gang. Van Buskirk had written a 1983 memoir, entitled *Tailwind,* which contains no mention of sarin. He said, however, that he had recovered the memory of sarin while speaking to Oliver. A few days before Abrams's report was released, the *New York Times* reported that Van Buskirk had been treated for post–traumatic stress disorder with "mind-bending drugs" and that he suffered "repressed memory syndrome." Abrams concluded that Van Buskirk was unreliable as a witness—a fact that, when coupled with his central role in the program, "put into issue not only what he said but the bona fides of the broadcast as a whole."[10]

Abrams found the corroborative information from other individuals associated with Tailwind to have been secondary and "often ambiguous or conflicting." Expert witnesses on the effects of chemical weapons had been sometimes given insufficient or incomplete information about the symptoms resulting from Operation Tailwind. As presented to viewers, the issue of nerve gas had been oversimplified and conflicting expert views had been glossed over. The Abrams report concluded, "The CNN broadcast was not fair. Information that was inconsistent with the underlying conclusions reached by CNN was ignored or minimized."

On July 21, Secretary Cohen announced that his investigation had found no support for either the nerve gas or defector elements of *Valley of Death;* he called the CNN program "irresponsible." By that time, Smith's and Oliver's careers were already finished. On June 23, Smith had been called to Atlanta for a high-level chewing-out from Ted Turner and other CNN officials. Smith would later tell Mary Murphy and Dennis McDougal, writers for a four-part *TV Guide* series on CNN's Tailwind fiasco, that Turner chastised them for failing to prove their point. Two days later Oliver was pressured by the news company to reveal her confidential sources, and shortly thereafter Pam Hill, CNN senior vice president and supervising producer of *NewsStand,* resigned, along with consulting producer John Lane.

CNN News Group chairman Tom Johnson issued an on-air apology for the story on the day the Abrams report was released, July 2. On the same day, Johnson asked Smith and Oliver to resign; when they refused, he fired them. Peter Arnett, who had read the *Valley of Death* story on the air, was retained but reprimanded.[11]

THE "SOURCES" DEFENSE

On July 23, Smith and Oliver called a press conference at which they presented a seventy-seven-page rebuttal of the Abrams report. The rebuttal began by pointing out the conflict of interest inherent in the fact that the chief investigator, Floyd Abrams, had been hired by their accuser, CNN. Abrams's position had compromised his independence and the validity of the report, they asserted. Moreover, the report had been based on two weeks of investigation, whereas Oliver and Smith had done eight months of original research for *Valley of Death*.[12] The fired producers also accused Abrams of using information selectively, and they objected to the report's implication that they had violated the canons of good journalism by "falling in love" with their story. Furthermore, Oliver and Smith pointed out that they had been given only eighteen minutes of air time for the show, which meant that interview material that would have strengthened their case was edited out. The additional material, they implied, would vindicate them.

Less than a counterattack, the rebuttal was first of all an attempt to defend the story by reasserting the credibility of their original sources and declaring that material cut from the broadcast would answer the questions raised by the critics. Second, it sought to defend Smith and Oliver against the charges that they had misused their sources to deceive the viewers.

On the matter of Admiral Moorer's credibility, Oliver and Smith wrote that his "memory and lucidity are excellent" and that the effort to discredit him because of his age was a "malignant insinuation" constituting "character assassination." In one interview Moorer was questioned about the historical context of sarin's alleged use in Vietnam. The sequence, as reproduced in the rebuttal, went as follows:

Q. [to Moorer] We are going to report the U.S. used nerve gas in combat during Tailwind. Will we be correct in saying this was the first time the U.S. used it?

A. You might want to qualify that a bit.

Q. How?

A. Well, I am not so familiar with the European theater. But I think there might have been a few isolated pockets where poison gas was used.

Q. You mean in World War II?

A. Yes.

Q. Really?

A. Yes, I think so.

Q. So we would be okay in saying first time in [the] Vietnam War?

A. Yes, I think so.

This segment, more compelling than some material that *was* used on air, had been cut; it was also not quoted in the Abrams report. Even so, Moorer did not answer "yes" to the first question in the sequence; when critically read and put in the larger context of other interviews of him, it is not clear what he is actually confirming. Is he agreeing that nerve gas was used in Vietnam? Or is he saying that *if* it was used on Operation Tailwind, that would have been its first use in Vietnam? Later in the same interview as quoted in the Abrams report (but not acknowledged by Oliver and Smith in their rebuttal), there is this exchange:

Q. So you are aware sarin was used?

A. I am not confirming for you that it was used. You have told me that. . . .

The bulk of the Oliver and Smith rebuttal takes the same form, that of trying to demonstrate that if we the viewers and readers could hear what they had heard, we too would believe. But like the sequence just quoted, some of those efforts seemed to tighten the noose around their own necks. On the question of defectors, for example, they refer to their May 1998 interview with Moorer and write, "The following passage is also *not* referenced by the Abrams Report:

Q. [to Moorer] We've been told, including by Singlaub [Maj. Gen. John K. Singlaub, the SOG commanding officer in Saigon from 1966 to 1968], that killing defectors, that defectors were always a top priority target for SOG.

A. Yes, I think so. You can rely on Singlaub. He was heavy into this from the start. He would have no reason to misinform you. You can believe him.

Oliver and Smith then append the following parenthetical note to Moorer's response: "(See quotes from Singlaub below on page 62 of this Rebuttal)." We turn to page 62 expecting to see that Singlaub confirms Moorer. Instead, we find the following:

> **Q.** [to Singlaub] So what are your options when confronted with defectors?
> **A.** You are reaching a logical conclusion. I would certainly hate to risk men's lives by going in and capturing them. It would be easier to go in with firepower and kill them.

Then, the Oliver and Smith rebuttal reads:

> Singlaub made the following statement during a telephone interview in April 1998: "It may be more important to your survival to kill the defector than to kill the Vietnamese or Russian. Americans can use the fact that they are Americans with their accent and knowing on the radio what to do. That can be damaging." Oliver called Singlaub again a week later and reread to him the above statement and asked:

> **Q.** [to Singlaub] I just want to make sure I got this right, that's what was said, wasn't it?
> **A.** Yeah, that's right. Of course, killing defectors was not in our formal mission statement. Our mission was to return evaders, escapees, and POWs.

This sequence doesn't say what Oliver and Smith say it does; Singlaub's response to their question about the options when confronting defectors—"you are reaching a logical conclusion"—could be interpreted as Singlaub's way of saying he doesn't accept the premise of the question. In fact, it actually confirms Abrams's charge that Oliver and Smith would misuse one source to leverage a response they wanted from another source. In this case, we find Oliver and Smith telling Moorer in May 1998 that Singlaub had said *killing* defectors was always a top priority for SOG, while their own report records that Singlaub had told them in April that killing defectors was *not* part of its formal mission.[13]

Oliver and Smith's defense against the charge of misrepresenting their sources in order to enhance their validity was just as troubling.

Responding to the criticism of the way they used Jay Graves, they came close to saying he was *not* a credible source and they had *never meant to imply that he was*. The *Valley of Death* program identified Graves as the leader of the SOG team that did the prelanding reconnaissance for Operation Tailwind. On camera, Arnett said Graves was "dropped in" to take photos and that from "this position his reconnaissance team spotted several Americans, roundeyes—either POWs or defectors." "We saw some roundeyes," Graves told viewers. His later testimony to the Abrams investigators that *he* had not seen them himself indicated that by letting his original words imply otherwise, Oliver and Smith had misrepresented him. In rebuttal, Oliver and Smith disavowed any intent to mislead the *NewsStand* audience. In a disclaimer that seemed to hinge on the definition of "we"—did Graves's use of "we" mean that he too had seen the "roundeyes"?—Oliver and Smith wrote that they "do not believe that the broadcast suggests that Graves himself saw Caucasians." Therefore, Oliver and Smith argued, they had not used Graves's testimony in a way that made it seem more valid than it actually was. Taking them at their word, one can only wonder why they had used Graves in the broadcast at all.[14]

Oliver and Smith's defense of themselves by pointing to their sources was, of course, standard journalistic practice. As will be seen in the following chapters, however, the "sources" defense was more problematic in this case than usual. Some of the sources had spent the years since the Vietnam war in government-sanctioned and privately sponsored covert operations, specializing in the arts of denial and disinformation. So practiced were they in deception, one reporter told me, that John Singlaub should be considered a professional liar. Singlaub and Moorer also had been associated with ultra-right-wing organizations holding conspiratorial beliefs that most observers say are paranoid.

Most damaging was that many of the sources backed away from the content of the broadcast; some even launched lawsuits against Oliver and Smith. The spectacle of Oliver and Smith trying to hide behind their sources while the sources scrambled to distance themselves from the fired producers adds intriguing questions to the Tailwind puzzle. Had the sources intentionally misled Oliver and Smith to believe their Tailwind tale and then backed away from it? If so, why? If not, what was so enticing about this story, that seasoned professionals had been unable to leave it alone? What had predisposed them to believe it so zealously that they were willing to jeopardize their careers by misusing their sources?

As it turns out, there are two layers to *Valley of Death*. The content of the June 7, 1998, broadcast—interesting as it was, with its elements of sarin and defectors—is only the surface. Scratch that surface, and what appears is a political phantasmagoria featuring a cast of paranoid characters and a script about conspiracies and betrayals, written with lines that, in some instances, are as old as time.

2

TAILWIND (TAKE I): COURAGE AND COVERT OPERATIONS

There really was an Operation Tailwind. On September 11, 1970, an elite unit of special forces troops crossed the border from South Vietnam into southern Laos. The mission of the 16 Americans and 140 Montagnard mercenaries was to divert the attention and resources of the North Vietnamese Army (NVA) from a battle site forty miles away where a large force of CIA-led Hmong mercenaries was conducting another operation. The Tailwind unit encountered heavy resistance from the NVA. For three days the men of Operation Tailwind were on the run, catching the enemy's eye, engaging briefly, and then running again. After destroying an enemy base camp on the third day, the unit came under heavy fire and was rescued by helicopter. During the extraction, tear gas was used to keep the enemy at bay. Nearly all the Americans had been wounded; three Montagnards had been killed and thirty-three wounded.[1]

This story, the real Operation Tailwind, was interesting, but the telling of it by CNN a quarter-century later was hardly a journalistic *coup*. Tailwind was but one of several such operations during the Vietnam War. It was an exciting story about secret military operations and the performance of duty in the face of fire, but by 1998 it was unlikely to be of interest to an American public sated with Hollywood images of barechested jungle fighters leaping into battle from helicopter skids.

If it wasn't the heroism and exposé potential of Tailwind that made it promising for the television news market, what was it? By packaging the real Operation Tailwind with the fictive elements of nerve gas and defectors, producers Oliver and Smith were able to construct a story that was as much about government secrecy and betrayal as it was about the fighting men of Operation Tailwind; its appeal was to the feelings of suspicion and fear left over from the war, sentiments intensified in the postwar decades by the prevalence of conspiracy themes in American political culture.[2]

Operation Tailwind's lure as a news story at the turn of the twenty-first century, however, cannot be understood separately from the history of which it is a part. It was a clandestine operation, the existence of which alone justified widespread speculation that the government wasn't telling the American people everything. Moreover, the origins of Tailwind itself lie in a subculture of paranoia that produced in Vietnam a hidden branch of military operations known as SOG, the Studies and Observations Group. In that sense, the real Operation Tailwind was both cause and effect, subject and object of its own mythologizing in the program produced by CNN as *Valley of Death.*

AMERICA'S SECRET WAR IN VIETNAM

The United States had been involved in Vietnam since World War II when it was allied with Ho Chi Minh's communist forces against the Japanese. When the war ended, the United States feared communist expansion and supported French efforts to recolonize the region. Following a major defeat of the French by Vietnamese independence forces at Dien Bien Phu in 1954, negotiations in Geneva led to a cease-fire agreement that required the French and their supporters to gather south of the seventeenth parallel while the communist Viet Minh grouped north of the line. General elections were to be held in July 1956 to reunify the country.

Those elections were never held because the United States feared the communists would win. Soon, the seventeenth parallel hardened into a political border. In the South, Washington put in place a repressive and corrupt client state led by Ngo Dinh Diem, whose regime, despite millions of dollars in aid from the United States, was never able to defeat its pro–Viet Minh opposition in the rural areas. U.S. analysts claimed

that secret agents from the North were infiltrating the South and stir-
ring up the peasants and that if that outside influence could be shut off,
political sentiments indigenous to the South would reassert themselves
and the people would rally to the Diem government.[3]

In January 1961, the U.S. Central Intelligence Agency (CIA) began
to monitor secretly northern influence in South Vietnam and it initiated its own infiltration of the North. The CIA operation was led by
William Colby, a veteran of the CIA's predecessor, the Office of
Strategic Services, for which he had carried out daring raids behind
enemy lines during World War II. Colby had joined the CIA in 1950
and was assigned as chief of station in Saigon in 1959. Based on the
maxim "If they can do it, so can we," the CIA began sending agent
teams North to collect intelligence, sabotage enemy activity, and conduct psychological warfare against the civilian population. Eighteen
months later, angered by the CIA's failed Bay of Pigs invasion of Cuba
in April 1961 and frustrated by the agency's lack of success in Vietnam, President John F. Kennedy decided to transfer covert operations in Vietnam to the military and ordered an expansion of the
mission.[4]

Between the summer of 1962 and the end of 1963, civilian and military leaders reassessed the U.S. situation in Vietnam and began, as the
president had directed, shifting responsibility for the covert war to
the military. The changeover was slowed by the assassinations of Diem
and President Kennedy in November 1963, but in late January 1964 the
Military Assistance Command Vietnam (MACV) took charge of the program.

The military covert-action organization in Vietnam was initially
known as OPLAN 34-A (Operations Plan 34-A); the title was changed to
Special Operations Group and then to Studies and Observations Group,
or SOG. SOG drew personnel from the army Green Berets, navy
SEALs, and the air force Air Commandos. Commanded by an army
colonel, SOG answered directly to the Joint Chiefs of Staff (JCS) in
Washington. SOG's mission went through several stages of refinement
but in the end it consisted of four main components: secret operations
inside North Vietnam involving intelligence gathering and sabotage;
cross-border operations against the Ho Chi Minh Trail in Laos and
Cambodia; psychological operations aimed at the North Vietnamese
leadership and populace; and seaborne raids on northern costal installations.

THE WAR ON THE NORTH: BLIND DROPS
AND THE DOUBLE CROSS

With little experience with covert operations, the SOG leaders adopted the techniques used by the CIA. The basic tactic was to insert agents or agent teams into North Vietnam. The agents were Vietnamese, sometimes northerners who had moved south during the cease-fire in the mid-1950s. They were recruited by SOG's counterpart agency within the army of South Vietnam and returned by SOG as spies to the areas in the North where they had lived. Others were South Vietnamese, inserted as "blind drops" and left on their own. Insertion was often done by parachute; once on the ground, the agents would maintain contact with their handlers in the South by radio. As described by Richard Shultz in his book *The Secret War against Hanoi*, the technique had been a "catastrophe of substantial proportions" for the CIA, having cost the lives of most of the 250 agents inserted during 1960–61.[5]

SOG had little more success; only seven of the thirty teams inserted still operated at the end of three years, some of those as double agents under the control of Hanoi. A team called Red Dragon, for instance, was inserted on September 21, 1967. Composed of seven members, it was located in the Red River Valley along the border with China. According to Shultz, who read the MACVSOG history of the mission, Red Dragon was to have conducted sabotage and intelligence activities, but U.S. personnel were soon convinced the team had been captured and was under North Vietnamese control. Red Dragon went off the air in 1969. No teams inserted by SOG were ever "exfiltrated," that is, recovered and safely returned to the South.

The possibility that Hanoi was actually capturing and "doubling back" agents was unnerving to SOG leaders. Doubling back meant that the North Vietnamese government was using the agents to transmit false or misleading information back to the South, thus compounding the intelligence problem confronted by the U.S. and South Vietnamese militaries. An internal investigation of SOG's espionage program found that Hanoi had total control of SOG's spies inside North Vietnam. SOG's response was to attempt a "triple cross," a double cross of the double crossers.[6]

The basic assumption of a triple-cross operation is that the enemy is paranoid. Applied to North Vietnam, the thinking was that the communist leaders were fanatical about internal security and political control.

Any hint that there were spies about would produce a witch-hunt that would soon impair the state Communist Party itself and produce such suspicion among the citizens that nobody would trust or believe anyone. As state repression against suspected spies mounted, people would begin to turn against the regime and each other, thereby destroying the country's capacity to wage war. SOG would exacerbate the paranoia by making the regime *think* there were more spies in the country than there actually were.

One SOG tactic was to air-drop radio transmitters into North Vietnam to broadcast phony material and make the regime think that actual teams of enemy agents were operating wherever the broadcasting came from. Sometimes, SOG would attach nothing more than a block of ice to a parachute. The North Vietnamese would find the abandoned chute, the ice having long since melted, and assume that a spy had chuted in and was loose in the area. A project code-named Borden involved recruiting prisoners of war from the North Vietnamese army as agents. "What the POWs didn't realize," writes Shultz, "was that those running Borden couldn't have cared less whether or not the NVA volunteers were sincere about becoming agents." In fact, it was assumed that many of them would reveal their assigned mission to the NVA leaders, thus inducing the paranoia that SOG thought would work to its advantage.[7]

PSYWAR: THE SACRED SWORD OF THE PATRIOT LEAGUE

Psychological warfare was the tactical common denominator of all of SOG's efforts against the North. Its logic was based on William Colby's assessment that communist regimes were police states with paranoid leaders. As Richard Shultz writes, Colby "wanted to play on Hanoi's obsession with counterintelligence—to take advantage of its excessive fear of subversion, deception, and conspiracy; to manipulate its fixation with perceived internal enemies and spies."[8]

The psywar was initially a CIA project, but like the other covert operations, it was transferred to SOG in 1964. The principle psywar technique, known as "black operations," was intended to cause the recipients of information distributed by SOG to attribute that information to false sources. The psywar consisted of four sets of activities: research and analysis; printed media, forgeries, and blackmail; preprogrammed radios; and special projects.

The research and analysis division was responsible for the collection and interpretation of information that could provide insight into Hanoi's psychological vulnerabilities. The printed-media division produced propaganda leaflets and forgeries of North Vietnamese military documents; these forgeries, containing false or misleading information, were then planted in the enemy's communications channels. This division also carried out blackmail activities. Letters would be mailed from third countries on the assumption that mail to North Vietnam was being opened by the police-state security people. Thus, a phony letter to a government official, that might cause censors to think he was not loyal, could be used to ruin his political reputation. The tactic was designed to breed distrust and paranoia within the leadership.

The radio division maintained three stations that broadcasted into the North. One of them was a false Radio Hanoi, which broadcast on a frequency very close to the real Radio Hanoi and copied its program formats. Listeners tuning into Radio Hanoi could easily be deceived into thinking they were listening to the real thing when in fact they were getting news and information that was slightly altered in ways that would discredit the Hanoi government. The other two stations were designed to give the appearance of stations operated by North Vietnamese resistance groups so that the regime would think it had an internal security problem to deal with.

The storybook cloak-and-dagger operations were conducted by the special projects division. One of those involved the production and distribution of booby-trapped NVA ammunition. It was the idea of John Singlaub, SOG's third chief, who was to be a prime informant for the CNN journalists thirty years later. Under Singlaub, SOG used the CIA to go to third-country sources and obtain weapons and ammunition used by the NVA. They doctored those items so they would explode and kill or maim enemy soldiers who tried to use them, and then planted them in enemy territory. In some cases whole caches of altered goods would be stored in areas known to contain real caches in hopes that the NVA would claim the wrong material. Since some of the bogus equipment was of Chinese origin, SOG also forged documents that would, for example, imply that Hanoi's Chinese allies were responsible for the malfunctioning weapons. The intended effect was to discredit the Chinese in the eyes of the NVA soldiers and undermine their confidence in their own weapons.[9]

The most bizarre operation run by the special operations division involved the creation of a nonexistent resistance movement called the Sacred Sword of the Patriot League, the SSPL. The idea behind the SSPL was that the CIA and SOG wanted the Hanoi government to think there really was a secret movement of political dissidents within the North. The Americans hoped that North Vietnamese officials would divert scarce resources to chase the apparition they had created.

The SSPL was the fabrication of Herb Weisshart, a deputy of the CIA's William Colby who had transferred to SOG. Weisshart knew the Vietnamese legend of Le Loi, a rich farmer who had led a fifteenth-century resistance movement against the occupying forces of the Chinese Ming dynasty. Le Loi had used guerrilla tactics, political trickery, and psychological manipulation to defeat the Chinese in 1428. He had assumed the throne, adopted the name Le Thai To, and established the Le dynasty, which was to rule Vietnam for more than three hundred years. According to the legend, which is known by all Vietnamese, King Le Thai To dropped his sword into Lake Thuy one day and a turtle carried it to the bottom of the lake. The king took this as a sign that the sword had been loaned to him by the gods so that he could defeat the Chinese; that heavenly mandate having been fulfilled, the gods were now taking it back. He renamed the lake Ho Hoan Kiem, the Lake of the Returned Sword.

Weisshart fashioned propaganda materials that made the SSPL sound like a reincarnation of the Le Loi movement. According to the story manufactured by Weisshart, the SSPL was a nationalist organization that had been repressed and forced underground—just like Le Loi. The story criticized the Vietnamese communist leaders for selling out to the Chinese who were using the Vietnamese as surrogates to fight the Americans. To add to the illusion that the SSPL was real, Weisshart created a radio station, the Voice of the Secret Sword of the Patriots League, which identified itself on air as broadcasting from Le Loi's home base in the mountains of Ha Tinh province. In fact, Radio SSPL was broadcasting from someplace outside North Vietnam. Phony documents produced by SOG and distributed by SOG-recruited pilots flying clandestine missions over the North suggested that the SSPL had ten thousand members and a military capability that had already liberated territory in parts of North Vietnam. The capstone of SOG's SSPL enterprise was the creation of a facsimile liberated area, called Paradise Island, to which SSPL "recruits" would be brought for training.

MARITIME OPERATIONS AND PARADISE ISLAND

The CIA had begun covert operations against North Vietnamese coastal installations early in 1961. The effort was based on the recognition that the small size of North Vietnam's navy left its shoreline poorly defended and its coastal infrastructure vulnerable to attack. Initially using motorized Vietnamese junks, the CIA's operation, generally referred to as Maritime Operations, or MAROPS, was later outfitted with state-of-the-art U.S. Navy equipment that included fast and stealthy Norwegian boats known as "Nasties." The Nasties had a range of 860 miles at thirty-eight knots. To run the boats into North Vietnamese waters the CIA recruited Norwegian and German mercenaries. Navy SEALs were assigned to train South Vietnamese commandos for sabotage operations along the North Vietnamese coast.[10]

Maritime Operations were taken over by SOG in early 1964 and given the code name Naval Advisory Detachment (NAD), with headquarters at Da Nang. NAD's missions included the destruction of North Vietnamese vessels, the interruption of supplies moving from North to South, bombardment of coastal targets, commando raids against military and civilian targets along the coast, insertion of agent teams into the North, and delivery of psychological-warfare materials such as propaganda leaflets and radios that would receive only stations operated by SOG. U.S. Navy and Marine Corps personnel trained South Vietnamese for the operations but were not allowed on the missions themselves.[11] On July 30, 1964, SOG/NAD boats shelled targets at Hon Me and Hon Nieu in North Vietnam, beginning what came to be called the Tonkin Gulf incident. In retaliation, Hanoi attacked the destroyer USS *Maddox* on August 2 but did not hit the ship. The *Maddox* was on patrol as part of an ongoing electronic surveillance program, Operation DeSoto. On August 4, The *Maddox* and another destroyer, the *Turner Joy*, were sent into the area as bait to provoke another attack. On the night of August 4, during a violent thunderstorm, sonar operators aboard the U.S. ships thought they detected attacking vessels and the destroyers opened fire. In the aftermath, it was concluded that there had been no attack, that erratic signals produced by the weather conditions had falsely indicated an enemy presence. In Washington, nevertheless, President Lyndon Johnson used the phantom attack as a pretext for escalating the war and ordered the first bombing raids on North Vietnam.[12]

NAD was also the key player in SOG's production of the Sacred Sword of the Patriot League. To make the SSPL seem real, SOG used a clandestine radio station to broadcast claims that the SSPL actually held occupied territory within North Vietnam. There was no SSPL, of course, much less a "liberated zone" within the North controlled by an indigenous anticommunist movement. So to lend credibility to its own story, SOG created such a zone—off shore.

Washington prohibited SOG from holding territory within the North, so SOG choose the island of Cu Lao Cham, just off the coast of Da Nang, on which to fashion a set of villages resembling those along the coast of North Vietnam, villages it would then claim were the home base of the SSPL—the SSPL's liberated zone. Beginning in May 1964, SOG boats flying the SSPL flag went into North Vietnamese waters, kidnapped North Vietnamese fishermen, and brought them to the island. The fishermen were told they were in the hands of the SSPL and were being taken to a secret liberated area somewhere along the coast. On the island, also known as "Paradise Island," the abductees were given good food and medical care, along with heavy doses of propaganda about how bad the Hanoi regime was. Before being sent back, the hostages were given gift kits of soap and other items as well as "secret" information about how to stay in touch with the SSPL, and radio sets pretuned to the SSPL station.

All of this was, of course, a form of guerilla theater; Washington policy prohibited SOG from organizing resistance movements within the North so the Paradise Island operation was only about producing illusions. SOG assumed that the fishermen, having been missing for three weeks, would be detained by North Vietnamese authorities upon their return and that most of kidnapped fishermen would spill all the "secrets" about the SSPL. Since there was no SSPL and no real secrets, the fishermen were thereby made unwitting accomplices of SOG's black operation to induce paranoia in the North Vietnamese leadership. According to Shultz, 1,003 North Vietnamese were brought to Paradise Island between 1964 and 1968.[13]

ON "THE TRAIL": SOG OPERATIONS IN LAOS AND CAMBODIA

The cease-fire agreement that ended the Vietnamese war against the French in 1954 had resulted in a demilitarized zone (DMZ) at the seventeenth parallel where a narrow strip of land between Laos on the west and the South China Sea on the east connected the wider parts of North and South Vietnam. Because Vietnam was very narrow in this panhandle, the DMZ could be easily sealed to prevent the movement of materiel and people in either direction. As the United States increased its military assistance to its client state in the South, North Vietnam sought ways to get support to its allies south of the DMZ. It did this by building a network of roads and paths that bypassed the DMZ, by looping west out of North Vietnam into Laos and then bending south and east back into Vietnam below the seventeenth parallel. Some of routes were later extended farther south into Cambodia before turning into Vietnam again. The network came to be known as the Ho Chi Minh Trail.

The CIA began monitoring traffic on the trail and using Special Forces–led units to attack enemy crossings into South Vietnam in the early 1960s. When CIA covert operations were turned over to SOG in January of 1964, cross-border operations by U.S. and South Vietnamese government troops were prohibited. But as the war heated up, U.S. military leaders began pressuring Washington for permission to "cross the fence" into Laos. Permission was granted for limited incursions in May 1964, but it was not until September 1965 that the first SOG-led units went over the border, in operations called Shining Brass.[14]

Code-named OP 35, SOG's trail operations were conducted by small reconnaissance teams consisting of three Americans and nine tribal minority soldiers, such as Chinese Nungs or Montagnards, and larger reaction companies of a hundred or more fighters. Eventually, there were 110 U.S. officers, 615 enlisted personnel, and at least a thousand indigenous troops assigned to OP 35. Washington limited the geographic scope of SOG operations to a few miles inside Laos and Cambodia, although there were exceptions to the rule.[15]

In *The Secret War against Hanoi*, Richard Shultz captures the surreptitious flavor of SOG's missions against the Ho Chi Minh Trail:

> By Fall of 1965 five recon teams were ready to cross the fence. The mission was completely covert; teams infiltrated into Laos were "sterile." They wore no rank or unit insignia, and their uniforms were made elsewhere in Asia specifically for SOG. The weapons carried were non-U.S. They had been acquired clandestinely and could not be traced. Teams had nothing on them that could identify who they were.

The first forays into Laos identified supply depots, truck parks, and fuel storage facilities, which were later hit and destroyed by U.S. bombers. Reconnaissance teams would provide on-the-ground direction for the air strikes. As a result of these successes, the number of missions increased in 1966, and the scope of operations was expanded to include taking prisoners and rescuing downed U.S. pilots, including pilots downed in the North. SOG teams also installed the seismic and acoustic sensors known as "McNamara's Fence" to monitor movement on the trail.[16]

Hanoi responded to SOG's incursions with countermeasures, placing spotters on the hills along the routes taken by SOG helicopters. The spotters would signal the landing locations and movement of SOG teams using a primitive but elaborate system of drums, bells, and gongs.[17] The North Vietnamese army employed local tribesmen and developed its own special forces units to track down and engage the SOG commandos. By 1968, according to Shultz, the NVA had committed twenty-five thousand troops to the defense of the trail. Fighting along the trail became fierce after 1968, and SOG casualties soared to as high as 50 percent.

The heavy losses taken by SOG led to speculation that its own security system had been breached. The espionage, it seemed, could have taken the form of spies infiltrated into the South Vietnamese units that SOG worked with, so that the details of forthcoming operations might have been known to the NVA well before their execution. At times the enemy seemed to know when and where the SOG teams would be inserted and be there waiting for them. Pete Hayes, a former SOG commander, told Shultz that on one occasion the waiting NVA actually "called the team by name and they named an individual [team member] by name."[18]

The decision by Richard Nixon's administration to withdraw U.S. troops and "Vietnamize" the war after 1969 put the brunt of the fighting on the South Vietnamese army. It was SOG's job to hold the NVA at bay while the Saigon army found its feet. In 1970 SOG executed 411 reconnaissance missions against the trail, some of them lasting only a few hours because of the intense fighting that resulted. Larger operations involving company-level forces and lasting a few days were sometimes mounted to extract trapped reconnaissance teams, rescue downed pilots, or support other operations. Operation Tailwind was one of those larger engagements.

In his *SOG: The Secret Wars of America's Commandos in Vietnam*, SOG veteran John Plaster provided a detailed account of Tailwind. A company-sized force of Americans and indigenous mercenaries, led by Capt. Eugene McCarley, departed from Dak To in South Vietnam's Central Highlands in U.S. Marine Sikorsky helicopters at noon on September 11, 1970. Escorted by twelve Cobra gunships, the airborne armada paralleled the border with Laos for fifty miles and then turned west, where it was met with heavy ground fire that claimed the mission's first casualties.[19]

The purpose of Tailwind was to distract the NVA from another operation forty miles away. Once on the ground, the commando unit basically offered itself as moving bait to attract the attention of the enemy. Encounters with NVA units would expose the enemy locations, making them easier targets for air strikes that the SOG team would call in against them. As the Cobras and A-1 fighters pummeled the enemy, the Tailwind troopers would take flight, running until they were encircled again. Fighting was intense at times, and along the way the SOG force killed dozens of NVA and destroyed a large cache of enemy ammunition.

The troops hit and ran for the next two days. On the third day, the unit came upon a bunkered base camp that Plaster describes as "a major logistical command center" for the NVA. The SOG men attacked the base camp, killing fifty-four North Vietnamese soldiers. In one bunker was a stash of hundreds of pounds of maps and documents, which the raiding party packed up and took. On the run again and burdened with the weight of the captured documents, McCarley's opportunities to save his battered company shrank as large units of NVA began to close in. The commandos fought their way to a landing zone where McCarley called in a massive air assault that Plaster says involved seventy-two U.S. fighters, nearly a half-million tons of bombs, rockets, and napalm, and CBU-19 tear gas bomblets. According to Plaster, all sixteen Americans had been wounded, but none had been killed. Three Montagnards had been killed. An estimated 432 NVA had been killed, and fifty wounded.

TOWARD THE SECOND TALE OF TAILWIND

It was Plaster's book, with its account of Operation Tailwind, that got April Oliver interested in the story. At the time she began working on

Valley of Death for CNN, it was the only source she had. What is remarkable in retrospect is that Plaster's version of Tailwind made no
mention of defectors or nerve gas. Nor was Plaster's account the story of
bravery and heroism that the CNN broadcast said it was. The operation
had accomplished its objective of diverting enemy resources, but no
Americans were killed so that, counting the three Montagnards who
were, the kill ratio had been approximately one SOG soldier for every
144 of the enemy. While those numbers might have indicated an effi-
cient military operation, they did not bespeak a tough fight.

Even with the additives of nerve gas and defectors stirred in by
Oliver, the story lacked the quality of a genuine exposé. The United
States had walked the fine line of international legality throughout the
war, and several informal proceedings, including those convened by
philosopher Bertrand Russell in Sweden in 1967, had indicted the U.S.
government for war crimes. The possibility that American military units
had used nerve gas would not warrant the attention of the average television viewer twenty-eight years later. The defector angle too seemed at
first glance to be a variation on an old story. It was widely known that
during the war GIs had defied military authority and even sabotaged
combat missions. At its height, in-service resistance by soldiers took the
form of "fragging," actual acts of violence against officers. Even if
the CNN report that some GIs had actually gone over to the other side
was true, it was no longer the stuff of a blockbuster news event.[20]

So if the particulars of macho derring-do, nerve gas, and defectors
were not likely to raise CNN's ratings, what were the preoccupations of
the American people that Oliver thought she could touch with the
material she had? In short, they were preoccupations about the U.S.
government's fidelity to the American people, fears born during the
Vietnam War of a recognition that the government had lied about how
the war was being fought, what it was about, and what the chances were
of winning. There were also suspicions held by some that the government had "sold out" the military mission in Vietnam by not fully
supporting the soldiers sent to fight, and then possibly abandoning prisoners and other men missing in action at the end of the war.

3

TAILWIND (TAKE 2): A GOVERNMENT BETRAYS ITS PEOPLE

On Tailwind, just *who were* the defectors killed? Are military officers sure no *POWs* were killed?

—Peter Arnett, narrator of CNN's, *Valley of Death*

Operation Tailwind was a diversionary action by U.S. commandos into Laos in September 1970. On the basis of documentable evidence, there has never been reason to believe that nerve gas was used on the operation or that the killing of American defectors was the object of the mission. As such, Tailwind has always been just another war story from the U.S. campaign in Southeast Asia, one of little more interest to the paramilitary community, which normally delights in such tales, than to the general public. With the elements of an illegal chemical agent and defectors added in, on the other hand, Tailwind became a means by which a story about something much larger and more important could be told.

This parable-like quality of Tailwind was not unique to it, of course. Accounts of other historical events convey meanings that are often unrecognized by the rest of us until someone interprets them for us. By connecting the event's details to other information and then telling us what it all means, the interpreter brings into view a picture that we had not previously seen. That story within the story, called a "subtext" by those who study literature, is sometimes the most inviting quality of the story being told. Unaware of its presence, we receive the subtext emotionally rather than cognitively and get "drawn into" its message before we have a chance to think about it.

Implicit in the account of Operation Tailwind as told by CNN on June 7, 1998, was a story about secrecy in government and the betrayal of national interests by political figures occupying positions of power in government and military institutions. We can bring the details of that implicit story into focus by looking at the interpretation of *Valley of Death* rendered by an organization that has defended the story since it aired.

IT'S ALL ABOUT THE POWS

For a day or so after the CNN broadcast, the content of *Valley of Death* was itself a news item carried by other outlets. But when Adm. Thomas Moorer, one of April Oliver's primary sources, declined to confirm key elements of the story to a Reuters reporter, most mainstream news organizations joined in calling for the claims made in the broadcast to be investigated. Beyond the mainstream, however, Oliver and Smith had defenders, the most strident of whom came from the far right. By looking closely at how supporters constructed their statements, we can better see just what political sentiments the program appealed to.

Michael Ruppert: Defectors or POWs?

The July 1998 issue of *From the Wilderness*, a newsletter published by Michael Ruppert, carried a story "The POWs, CIA and Drugs: Uglier Truths behind the Sarin Gas Stories." Written by Ruppert, the story defended April Oliver's findings and said her report "pointed to much uglier and deeper truths about CIA covert operations than the fact that the CIA used nerve gas to kill defectors and deserters in Southeast Asia." According to Ruppert, there is "a high probability that sarin gas was used not only against defectors but also against prisoners of war whom the government had decided would be a major embarrassment if they came home alive." Ruppert went on to provide what Oliver had not—a motive, an explanation for why the government thought the defectors were important enough to kill, and why, in his view, some in government would have wanted POWs killed.

Ruppert believed there were POWs in Southeast Asia long after the U.S. government said there were not, and that some of them had been captured while on covert operations in Laos. The government had always denied conducting those operations, and should those POWs ever be allowed to return home, they would provide living proof of the U.S. military's illegal cross-border missions. Moreover, those secret and illegal missions were often carried out by the CIA and, according to Ruppert, were paid for with money the CIA raised by trafficking in heroin.[1] Defectors, having gone over to the other side, would have had the freedom of movement to learn about the drug trade and the existence of live POWs. That information, contended Ruppert, could have been "their ticket home" at some later time. So, rather than run the risk that defectors would eventually "reveal the U.S. government to be as morally bankrupt as the Third Reich," the government, he said, ordered them killed.

Ruppert's claim that the CIA was involved in running heroin might be true. In order to gain the support of opium growers in Laos for its clandestine war in their region, the CIA probably used its secret civilian airline, Air America, to transport opium products to market. The agency may also have used the shuttle service to raise money to support its off-the-books military operations in denied areas. But there is no reason to believe that the CIA or Special Forces assassinated POWs in order to keep those activities hidden, nor is there evidence that the drug running was part of a larger scheme to destroy America from within through the proliferation of drugs—which is where Ruppert's line of thinking leads. His views on the CNN broadcast of *Valley of Death* could easily be dismissed as inconsequential but, as a window on the political culture that CNN thought it could attract with the show, it is invaluable.[2]

The clue that CNN (or at least Oliver and her cohorts) was targeting emotions connected to the POW issue with the defector part of the story is found in the text of the broadcast itself. The quote from *Valley of Death* used as an epigraph for this chapter—Are military officers sure no *POWs* were killed?—strongly suggests that the program was pitched to far-right-wing political sentiments, to a community that kept the POW issue alive well after there was any credible evidence that live POWs remained in Southeast Asia. Arnett's voice inflection giving emphasis to the word "POWs" is additional proof that this is the issue the producers wanted viewers to pay attention to. The abandonment of the POWs, always a cornerstone of the Vietnam war's "great betrayal" narrative, could now, with the information revealed in *Valley of Death*, be pushed to the end point: perhaps the POWs never came home because they had been assassinated by their own government.

If the proof of the pudding is in the eating, the fact that the more center-leaning spokesmen for American conservatism also picked up on the betrayal narrative in the Tailwind story indicates that Oliver's targeting was accurate. One of those mainstream commentators who swallowed the subtext of *Valley of Death* was Chris Matthews, the popular host of the CNBC news magazine *Hardball*. On July 7, 1998, just days after they had been fired, Matthews had Oliver and Smith on his show.

Chris Matthews: The Government Gases Its Own

Matthews framed the controversy surrounding the Tailwind story as a betrayal issue, ending his introduction of Oliver and Smith with the question, "Do either of you know for a fact that the U.S. used nerve gas to kill Americans?" Americans? Since all news coverage of the CNN controversy to that date had alleged that the target of the nerve gas attack was defectors, Matthew's choice of words seemed odd. Soldiers who are defectors have gone over to the other side; they could be thought of as having renounced their claim to being American. Americans? Patriots might say they were anything but. Why, when month-long journalistic practice had established "defectors" as the subject of the story, was Matthews suddenly changing terms? Why was he using the term "Americans" rather than "defectors"? Was he being careless, perhaps using his words loosely? No.

Moments later, responding to a rambling statement by Oliver implying that the nerve gas had been used only to rescue the Tailwind commandos from enemy fire, Matthews again cast the alleged defectors as Americans, saying, "But [gas used to extract the raiders is] not aimed at killing Americans, that's aimed at saving Americans." And so it went. Matthews hammered the point throughout the program, using the words "nerve gas to kill Americans" (or some combination of those words) nine times in the fifteen-minute broadcast. At one point he said, "The blockbuster story is that American military guys sat around and said, 'Let's kill Americans and let's use nerve gas to do it.'"

The other rhetorical twist given the story by Matthews was that the perpetrator of the nerve gas crime became not *just* the military or even a smaller subset of it, the Special Forces, but "the United States," as in, "the government." Near the end of the program, Matthews delivered his coup de grace: "The [figurative] headline coming out of your report was the United States used nerve gas against its own Americans and that was what was so heart-stopping about this piece." Referring to the defectors as "[the government's] own Americans" was clearly a way of pointing viewers to an issue that went beyond either the violation of international law implicit in the allegation of nerve gas use or the charge that GIs might have defected to the enemy during the war.

In effect, Matthews was baiting Oliver and Smith with the far-right betrayal theory advanced by Ruppert in *From the Wilderness*. The fired producers didn't exactly take the bait, but neither did they say anything to discourage Matthews's fear-mongering. In fact, in the exchange just recalled, Oliver could have agreed with Matthews's proposition that the nerve gas was used just to extract the Tailwind commandos. Agreement would still have allowed her to defend the blockbuster quality of what were, ostensibly, the two main components of the story—the illegal use of nerve gas (its use was, after all, illegal for any purpose, even extraction operations) and the defectors—while disassociating herself from the more conspiratorial plot hinted at by Matthews. But she didn't take that way out. Instead, she maintained that "this particular weapon [the nerve gas] was used offensively on a target village base camp in which there were enemy present and there appeared to be American defectors as well in this camp." Still later, given another chance to disconnect the use of nerve gas from the defectors as the target, Oliver's verbatim reply as reproduced in the CNBC transcript of the program was: "That—what was said—it was used pr—preemptively, offensively on a village in which Americans went in as—and were targeting these defectors, but we have no way to know for sure whether it meant."

From Oliver's exchanges with Matthews (Smith was silent for most of the program), we can see that Oliver was drawn to the story's conspiratorial nerve-gas-against-Americans subtext. If she had not wholeheartedly bought into the theory of a larger plot, she was nevertheless willing to help Matthews suggest just such a possibility to his conservative audience.[3]

Matthews's spin on the CNN Tailwind story had political and normative implications, and both kinds abetted the conspiratorial agenda of the far right. His substitution of the generic term "Americans" for defectors was, of course, an identity-less blank space that could be filled in by anyone's fancy (or fear). We're all Americans, so what was

Matthews implying about the logic of the supposed gassing? That just being an American was enough to warrant a gas attack by the government? The lack of specificity in Matthews's framing was useful for the purposes of spreading right-wing paranoia about government conspiracies, but he was actually pointing his viewers toward the far right. Without actually saying so, the mischievous Matthews was telling his audience that the *real* question here was whether or not POWs had been gassed by their own government.

By his reframing of the story, the defectors, hardly embraceable figures to a wide band of television viewers, became just that, "good guys," Americans who, like the POWs, had been betrayed by their own government. For some viewers, Matthews's reiteration of the nerve-gas-against-Americans phrase probably had the effect of simply displacing the defectors from the story altogether; those who had tuned in to *Hardball* that night without any prior exposure to the story, for example, were likely to have "heard" a story about Americans gassed by their own government. Even viewers who were conscious of the discrepancy between the terms "defectors" and "Americans" may have tended to subsume the former into the more inclusive category "Americans," thereby erasing the image of defectors and the need to think about how to think about them.

Something still more interesting was probably going on in the minds of the far-right-wing members of Matthews's audience, however. For them, the implicit rehabilitation of the defectors to the status of Americans, even *heroic* Americans, if their equivalence to POWs could be established, was a bold stroke, and one seemingly incongruent with their own views. A defector, after all, would be the patriots' Antichrist, the embodiment of national betrayal. But the meaning of defection is relative; whether it's good or bad depends on what the defectors are defecting from. If the government has acted in an un-American fashion, might not defection be virtuous? The legacy of the far right's ambiguous relationship to the war in Vietnam left the door open for it to accept defectors as victims of the country's misbegotten wartime policies.

During the 1960s, far-right organizations like the John Birch Society supported the war in principle, but opposed the way the government conducted it. According to the Birch Society, communists in government, referred to as "insiders" by the society, were prosecuting the war but intentionally preventing the military from pursuing a winning strategy. The result was that chaos reigned in the streets of America, world opinion was turned against the country, and Ho Chi Minh was able to exploit anti-American sentiment that the war produced in Vietnam. So, for the Birchers, a war that was supposedly an *anti*-communist endeavor was actually furthering the interests of international communism. It is not entirely surprising then that those who could twist a war *against* communism into a war *for* communists could thirty years later find a way to remember defectors as victims of political conspiracy if not, indeed, loyalists in their own cause.

There was one other feature to the Chris Matthews show that is a dead giveaway to the idea that Matthews recognized the right-wing narrative contained in the Tailwind story. The headline for the *Hardball* edition on which Oliver and Smith appeared announced that Arnaud de Borchgrave, identified as a "former foreign correspondent," would also be on the program. De Borchgrave's name would have elicited a puzzled "Who's that?" from most television viewers. But Matthews was gambling that enough of his conservative audience would know who de Borchgrave was and be attracted to the program by his name.

De Borchgrave's credentials as a figure on the hard right are in order. In 1980, after resigning from *Newsweek* where he had been a foreign correspondent, de Borchgrave coauthored a best-selling novel, *The Spike*, about Soviet influence in the U.S. media. In 1985 he was appointed editor in chief of the *Washington Times*, a newspaper owned by the Reverend Sun Myung Moon's Unification Church, popularly known in the United States as "the Moonies." De Borchgrave's ascension to the leadership of the *Times* was applauded by conservatives who had rallied to the paper when it was founded in 1982, but professional journalists had another view.[4] Lars-Erik Nelson, Washington bureau chief of the *New York Daily News,* remarked to the *Washington Post* that de Borchgrave was talented but seemed "to have gotten hung up on a philosophy that the KGB, the Soviet secret police, has become a dominant influence in American journalism through disinformation or suppression of vast numbers of stories about a communist plot."[5]

De Borchgrave's role as editor of the *Washington Times* connected him to other Moon-backed organizations such as the reactionary Confederation of Associations for the Unity of the Societies of America (CAUSA), which was a front for Moon within the militant World Anti-Communist League, an organization headed by John Singlaub, one of Oliver's sources for the Tailwind story.[6] De Borchgrave was also a member of the U.S. Global Strategy Council, created by former CIA deputy director Ray Cline to advise the Reagan administration on foreign policy, and he was a senior associate of Cline's at the Georgetown Center for Strategic and International Studies.[7]

Charges that the "Moonie" organization controlled the content of the *Washington Times* dogged de Borchgrave throughout his tenure at the paper. In 1987, *Times* editorial-page editor Michael Bonafield and four staff members resigned in protest of de Borchgrave's fealty to the Moonies and his defense of the South Korean government's repressive political practices. In 1988 members of the prestigious National Press Club protested the candidacy of Peter Holmes, a *Times* editor, for the presidency of the club, citing the *Times*'s affiliation with "the evangelical mission of the Rev. Sun Myung Moon." De Borchgrave resigned the editorship of the *Times* in 1991 but stayed on as a writer. In 1998 he became CEO of the all-but-defunct United Press International and, a year after that, joined NewsMax.com, a right-wing Internet organization.[8]

April Oliver: Did She "Read" the Subtext?

On the *Hardball* show with Oliver and Smith, de Borchgrave spoke only once, at the very end of the program, so his role there seems to have been purely symbolic, perhaps Matthews's way of signaling to right-wing America that "Hey, this story's for you." But Matthews's recognition of where the story's market lay doesn't mean that Oliver too was fully cognizant of what others might read in it. If, after the fact, she recognized but did not disassociate herself from the conspiratorial narrative that Matthews amplified, it doesn't necessarily mean that she constructed the show's subtext intentionally.[9]

In her behalf, then, one could offer the suggestion that during the months of preparation for *Valley of Death* April Oliver did not recognize the dubious conspiratorial narrative embedded in the story. It is the nature of subtexts, after all, that their content is hidden, sometimes making the storytellers themselves the unwitting purveyors, even victims, of their latent meaning. Is it possible that Oliver was bushwhacked by her own innocence? Not exactly.

Unbeknownst to viewers who saw *Valley of Death,* Oliver had already been criticized for a piece about SOG that she had produced for CNN nine months earlier. On September 14, 1997, CNN's *Impact* show had used interviews done by Oliver with SOG veterans to relate what moderator Bernard Shaw called "the untold story of U.S. soldiers used as bait, chemical agents used, though banned by international protocol, and American troops killed, possibly by U.S. air strikes."

The program had a lurid quality to it. One of the SOG vets, John Plaster, although well into his retirement years, was shown on camera in black fatigues and a black beret adorned with an ominous but odd-looking X-shaped patch.[10] Ed Wolcoff, another former SOG member, shown with a black patch over one eye, was said by the narrator to have carried a meat cleaver on his missions. Later he tells the camera, "The kind of things you see on the screen that Schwartzenegger might do or Sylvester Stallone might do, I actually got to do. It was the greatest adventure of my life." Wolcoff also recalled that B-52 strikes would be ordered to cover areas where missing Americans were last seen. According to him, "[U.S. leaders] didn't want the Americans to be captured for political purposes and then paraded in front of news cameras." Former SOG commander John Singlaub's answers to follow-up questions seem to confirm Wolcoff's suggestion that the U.S. military may have itself intentionally killed POWs. Narrator Peter Arnett said that SOG had been issued experimental weaponry that included darts with chemical agents, and Singlaub told of having requested that an "incapacitating agent" be made available to SOG.

Viewed in retrospect, the September 1997 *Impact* show pretty clearly belies Oliver's innocence. A meat cleaver? A uniform and beret that were more costume than military-issue gear? Poison darts? Why, as editor, would she load these images into the program except for their emotional appeal? And what emotions was she appealing to? By using Ed Wolcoff's words invoking Hollywood's Ramboesque portrayals of the war, Oliver was obviously targeting an audience familiar with filmic fiction, while the program's suggestion that soldiers missing in action may have been killed for political purposes was certainly expected to resonate with Americans drawn to the mythology surrounding POWs and MIAs.

Here, then, was a tabloid-quality prototype for Oliver's *Valley of Death*, with rough-hewn versions of the later story's twin pillars: the use of nerve gas and the deployment of military firepower against other Americans. The September broadcast did not receive the criticism that *Valley of Death* did, perhaps because it had not received the prebroadcast ballyhoo that CNN gave the Tailwind story. But privately, Oliver was clearly warned that she was heading down the wrong path.

That warning came in letters from Alfred H. Paddock, Jr., a retired army colonel and military historian. Paddock was a SOG veteran and a specialist in psychological operations who had first met Oliver over lunch on May 21, 1997. They talked about her research for the story on SOG that would air in September. The day following that meeting, Paddock wrote to Oliver wishing her "good luck" with her project but cautioning her to "do your homework well and don't rely on just one or two veterans' versions of the 'truth' to tell your story or to draw your conclusions."[11]

On September 16, 1997, two days after the SOG story aired, Paddock wrote to Oliver. "Overall," he said, "I thought that the program focused on sensationalism rather than a thoughtful, balanced examination of MACSOG's role." He called the inference that U.S. POWs may have been victims of B-52 strikes "irresponsible journalism" and chastised her for the reference to a meat cleaver being used for a weapon and for allowing Plaster to pose in black fatigues. The primary mission of SOG teams, he emphasized, had been reconnaissance, not "direct action," as the image Oliver had constructed for CNN viewers suggested.

In an undated response, Oliver said she had adequate confirmation of the information aired and thanked Paddock for his interest. On September 29, Paddock wrote again, complaining that Oliver was ignoring his criticism. "Your show," he said, "just perpetuated the myth that Special Forces is a commando or Ranger-type 'warrior' organization, when in fact their capabilities and roles are much more flexible and sophisticated." Paddock acknowledged that there are "legitimate issues about MACSOG activities that warrant scrutiny . . . but gas and B-52s???" He accused Oliver of "hyping" those issues and ended the letter saying CNN (and Oliver) seemed to be more interested in "titillating than educating."

Paddock's letters are valuable because they prove that Oliver had her reality check while *Valley of Death* was still in production. She was trafficking in the symbolism of legends and myths, and Paddock called her on it. Paddock even anticipated Oliver's metamyth of the government's betrayal of its own POWs. Oliver had grounded her government-bombs-its-own narrative by having John Plaster tell about his friend Pete Wilson, also known as "Fat Albert." On one mission, Fat Albert had stayed behind to help a wounded team member. Choking back his tears, Plaster tells the camera, "The last thing ever heard was his voice on his emergency radio calling Mayday." Peter Arnett takes the sobbing Plaster off the hook, reminding us that, "[because] SOG members [were] not to be captured *alive* by the enemy, questions *still linger* about Fat Albert's ultimate fate." In other words, Fat Albert had probably been bombed to smithereens by the U.S. Air Force. In his September 16 letter, Paddock told Oliver that her use of the Fat Albert story in this way struck him, an "old psywarrior," as "a good propaganda technique."

Words tell only part of a story; *how* those words are spoken tell the rest. In the epigraph, Peter Arnett asks who were the defectors who were killed by Operation Tailwind. The obvious answer is, "Well, they were just defectors." But the intonation of his voice suggested a different answer. By altering his pitch, he put emphasis on the words *who were* as if to imply that those killed really weren't defectors. Likewise, his intoned phrase "questions *still linger*" about Fat Albert's death suggest to us that the commonsense answer—he was killed by the enemy—is not the right one.

On one level, Oliver and Arnett were employing a simple propagandistic device typically used by the political right, which is to put questions in people's minds that unsettle them, and then offer misleading answers to the bogus questions. But Oliver and Arnett were playing at a still deeper level of deception, because while their own reportage did not satisfactorily answer the question of whether *anyone* had been killed, they proceeded to raise questions about who the dead were, how they had died, and who had killed them. It was this level, hidden beneath their own story, that constituted the true subtext of *Valley of Death*.

THE SEDUCTIVE SUBTEXT OF *VALLEY OF DEATH*

The hidden appeal of *Valley of Death* was made clear to me while visiting with a graduating college senior and her family. The parents wanted to know what I would be doing during the summer; when I said I was writing a book, they wanted to know what it was about. I began by asking if they remembered the story that CNN aired in 1998 about the U.S. military using nerve gas to subdue some GIs who had defected and gone to Laos to fight on the North Vietnamese side. They did, so I continued, saying that my book asked two questions: where did this story come from, and who believed it? I explained that I thought the story came from popular culture and male imaginations and that it had been nourished in fundamentalist Christian institutions. At that point, the family was listening attentively but showing no sign of anticipating where my analysis was headed.

I then said that the attraction of the story seemed to be in its conspiratorial subtext that implied that the supposed defectors were actually POWs who the U.S. government did not want to come home. Before all the words of that last sentence were out of my mouth, the parents, their graduating daughter, and her younger sister were shaking their heads in recognition of what I was referring to. They began talking as I finished the sentence, declaring not just that they could understand how someone could believe the story, but that its subliminal dimension sounded right to them. There was a hasty exchange of comments and affirmative nods between them indicating that they believed the subtext could be true; a mention by the mother that "it's like in *Captains and Kings*," a novel by Taylor Caldwell that they all seemed to have read, produced confirmation of my perception that they too felt drawn to the story of political intrigue that lay beneath the surface of the story broadcast by CNN.

It was an uncomfortable moment for me because my social instincts tell me that sensible people are usually repelled by conspiracy stories. The typical response to my suggestion that CNN's producers had actually spun a yarn about a government cabal to kill Americans would have been to scoff at their stupidity. All the more so, I thought, because my representation of the issues (my word choices, voice inflection, body language, et al.) should have made clear that *I* thought the CNN Tailwind production was pretty implausible. So much for my instincts. The reality, I knew then, was that, even in the face of a discrediting presentation of the story's meaning (like I thought I had just given), the story itself was so compelling that very reasonable, middle-of-the-road people were drawn to it. The answer to one of the questions that was motivating my research—who would believe this story?—was that just about anyone from the American mainstream could be a believer. The question of *why* the story was so appealing now loomed all the more important.

Recognition of the preconditioning provided by *Captains and Kings* for this family reinforced my initial hunch that popular culture had paved the way for tales of the Tailwind type. But literature and film are also reflections of their times; *Captains and Kings*, for example, is about the Kennedy assassination in 1963, and the conspiracy theories it spawned. The "times" themselves are, of course, implicated in their own subsequent representations, and they are accomplices to the formation of worldviews that are receptive to certain kinds of information as probable truth.

The extraordinary nature of the war in Vietnam and the volatility of domestic politics during the 1960s and 1970s opened up the possibility that things that would be unbelievable if said to have happened in another time could be accepted as believable when placed in the context of the Vietnam era. The next three chapters—on the grist that the war itself provided, the popular culture of the postwar period, and the identification of the religious themes that are encoded in *Valley of Death*—provide an account of how a story like this might have started, and why some people believed it.

4

LIES AND LEGENDS, MEN AND REMEMBERED METTLE

The most common single response I get when telling people about my interest in *Valley of Death* is: "I'm surprised *you* don't believe it. After all, a lot of weird stuff happened in Vietnam, and the government lied about all of it." People sometimes continue with their own recollections about chemical defoliants having been used in the war and reports that some GIs refused orders to fight, fled their units, and were sheltered by friendly Vietnamese people. One woman who had protested the war expressed exasperation at my thesis, saying, "Hey, I was gassed by the government in the 1960s so why wouldn't they have used nerve gas in Vietnam?"[1]

The "why not?" question is table-turning rhetoric that effectively puts the myth buster on the defensive. Instead of asking for a more convincing account of what *did* happen, the reversal of inquiry asks the critic for proof that the story did *not* happen as reported. April Oliver resorted to the device more than once when pinned down in public about the logic of the connections she was making between events. As it turns out, the "why not?" question is not so easy to answer.

To begin with, the government did lie throughout the war, making the fact that the Pentagon now denies the validity of the *Valley of Death* somewhat pointless. It is also true that the U.S. military used the chemical defoliant Agent Orange in Vietnam (and was less than forthcoming about it), and that rumors of nerve-gas use circulated in the U.S. press as far back as 1965. The large number of U.S. deserters in Vietnam likewise fed speculation that some GIs were cavorting with the enemy. Finally, the eyewitness accounts of the men of Tailwind are powerful testimony to the truth of what the CNN producers put on the air.

What can be shown, however, is that each of these would-be bases for *Valley of Death* has a qualified relationship to the story that was produced. Although there are varying amounts of truth in each of them, they amount to little more than suggestive lures for the tale of Tailwind told by April Oliver.

A LITANY OF LIES

Valley of Death's metanarrative, the thread that is common to all its main components, is that the U.S. government lied to the people about the war. That part of the story is so believable because, in fact, the government did lie about everything that was important to the conduct of the war.

The lying began when the French departed Indochina after their defeat at Dien Bien Phu in 1954. The settlement that ended the French war, reached in negotiations at Geneva, called for elections to decide who would govern Vietnam. Until the elections could be held in July 1956, the Vietnamese military forces who had fought on the side of the French were grouped below the seventeenth parallel, and those who fought for Vietnamese independence as the Viet Minh gathered north of the line. When it became apparent that communists running for office as part of the Viet Minh faction would win the elections, the U.S.

government blocked the elections. When fighting resumed, the United States claimed that North Vietnam was invading a sovereign South Vietnam and justified U.S. military support for the South on that basis. The image of the North as a foreign aggressor was a lie constructed to cover the Washington's own aggression and was a mainstay of U.S. government propaganda throughout the war period.

The biggest lie of the war was probably the one told about the so-called Tonkin Gulf incident. To justify the first bombing strikes against the North and the sending of ground troops into the South, the U.S. government claimed that North Vietnam attacked the American destroyer *Maddox* on August 4, 1964. In fact, U.S.-backed commando raids on the coastline of North Vietnam (see chapter 2) had provoked the North to respond defensively. In the days before August 4, the *Maddox* had been playing cat and mouse with North Vietnamese gunboats, and gunfire between the parties had been exchanged. But there had been no attack on August 4. President Lyndon Johnson, nevertheless, used the phantom incident to escalate the war and leverage approval for his action from Congress through passage of what came to be called the Gulf of Tonkin Resolution. With this contrivance, the U.S. war in Vietnam began in earnest.

Implicit in the lies that got us into the war was a third lie about the amount of support our troops could expect from the Vietnamese people. In a war portrayed as North Vietnamese communist aggression against the South, the people of South Vietnam were understood by Americans as the victims who welcomed U.S. intervention on their behalf. In that script, the people of the North were hostages of communist tyranny who awaited liberation by the freedom fighters from the South and their American allies. The reality was that all but the landlords and comprador bourgeoisie, and the government bureaucracy they propped up with money and arms from the United States, sided with the communist-led movement for national independence. As a result, U.S. troops faced not only an armed resistance movement in the South, backed by the force of North Vietnamese regulars, but a civilian population that was hostile to its very presence.

The U.S. military mission to Vietnam was, in other words, doomed from the outset. But that's not what the American people were told. In one of the signature phrases of the war, Americans were reassured at various turning points that there was "light at the end of the tunnel," that victory over communism in Southeast Asia was just around the corner. To support their optimistic spin, political and military leaders offered one-sided body counts that showed we were winning all the battles. The body counts were lies too, reflections of U.S. commanders' needs to document the mettle of their troops and justify their own existence in the field. The kill ratio was indeed disproportionate (about thirty Vietnamese to one GI), but many of the "enemy" were civilians, a fact that only hardened the resolve of the populace and added to the certainty that we would lose. A secret collection of Pentagon papers published by the *New York Times* in 1971 revealed that not only had the war been unwinnable since its start but that U.S. officials acknowledged that fact to themselves while covering it up to deceive the American people. They had lied.

There were many lies about the conduct of the war. Some of those involved lies about the kind of weapons being used—the use of both herbicides and cluster bombs were denied at one point or another—and lies about where U.S. troops were operating. Laos and Cambodia, for example, were both called "denied areas" by U.S. officials, which meant not that operations there were forbidden but that the government was unwilling to admit that it was actually conducting operations "over the fence" in those countries.

There were many lies about the treatment of prisoners, both ours and theirs. In order to prolong the war, the Nixon administration regularly lied about what it knew about the number of POWs held by the Vietnamese and how they were being treated. In his book *M.I.A., or Myth-making in America*, H. Bruce Franklin recalls that Washington helped create the myth that American POWs were being held long after the war was over by publicly alleging that the Vietnamese held more prisoners than they had. When the Vietnamese would report POW counts lower than U.S. claims, the government would say the Vietnamese were lying—when in fact it was U.S. leaders who were lying. They also lied about the treatment of prisoners. In *Traveling to Vietnam*, a history of the liaison work that U.S. peace activists carried on with North Vietnam during the war, Mary Hershberger portrays the North's treatment of American POWs as far more humane than the U.S. government ever acknowledged publicly. American leaders, on the other hand, secretly prevented the ready passage of mail between POWs and their families, using the U.S. Postal Service to hold letters for up to two years after Hanoi had allowed them to leave. When U.S. veterans began testifying about the treatment they and their South Vietnamese allies had dished out to captured Viet Cong and NVA troops, it became clear that the U.S. government had lied about that too.

These were major lies, and each had variations to fit the time and occasion. It was not uncommon, for example, for the United States to dispatch bombing missions or covert operations from locations far outside the Southeast Asian theater using troops who were, on paper, stationed in Germany, Korea, or Omaha, Nebraska, and then deny that these men had ever been in (or over) Vietnam (or Laos or Cambodia). When those soldiers were shot down or captured, the government had to lie to their families about the circumstances of their disappearances—lies that fed the cynicism of the American people about the war and their government.

GAS FOR GRIST

The widespread distrust of government was one of the legacies left by the war in Vietnam. The memory that the government had lied, more or less unremittingly during the ten years of the war, preconditioned many Americans to believe that just about anything the government denied was probably true. A story like *Valley of Death*, moreover, had all the suspect categories: covert operations in a denied area (Laos), an exotic and illegal weapon (sarin), betrayals (running in two directions, at least), and, of course, government cover-up of all of the above (which in some minds makes all of them *true*).

Not all that made *Valley of Death* sound true was of such ephemeral nature, however. It is often said that myths are made of things that really did happen and resemble the story later told as a myth. In that sense, myths can be partially understood to be exaggerations of actual historical events; the figures in myths are often demonized or lionized facsimiles of real-life people. The presence of sarin nerve gas in *Valley of Death* probably falls into the category of something the plausibility of which is based on its close approximation to something that actually happened. As it turns out, though, the approximation is not close enough.

The part about sarin in *Valley of Death* would maybe have been more believable had there never been previous allegations of "gas warfare" in Vietnam. But there had been—sort of. In a December 1964 operation bearing similarities to Operation Tailwind, U.S. forces used something described as "nausea gas" in an attempt to free four U.S. prisoners of the National Liberation Front. The plan was to "incapacitate everyone, prisoners and captors alike, then send in a masked Special Forces Unit to rescue the Americans." The mission failed because the gas was sprayed from helicopters and didn't penetrate the dense foliage.[2]

The story is interesting in several ways. First, its details are close enough to those of Tailwind to confirm that in its broad outlines (*sans* defectors and sarin), operations like the one remembered by some Tailwind veterans probably happened. Second, the story provides support for the idea that gas was used for tactical purposes in Vietnam, not just for crowd control by civilian police. But the differences are more important. The gas is not described as *nerve* gas, much less sarin, and news reports on the incident emphasized that the gas was *non*-lethal. The failure of the operation is also important. Critics of *Valley of Death* have said that its claim of gas use made no sense because, in that situation, gas of just about any type would be tactically ineffective—something the military had apparently learned from experience.

There were other reports of gas use in the early months of 1965. One was an attempt to flush NLF guerillas out of tunnels using gas; another was to free some civilians hostages from guerilla fighters. The gas was ineffective in both cases. In late March, Associated Press photographer Horst Fass stumbled across a South Vietnamese unit preparing to deploy gas. The operation was called off, but Fass relayed what he had seen to reporter Peter Arnett, and the AP was soon reporting that "U.S. and Vietnamese military forces are experimenting with nonlethal gas warfare in South Vietnam." While the AP's use of the phrase "gas warfare" is clearly a tantalizing basis for belief thirty years later that *nerve* gas might have been used, the qualification that it was a nonlethal substance makes it just as clear that Horst's story and the others could have been grist, but nothing more, for the story produced by April Oliver.[3]

The oddest thing about the 1964–65 stories in the *Valley of Death* fiasco is that they played no apparent role. April Oliver's work would have had far more credibility if she had begun her investigation with that cluster of stories and then worked outward from them. Indeed, her CNN colleague Peter Arnett, the on-air narrator of *Valley of Death*, having been a figure in the original AP report from Saigon, makes one wonder why Oliver and her team shied away from investigating the 1964–65 stories. Could it be that Oliver and Arnett knew that there was nothing more to them than was reported at that time and opted instead for a story cut from the whole cloth of veteran memories and their own imaginations?[4]

There are, of course, lingering questions about the nature of the gases used in Vietnam.[5] Gases of the Vietnam War era could be divided into "disabling" gases and "lethal" gases. In the first category were the tear gases known as CN and CS, vomiting gas (or DM), psychochemical gas that could cause hallucinations, and so-called knockout gases that could produce temporary paralysis. In the second category were nerve gases that kill quickly through inhalation or touch, blood gases that enter the blood stream and paralyze the central nervous system, blister gases (of World War I vintage) that are absorbed through the skin, and choking gases that cause inflammation of the lungs. None of the gases was called sarin in the press, although the term may have been used in the technical literature.[6]

An argument can be made that *any* war gas is a nerve gas. The tearing and stinging effects of CS, for example, result from the involvement of nerves carrying sensations from the skin and eyes to the brain and returning the brain's response to the appropriate organs. Also, surely the gases referred to as psychochemical or knockout agents would be considered nerve gases in the sense that they contain chemicals that affect the nervous system. But that is not what is meant by the conventional use of the term "nerve gas," nor did the CNN crew that produced *Valley of Death* mean it that way. Oliver, Arnett, and the other narrators of the program repeatedly used the terms "lethal," "nerve gas," and "sarin" in combinations that left no doubt that they meant exactly what nerve gas is usually understood to mean.[7]

DESERTERS—BUT NOT DEFECTORS

The defectors in *Valley of Death* are simultaneously the most plausible and implausible figures in the story. By 1969 discipline was a major problem in the U.S. military. Almost every military training facility in the United States had an organized group of GIs who actively resisted authority and acted as a liaison to the antiwar movement at large. Coffeehouses opened near the bases by war protesters provided friendly spaces where dissident soldiers could meet to plan actions against the brass, produce radical newspapers, and get advice on their legal rights.

When the military tried to crack down on the GI movement, the result was outright rebellion that sometimes turned violent. During 1968 and 1969 rebellions led by antiwar troops swept through military lockups at the Presidio, California; Fort Dix, New Jersey; Fort Bragg, North Carolina; Fort Leavenworth, Kansas; Quantico Marine Corps Base, Virginia; and Fort Hood, Texas. One of the largest and most violent occurred at Travis Air Force Base, California, in May 1971, when five hundred rioting soldiers burned the bachelor officers' quarters to the ground.[8]

Enlisted men fighting their own officers—making war on the war leaders, in a sense—is itself a kind of defection and, in any case, certainly more than enough foundation for the construction of a thirty-year-old memory about GIs going over to the enemy. When coupled with stories of absenteeism, the images of defection become even more vivid. In his book *Winter Soldiers,* about GI and veteran dissent during the war, Richard Moser writes, "By 1967 absent without leave (AWOL) and desertion rates began to climb precipitously. Army AWOL rates climbed from 57.2 per thousand in 1966 to 78 per thousand in 1967 while desertion grew from 14.9 to 70 per thousand between 1966 and 1971, the highest in modern history."[9]

Data on the number of AWOLs in Vietnam itself are hard to come by, but by 1969 the problem was so serious that U.S. authorities would periodically issue new military payment certificates, scrip that GIs used for purchases on the local economy, in order to render the MPCs held by AWOLs valueless and thus force them out of hiding and back to their units. A large number of soldiers walked away from their units just to spend an unauthorized weekend with a Vietnamese girlfriend, but others left more permanently to live underground in Saigon or some other large city. Some soldiers failed to return to Vietnam following out-of-country rest and recreation or trips home for family reasons. Technically, AWOLs were classified as desertion cases after thirty days, but the army was reluctant to reclassify long-term AWOLs for public relations reasons.[10]

The AWOL and desertion problem in Vietnam was greater than in either World War II or Korea but not strikingly so. The controversy surrounding the war, however, and the high level of overt GI resistance to it politicized the issue of desertion, fueling speculation that some of the "missing" were actually defectors. The nature of the war, moreover, encouraged suspicion about the loyalties of friends and enemies on all sides. U.S. military leaders were virtually paranoid about their Vietnamese allies, always suspecting that someone they trusted today would defect to the enemy tomorrow—or that a recent defector from the other side was actually a double agent. Undoubtedly, many of the long-term deserters were, like Nick in *The Deer Hunter*, defectors in a cultural and political sense. Yet evidence that more than a couple GIs actually took up arms against their former comrades is almost nonexistent.[11]

Concern for the welfare of missing personnel understandably led men in Vietnam to speculate on the circumstances under which they disappeared and why they remained unaccounted for. Best-selling author Nelson Demille was an infantry officer in Vietnam in 1968. At the Phu Bai air base, he says, a pilot told him that pilots had been seen bailing out but had never shown up on the POW lists because they were being traded by Hanoi to the Soviets for surface-to-air missiles. Demille claims the pilot then told him, "The Red Air Force is using these guys to train their pilots in American tactics." Demille comments, "It made sense."[12]

That such rumors "made sense" means they cannot be discounted as playing parts in stimulating the imaginations that created *Valley of Death* thirty-three years later. In fact, Demille went on to pen the 1988 political mystery *Charm School*, which has all the ingredients of the story April Oliver fed to CNN.

THE LEGEND OF THE LOST COMMAND

The ambiguous identity of the defectors is what gave *Valley of Death* its intrigue. Were they *really* defectors, or were they POWs? The possibility that they were POWs, of course, went to the inner core of conspiracist beliefs that the U.S. government had not only abandoned POWs in Southeast Asia but had actually assassinated them. It is the ambiguity per se in the defector/POW identity issue, however, that lends the story its mytho-poetic quality and makes it appealing even to less political listeners. Interpretations of how similar stories have functioned in other times and places point to the likelihood that the power of myth is at work in CNN's version of Operation Tailwind.

Most references to stories about missing soldiers seem to come from World War I. This is no surprise, because the war took such a terrible human toll and was fought in ways that were so graphically bloody that escape into the realm of the *un*known was probably necessary emotional relief from the terror and trauma of the war's reality. As the first war of the modern era, moreover, World War I combined technologies of the past and future, pitting horse-drawn equipment against airplanes, trench warfare against poison gas, and foot soldiers armed with bayonets against artillery. Those ambiguities in the identity of the *kind* of war it was made it hard for soldiers and civilians alike to get their minds around what it really meant. Also, the war was very controversial. There was large-scale opposition to it in the United States, where many labor and social reform groups openly resisted U.S. involvement. Thousands of dissenters were to be arrested and deported in the Palmer Raids that followed the war.

Literary references to missing soldiers most commonly evoke the legend of "The Lost Battalion," a story that was born in the battle of the Argonne Forest in 1918. Between October 2 and 7, the First Battalion of the 308th Infantry Regiment, commanded by Maj. Charles W. Whittlesey, lost contact with its supporting units. In the absence of communication from Whittlesey's men, speculation began about what had happened to them. Perhaps they were lost or had been wiped out by the Germans. On September 8, contact with the unit was restored, and eventually a more or less official version of the event evolved, explaining that the battalion had been cut off by the enemy. But when Whittlesey disappeared from an ocean liner three years after the war, speculation resumed that in fact the battalion had gotten lost due to poor leadership by the major and that he had committed suicide out of guilt.

An interesting subplot of the legend is that on October 7, Pvt. Lowell R. Hollingshead and some others left the "lost" battalion and ended up in German hands. In his written report for the day, Whittlesey reported the men AWOL and according to Arch Whitehouse in *Heroes and Legends of World War I*, other versions of the story confirm that the men left without permission. Did they just desert and end up captured, or did they intentionally go out looking for a chance to surrender or even defect? Whatever the case, all of them were declared to have been killed except for Hollingshead who later said he had been interrogated for information about his unit and then befriended by a German lieutenant named Prinz who, according to Hollingshead's account, claimed to have formerly lived in Seattle. According to Hollingshead, the German commanding officer typed a letter for the private to carry back to Whittlesey demanding that the U.S. unit surrender. The letter also praised Hollingshead as "an honorable man." In a volume later published as *History and Rhymes of the Lost Battalion* by a member of the unit, L. C. McCollum, Hollingshead claimed that the group he left with had been dispatched by Whittlesey as part of an effort to break out of the trap the Germans had them in. Whittlesey was rewarded with a Medal of Honor after the war, while Hollingshead got nothing—which, coupled with Whittlesey's disappearance through possible suicide, was to keep alive the questions about what had really happened during those early days of October 1918 when First Battalion was "lost" in the woods of the Argonne.

No-Man's-Land

The story of the Lost Battalion was carried in the *New York Times* for several days in October 1918 and, according to Whitehouse, has since been told by scores of writers.[13] Hollingshead's role in the story is typical of the deserter stories that proliferated during World War I, many with mythical elements. Together, those stories constitute what Paul Fussell, in *The Great War and Modern Memory*, calls the "finest legend" of the war.

> The rumor was that somewhere between the lines, a battalion-sized group of half-crazed deserters from all the armies, friend and enemy alike, harbored underground in abandoned trenches and dugouts and caves, living in amity and emerging at night to pillage corpses and gather food and drink. This horde of wild men lived underground for years and finally grew so large and rapacious and unredeemable that it had to be exterminated.[14]

Stories like these functioned, according the Fussell, to project the tellers' fantasies of rebellion against authority and military order onto fictional others. The stories also convey the point that soldiers everywhere, despite the uniform they wear, have a common enemy in the war. The figures in the stories are liminal characters who bridge life and death and cross the boundaries of wartime conventions and national loyalties. They are loyal to something larger than Nation, something that finds its expression in "no-man's-land," the space between the trench lines, ground unidentified with any flag.

Some of the stories have ghostlike figures who travel behind enemy lines to inquire of frightened soldiers about their units. Later, someone remembers that the apparition wore a bit of odd clothing—a cap or collar that did not fit the uniform—and that on the same night men were killed in an unexplained manner. The truth is now known: the mysterious man was actually a spy. Fussell speculates that such stories help preserve notions of national and racial superiority by confirming that the enemy can win only with the complicity of our own naïvete or treason.

That Vietnam would spawn rumors and legends resembling those of World War I is not a surprise. Like the Great War, the Vietnam War was set in a transitional period of history. Sometimes called the first postmodern war, it pitted the advanced technology of the mid-twentieth century—fighter-bombers, napalm, electronic communications—against premodern technology and guerilla warfare tactics. Vietnam, being in some ways as incomprehensible to Americans in 1970 as World War I was in 1917, produced an unprecedented level of protest that challenged the certainties of what was good and bad, right and wrong, and the conventional meanings of loyalty.

Nor is it a surprise that legendlike stories with components matching those of World War I would circulate in the postwar period. Helicopters, at least as awe inspiring to civilian Americans in the Vietnam era as long-range artillery was a half-century earlier, are staples in Vietnam War lore. Gas, needless to say, held its mystique across the decades. Both wars had their liminal characters in deserters and, à la *Valley of Death*, the defectors. Finally, both wars had their liminal space, their "no-man's-land," which became the blank slate on which postwar imaginations could project the war's unsettled sentiments.

LAOS: THIS LEGEND'S NO-MAN'S-LAND

I smiled when I heard CNN's report about nerve gas being used against defectors in Laos. Laos, of course. Laos, I thought at the time, works in this story the way San Francisco works in the stories about spat-upon veterans. For most Americans, the San Francisco of the 1960s is a land of exotica, a place in the long ago and far away where college kids rioted on a daily basis, hippies lived on dope, and topless women roamed the bars of North Beach. Told that GIs returning from

Vietnam were regularly spat on as they passed through the San Francisco airport, many Americans will nod as if to say, "San Francisco, I can believe it." San Francisco is the cliché. Want to say something weird happened? Saying it happened in San Francisco will make the story more believable for folks beyond the Bay Area.[15]

Laos works the same way—only better—for war stories. Given that the press speculated about illegal gas (not sarin, however) being used as far back as 1964 and that hundreds, if not thousands, of U.S. deserters lived underground in Saigon by the end of the war, why did April Oliver not begin her investigation with those historically grounded reports? The answer has to be that Laos works better for storytelling purposes. Just as San Francisco lends the stories of spat-upon veterans a cultural cachet that St. Louis wouldn't, Laos evokes a set of emotions and images that "work" for *Valley of Death*'s subtext in ways that Saigon would not. It's there, in other words, not for its contribution to historical accuracy but as a storytelling device.

As I became acquainted with the legends and myths of war, I recognized that Laos was the Vietnam War's no-man's-land. It was officially off limits to the United States and North Vietnam, and both sides denied conducting activities there. But both sides did go there—which created a special identity for Laos and the soldiers who ventured into it. Like the legendary World War I deserters who supposedly shucked their commitments to the homeland and moved onto ground between the warring nations, the soldiers who moved along and around the Ho Chi Minh Trail in Laos had a kind of transcendent identity that simultaneously defied officialdom and the rules of conventional warfare and embraced the highest ideals of patriotism. Whatever sensibilities in the Western subconscious are touched by legends like the no-man's-land of World War I, they are also touched by characters like Captain Willard, who plunges into the Cambodian wilderness in search of the renegade Colonel Kurtz in Francis Ford Coppola's 1978 film *Apocalypse Now*. (Who, after all, could read Fussell's reference to a "battalion-sized group of half-crazed deserters" and not think of the private army assembled by Kurtz?) The ease with which the figures and story lines from World War I legends translate into the images we've used to represent the war in Vietnam suggests the presence of universal sentiments that were agitated by the war and never settled in the years that followed.

Go West, Young Man—to Laos

The deepest appeal of Laos, however, has to do with the way it fits into the foundational myth of the United States as a nation of people always moving, seeking, unable to resist the temptations of the unknown or the challenges of conquest. It is the unknown that holds particular allure for people and nothing is more unknown than the future. For Americans, the future has always had a directional representation— westward. Expansion to the west during the eighteenth and nineteenth centuries responded to a missionary imperative, as the nation sought to tame the wilderness, Christianize its inhabitants, and render its natural resources into saleable commodities. The West meant unforeseen risks and unimagined possibilities, adventure and opportunity. The future belonged to those who dared to venture into the forests, cross the prairies, ford the rivers, and climb the mountains; it belonged to those who went west. For those who didn't go, the West became a place in the imagination, a place filled with delights and terrors, heroes and heathens, success and failure. Well into the twentieth century, the West was where young boys went in play and adults went in their daydreams.

For GIs in Vietnam, the West, both literally and allegorically, became Laos and Cambodia. They were the enchanted lands beyond the boundaries of their maps, known only to a special few soldiers who returned from missions that were so secret that no one dared ask about their purpose. Having driven west across the Central Highlands on Highway 19 as far as Mang Yang Pass many times, and spent a couple of nights on firebase Schuller near An Khe, I developed my own fascination with the unknown that lay farther west.[16]

It was my memory of those mental wanderings that later hooked me on Tim O'Brien's novel *Going After Cacciato*. Resistant to fictionalized portrayals of the war in Vietnam, I had passed up the book until my comments about Laos being the perfect setting for an imaginative story like *Valley of Death* prompted a colleague to insist that I read it. The story begins after Cacciato has walked away from his unit; his squad is dispatched to find him and bring him back. The early pages suggest enough of a hunter-killer theme to have made this 1975 bestseller yet another inspiration for CNN's version of Tailwind, but as it develops, the hunt of Cacciato becomes a slapstick chase story. There are any number of directions O'Brien could have sent his AWOL character. Since Cacciato is a runaway, O'Brien could have had him disappear into the Vietnamese underground like Nick in *The Deer Hunter*, but Cacciato wants to get out of the war zone, not just Western culture. O'Brien could have had him stow away on a container ship or steal a Vietnamese fishing boat and go *east*. But he didn't because the story is fantasy; it's about the *imagined* flight from Vietnam of another character in Cacciato's unit, Paul Berlin, who is only pretending, in his mind, to be someone named Cacciato. Container ships and fishing junks are real and the East is known; those elements won't stimulate readers' imaginations. O'Brien wants us to think about the unknown. The unknown is *west*. Cacciato goes west. He goes to Laos—and then to Burma, India, Pakistan, Afghanistan, Iran, Greece, and eventually Paris.[17]

THE DEFECTORS: SOME LIMINAL FIGURES FOR A LIMINAL LAND

The defectors are the critical characters in *Valley of Death*, not just because of their interesting fictional quality but because of the role they play in the subtext that makes the story so seductive. Defectors play into the feelings that many Americans have that something yet unidentified has to account for why we lost the war. There was something stealthy and unfair about the opponent that made this war different and ultimately can explain why we didn't win. Those feelings, recall, were the basis for the creation of special-operations units like SOG. The sense was that the enemy was dealing in subversion and trickery and that the United States had to fight fire with fire. When operations failed, the first assumption of military planners was that there had been a security breach such as a leak of classified information, perhaps even an enemy agent working undercover in our own intelligence branch. According to a *Time* magazine story on former Nebraska senator Bob Kerrey, Kerrey was awarded a Medal of Honor for leading his SEAL team on an operation that failed when information from Vietnamese defectors led them into a trap.[18] The extent to which U.S. fears of intelligence sabotage accorded with reality, versus being products of political paranoia is, of course, debatable, but the fact is that Vietnam became a war where psychological operations, countersubversion, and double and triple crosses became the orders of the day.

Stories about U.S. defectors crossing to the communist side dove-
tailed with the paranoia generated by the unwinnable nature of the war.
The most common stories were those of "The White Cong," the Cau-
casian male occasionally seen traveling with a VC unit, or "Salt and Pepper," the white and black renegades spotted with enemy units. These
stories were investigated by writer Christopher Feola who declared
them to be a kind of folklore of which the origins predated Vietnam. According to him, the same stories were told during the Philippine-
American war of 1898 when an American traitor was supposedly
involved in the Blaingiga massacre. The turncoat was sometimes reported to be white, sometimes black, and to be wearing the West Point
class ring belonging to an American captain who had been killed in the
massacre.[19] Feola says that similar stories followed the American-Indian
wars and argues that they have a racist subtext that treats people of color
as inferiors who cannot win without the help of the "white man."[20]

Transported into the Tailwind story, defectors supply the same kind
of alibi for why missions were failing and the war was going badly. Perhaps, as some versions of Tailwind had it, the defectors holed up in
Laos were operating some sort of communications system that could
eavesdrop on U.S. military intelligence and tip off the North Vietnamese that raids were coming. It may have been such tips that foiled
the recovery of POWs, since, according to some accounts, POWs
seemed to have sometimes been moved out of targeted sites just before
raiders arrived.[21]

At this level, defectors explain away failed missions and the lost war.
They shore up myths about national and racial supremacy and, in a
sense, rewrite the history of the war as a story about America at war with
itself. We were defeated in this narrative, not by an upstart nation of
Asians but by the betrayal of our own kind. But there is another and
more subtle way in which Tailwind's defector story works. Note that in
Van Buskirk's description of the "longshadow" whom he chases into the
spider hole, the traitor has long blond hair and "looks like he's running
off a beach in California." Symbolically, the long hair and its blond hue
have the effect of feminizing the image; a beach implies leisure—make
that a *California* beach—and it suggests decadence.[22] Van Buskirk's image of the betrayer, in other words, is as much a *what* as a *who*. In his
mind, the betrayal is cultural; it is the soft, effeminate side of American
life that has eroded the masculine warrior culture needed to prosecute
the war.[23]

Remember also that even for the veterans of Operation Tailwind, there is some ambiguity about who the "longshadows" were. In Van Buskirk's mind the man he chased was clearly *not* a POW—"This is a GI, boots on, not a prisoner, no shackles, no chains, nothing"; but Jay Graves, leader of Tailwind's reconnaissance team, told CNN's camera, "We don't know whether they're prisoners or whatever."[24] The uncertainty about who the targeted Americans were allows the story to work as a betrayal narrative that runs in multiple directions—either the U.S. government, the CIA in particular, has betrayed the POWs, or some of our own troops have betrayed the nation's anticommunist mission by joining the enemy. In some ultra-right minds, of course, version number two can be bent back as a story about rebel GIs turning against an unwinnable war prosecuted by an illegitimate government.[25]

Questions about the deaths of Americans at the location of Operation Tailwind could possibly be answered if the site were excavated. If, in fact, as many as twenty Americans died there, as Robert Van Buskirk claims, a forensic team should be able to find some evidence of their deaths as well as evidence that would clarify what type of gas canisters were dropped. I contacted Susan Dutton, deputy chief of mission at the U.S. embassy in Vientiane, Lao PDR, to ask if research efforts of that type had been conducted or planned. She had "no information on the subject" and referred me to Jerry O'Hara with the Joint Task Force–Full Accounting, the agency working to recover American personnel missing since the war's end. O'Hara said his group had "been in the area [of the Tailwind raid] but have investigated or excavated nothing related to the incident." Responding to a second inquiry from me, he said, "There are no missing or unaccounted-for Americans as a result of Operation Tailwind."

THE MAKING OF MILITARY MEMORIES

The superficial answer to how nerve gas and defectors appeared in the CNN version of Operation Tailwind is that the Tailwind veterans put them there. When April Oliver interviewed Robert Van Buskirk, he told her that nerve gas had been used in an effort to kill GIs suspected of having gone over to the enemy. The disparity between what those former commandos remember and what the historical record shows, however, plus the fact that Van Buskirk, for one, had never included nerve gas and defectors in his previous recollections of Tailwind, makes it necessary to inquire into the construction of veterans' memories of their wartime experiences. In effect, we need to ask, how did nerve gas and defectors get into *their* stories?[26]

Most of us use the word "memory" to refer to the act or facility of remembering—"John has a good memory," for example—as well as the memory itself, as in "summer vacation is a pleasant memory." Both usages imply that that which is remembered is fixed, something objectlike that is retrieved by the act of remembering. However common it is to think of memory in this way, it is probably not accurate. Memories are not like snapshots, images imprinted in the mind at the moment something is experienced or information is received, that can be periodically retrieved, looked at, and then returned to storage for later reference. Memories are more fluid than fixed. In the first instance, the experience or information to be remembered is constructed only in part from what the senses receive. Unlike the camera, which simply records, the mind begins to interpret information as it comes in, making decisions about "what" this is that will be remembered. The mind uses prior knowledge and experience to make those choices, which means, in a sense, that the mind remembers the past in order to process the present that will be remembered in some future. Memory, in other words, is implicated in the construction of memory.

Writing in the *New York Times* about the unreliability of eyewitnesses to catastrophic events, Matthew Wald notes that the mind of a witness will instinctively try to match events with its record of past experiences and, when it finds no match, turn to other recorded images like those remembered from films. Thus, it is entirely normal for men in war to remember their experiences through their existing impressions of war collected from movies, comic books, and other sources.

Going forward from their time in service, veterans' memories remain pliable, constantly being reconstructed by their exposure to other representations of the war. Experiences are always remembered in different contexts, which means that the remembered images are made to interact with new information and are tasked with making sense out of a new and different situation each time. That interaction changes the memory, adding to or subtracting from what was previously remembered. Frequently, for example, conversations occur around memories and those conversations merge the recollections of others with our own to create a new edition of the memory.

Memory is also mediated by the symbols used to represent events so that we reexperience important occasions through memorials, photographs, film, music, and literature. Thus, when we view the Vietnam Veterans Wall in Washington, D.C., we remember the sacrifice that U.S. soldiers made in that war but when we view a photograph of Vietnam veterans throwing their medals on the Capitol steps in protest of the war, we are reminded that GIs were political actors, not just victims. The exposure to both of those images over time ensures that what we remember about Vietnam veterans is very complex, perhaps even contradictory. Likewise, newscasters can use an image like a meat cleaver, as the producers of *Valley of Death* did, to conjure a bloody hand-to-hand war that we then "remember," and play strains of Buffalo Springfield to call up the emotions of paranoia whose limits, as the song goes, "ain't exactly clear." The meat cleaver and popular culture may both be quite different representations of the war, however, from what actually happened.

The more frequent and intense the interaction between our past and present, the more problematic the conventional, snapshot sense of memory becomes. The Vietnam War was America's first lost war, and for that reason the country has had a hard time letting go of it. The war keeps being played and replayed on the screen, in public debate, by scholars in academic journals, and, as with Operation Tailwind, via televised investigative reports. More than most events of the last half-century, the war in Vietnam has been remembered and *re*-remembered, its symbolic representations now layered with three decades of personal and political emotion.

Male Fantasies

The tendency of men to exaggerate their accomplishments in war is widely recognized. War is a rite of passage, the defining experience that separates men from boys, which means that the society demands an account of the years that men spend in the military. "What did you do in the war, Daddy?" is the paradigmatic question that veterans are asked. The right answer, they soon learn, is to talk about the combat they saw or, if they didn't see combat, make something up. That's what

Vietnam veteran Bill Stroud did. When he was interviewed by screen-writer Waldo Salt who was working on the script for the 1978 film *Coming Home,* Stroud said he had started telling "war stories" in order to conform to what was expected of a veteran. "I started tellin' war stories, things that didn't happen to me," Stroud said, "but then the kids, who were really excited about it, kept asking me to repeat it. And every time, I knew it was a lie, so then I'd feel really strange cuz I'd tell it again and I knew I'd just told this lie again and I didn't necessarily want to tell a lie."[27]

For many men, military service is the high point of their lives and, whether they "saw action" or not, it produced formative experiences that they like to tell about. The problem is that in a culture sated with Rambo-like images of war, no one wants to listen to what a cook or payroll clerk did; in a war like Vietnam, where a large majority of the men did not see combat, that means that the audience for stories about Vietnam as it was actually experienced by most GIs is pretty small. The dominant culture, in other words, leaves many veterans choosing between reticence and revisionism.

During the 1990s, a raft of Vietnam-era veterans were exposed for claiming false service records. The more captivating cases involved men with prominent public identities like Admiral Jeremy Boorda, the chief of naval operations who committed suicide in 1996 when he was revealed to have awarded himself a medal for heroism that he did not deserve; and Mark Fuhrman, the Los Angeles police officer involved in the O. J. Simpson case, who boasted of clandestine commando duty in Vietnam when the closest he had been to land was a ship in the South China Sea. Toronto Blue Jays manager Tim Johnson made the list when the team fired him in 1999 for telling tales about his Marine service in Vietnam when he had never been there.[28]

In some cases, the adoption of false military identities seems to be a strategy, part of an attempt to get into treatment or service programs. The diagnostic concept "post–traumatic stress disorder" (PTSD) developed during the 1970s out of a search by mental health professionals and journalists for a way to describe and talk about wartime trauma and the coming-home experience of Vietnam veterans. By the 1990s there was a growing body of professional literature on "factitious PTSD," in which noncombat veterans fooled clinicians with false but convincing symptoms and personal stories about battlefield terror.[29]

B. J. "Jug" Burkett, a Dallas, Texas, businessman and Vietnam veteran, made a hobby of tracking down the real identities of so-called troubled veterans and discovered that about 70 percent of them were not who or what they claimed to be. One of them, "Steve," claimed to have been a Navy SEAL who now carried the guilt of having killed civilians in Vietnam. Steve was the subject of a CBS special, *The Wall Within,* about psychologically damaged veterans. The truth, as Burkett found out, was that Steve had never been a SEAL.[30]

Veterans who served during the Vietnam era but nowhere near the war zone also concocted phony biographies to gain access to homeless shelters and other social services. In his book *House of Purple Hearts,* author Paul Solotaroff reported that as many of two-thirds of homeless vets were sporting false military identities. Other veterans seem to reconfigure their memories to suit personal, perhaps emotional, needs. One study found that Vietnam veterans with marital problems are more likely to exaggerate their combat experience, apparently in an effort to explain to themselves and others why their marriages are failing.[31]

For some men PTSD became a useful legal alibi. Some of the more interesting cases involve men who choke or beat women during nighttime fits they describe as "flashbacks." "It was like I was back in Vietnam and I thought she was Vietcong," is the common explanation offered by the offending husband or boyfriend. The most notorious use of PTSD for a legal alibi was Joseph Yandle's. Yandle was convicted of murder for his role in a 1972 robbery. Sentenced to prison in Massachusetts, Yandle got the attention of reporters with a claim that he was a decorated Vietnam veteran with a heroin habit. The drug helped suppress the nightmares he had from the war and his addiction had driven him to crime. The press bought it and CBS aired his story on a 1994 episode of *60 Minutes.* Republican governor William Weld bought it too and commuted Yandle's sentence in 1995. Four years later Yandle was back in the pen after investigations into his background disclosed he had never been in Vietnam.[32]

The most curious of the stories were those seeking recognition through association with some ignoble act like the killing of innocent civilians. In 1997, John Plummer claimed he had ordered a napalm attack on Trang Bang in 1972. Kim Phuc, then nine years old, had been badly disfigured in that bombing, her agony captured in a Pulitzer Prize–winning photograph. When Kim and Plummer met at the Vietnam Memorial in Washington, she forgave the former soldier. Then, Plummer, a preacher, began using the story in sermons and public lectures. He was featured on ABC's *Nightline*. But the story wasn't true. Plummer had been a junior officer in Vietnam with no authority to order air strikes.[33]

The line between outright fabrication and the mental disorder known as "false memory syndrome" is, of course, difficult to discern. One of the more interesting cases of this type arose out of an incident from the Korean War. As reported by the Associated Press in a September 30, 1999 story that won a Pulitzer Prize, U.S. troops massacred civilians hiding under a bridge near No Gun Ri, Korea in 1953. The story was initially based on what a Korean War veteran, Edward Daily, had told the reporters. Daily said he had been a machine gunner at No Gun Ri and was now haunted by the cries of the children as they were killed. He also claimed to have been awarded the Distinguished Service Cross, Silver Star, and several other medals. Reporters outside the AP circle used the Freedom of Information Act to request Daily's military records and discovered that he had not been at No Gun Ri and had won no medals.

Further inquiries into Daily and his story revealed him to be a classic case of false memory syndrome. After initially defending his story against critics, Daily eventually became convinced by the newly released documents that indeed he had never been at No Gun Ri; amazingly, he expressed bafflement at how he had come to believe his own false story. While deceiving others, it seems he had also deceived himself by creating over the years a network of "buddies" who, hearing him talk about his role at No Gun Ri, had come to believe he had been there and then fed back to him the confirmation of the identity that he sought. *New York Times* reporter Michael Moss said Daily had "managed to airbrush himself into the fragile memories" of other Korean War veterans to the point that one of them maintained, even after Daily had been exposed, "I know Daily was there [at No Gun Ri]."

Attempts to understand Edward Daily pointed to his need for the attention that his story got him, but there seems to have been more to it than that. Like John Plummer, who embraced Kim Phuc, a victim for whom he was not responsible, Daily was captured in a 1999 AP photo embracing a No Gun Ri victim at a Cleveland prayer service. Prior to that, in 1993, he had attended a peace ceremony in South Dakota with members of the Lakota Sioux tribe. On that occasion, he had made apologies for the 1890 massacre at Wounded Knee by the Seventh Cavalry—the same Seventh Cavalry that he had falsely claimed to have been with at No Gun Ri.

The images of clandestine hands-on killing, like those told by Mark Fuhrman, are undoubtedly traceable to the silver screen, as are the stories told by wannabe ex-POWs who describe scenes of torture right out of *Hanoi Hilton*. What is even more fascinating is the degree to which film mediates not only the memories of veterans but the work of psychiatrists as well.[34] Journalists are, of course, subject to the same forces of popular culture, making it difficult to establish the provenance of stories like *Valley of Death*. The feedback loops ensnare all the players—veterans, mental health professionals, reporters, screenwriters, and novelists—to the point where it becomes virtually impossible to authenticate a "source." What can be shown, though, is that the central themes of *Valley of Death* all appeared in films and novels long before April Oliver began her work and, for the most part, before her principal sources began telling their tales.

5

TWO PARTS *APOCALYPSE NOW* AND A PINCH OF SARIN: POPULAR CULTURE'S RECIPE FOR *VALLEY OF DEATH*

I didn't see *Valley of Death* when it aired and it was several weeks before I acquired a taped copy of the broadcast. When I watched the tape with Laura Hogan, a student in my seminar on myth, memory, and Vietnam, we were jolted by the story told on camera by Robert Van Buskirk. As recounted at greater length in chapter 1, Van Buskirk tells how the men of Operation Tailwind landed at a village base camp in Laos and spotted "longshadows" living there. Judging them to be defectors, Van Buskirk says he chased a man with long blond hair who disappeared down a spider hole. When Van Buskirk told him to come out, the supposed turncoat replied, "F—— you," to which Van Buskirk responded, "No, f—— you."

As the "f—— you" line parted Van Buskirk's lips, Laura and I looked at each other as if to say, "Oh, really?!" Could such made-for-Hollywood lines have really been manufactured on site by a terrified defector and his hunter-killer? More likely, I thought, they had been manufactured *in* Hollywood by a well-paid screenwriter. But could I find the source? I imagined there being a film or novel with a hunter-killer/defector scene much like the one described by Van Buskirk in which the characters utter those lines. But searching films and novels for snippets of dialogue is a hunt for a needle in a haystack, and, having no way to systematize the task, I wasn't confident I could identify where in popular culture Van Buskirk might have seen or heard those phrases.[1]

Van Buskirk's "f—— you," in any case, was only the most obvious suggestion that fictional images ginned up by professional wordsmiths had probably interacted with the fecund imaginations of aging veterans to spin the yarn that CNN aired as *Valley of Death*. Moreover, to make the point that popular culture and political imagination were driving forces in the construction of the story, I would have to account for more than Van Buskirk's plagiarism. In particular, I would have to show that nerve gas and defectors had been elements of popular culture before April Oliver began her work and that there was reason to believe that people working on the show had been familiar with those films and books. As it turned out, the quantity and quality of fictional material related to what Oliver produced exceeded what I initially suspected, and interviews done with CNN staffers and other journalists provide clues that this material had indeed influenced the production of the story.

NICK AND KURTZ: OVER THE CULTURAL FENCE

Few Americans remember much about the actual war in Vietnam. The history of how the United States became involved and why the war was unwinnable, despite being the longest war we had ever fought, has been all but forgotten. In place of the war's actual history many Americans "remember" that North Vietnam invaded the South, that the United States went there to repel the invasion, and that we were unsuccessful because liberals in Washington and radicals in the streets would not let us win. Many people also remember how badly "their boys" were treated when they returned from the war. Most of these beliefs, wrong though they may be, were popularized by feature-length films.

In the earliest years of Vietnam, America was still dominated by the post–World War II culture. As a result, films like *The Lively Set* (1964) and *Bus Riley's Back in Town* (1965) were really 1950-ish slice-of-life films with coming-home narratives substituting Vietnam veterans for World War II returnees. By 1968, though, it was becoming apparent that Vietnam was "not our father's war," and the silver screen began to reflect that change. A few films, like *Alice's Restaurant* (1969), which featured Arlo Guthrie playing himself, captured the mutuality between the antiwar movement and Vietnam veterans, while others, like *Hail Hero,* with Michael Douglas, and *Getting Straight,* with Elliot Gould, both released in 1969, began the trend toward films that discredited the opposition and displaced the existence of antiwar veterans with images of physically disabled and mentally dysfunctional men home from the war. With the exception of the cartoonish *Green Berets* (1968), which starred John Wayne, no Hollywood-made film was actually set in Vietnam until the late 1970s.

If Hollywood refused to deal with the war per se prior to 1970 (perhaps because it was a war that simply could not be understood within the frameworks of Great Wars past that film makers were used to), it certainly was not going to deal with a lost war for which there was *no* paradigm. So beginning in 1970 and continuing for eight years, filmdom cranked out dozens of stories about damaged vets back home.[2] Many, like Lipper in *The Stone Killer* (1973), were pathologically violent, having been "trained to kill" in "the 'Nam," while others, like Travis Bickle in *Taxi Driver* (1976), had returned with twisted masculinities and sexual fixations. A host of avenger films portrayed vigilante vets as righters of wrongs done to them or their country, the wrongs done to them usually being stand-ins for the war they had not been allowed to win.[3]

In general terms, the conventional memory of what the war in Vietnam had been was established by Hollywood prior to 1978. It was widely viewed as a war that "happened to" the United States, particularly to the veterans, a war with an invisible "enemy" who was alien even to Vietnam, a war fought by commandos (Green Berets all) and that "could have been won" had it not been for the sellout on the home front. These are the images of the war that have formed the background assumptions of American thought and memory on the war, and any story produced in 1998, such as *Valley of Death,* would have to be consistent with them if it was to resonate with an American audience. Hollywood began to deal more directly with the war itself in 1978, with Michael Comino's *The Deer Hunter,* where the foreshadowings of CNN's *Valley of Death* became a little more explicit. Two themes that would dominate portrayals of the war throughout the 1980s first appeared in this film: betrayal and the hunt for unaccounted-for personnel. In *The Deer Hunter,* Mike, Steve, and Nick from Clairton, Pennsylvania go to Vietnam. All three are captured by the Viet Cong but get separated in their attempt to escape. Mike and Steve return to the States without Nick, then Mike goes back to find him. Nick, however, has deserted. Mike finds him living in

Saigon, apparently acculturated to the dehumanized existence of the Vietnamese underground. When Mike tries to bring him back to the United States, Nick spits on him, rejecting everything that Mike stands for. The scene ends with Nick dying from a gunshot wound suffered while playing Russian roulette.

In a military sense, nothing in *The Deer Hunter* implies that Nick had gone over to the enemy; he was not a defector in the usual use of the term. But he had abandoned his unit, and the patriotism that Mike stood for, in favor of the enemy's values and way of life (as those are portrayed in the film). Deeper than a changing of military sides, Nick's defection was a thoroughgoing rebuke of Western culture. Mike's pursuit of Nick, moreover, established the precedent in mainstream film fare that Americans do not leave unfinished business behind. Mike's quest is for closure. He has to know: Is Nick dead or alive? Has he been recaptured? Is he waiting for someone to come for him? Is he still one of us? Or is he one of them? Nick's death clears the stage for a new beginning, which is heralded by friends and family singing "God Bless America" at his funeral.

The Deer Hunter's relationship to *Valley of Death* is close, but the gap between Hollywood and what April Oliver scripted for CNN becomes even narrower with the release of *Apocalypse Now* a year after *The Deer Hunter*. The film's hero, played by Martin Sheen, is Captain Willard. Willard's unit: SOG. His mission: to hunt down and kill Colonel Kurtz, who has formed his own army of defectors and is operating out of a secret base camp in Cambodia. Add nerve gas, and this Francis Ford Coppola film could pass for CNN's variation of Operation Tailwind.[4]

Willard's identity as a SOG operative is especially interesting. The existence of Special Forces troops, Green Berets, was widely known and even publicly celebrated throughout the war years. But SOG was different. Green Berets were assigned to special duty with SOG, as were navy SEALs and their air force and marine counterparts. SOG itself, though, was a secret, its very existence unconfirmed and virtually unacknowledged when *Apocalypse Now* went into production in the mid-1970s.[5]

Even more important is that as SOG begins to creep into public consciousness with *Apocalypse Now*, it does so in connection with a mission to *hunt down and kill other Americans*. Given the absence of evidence then or now that SOG ever had any such mission, it is virtually impossible not to believe that this film somehow stimulated the imaginations of individuals involved in the telling of *Valley of Death*. In a search for reasons why people who had no other reason to do so believed that a secret mission really existed to kill renegade soldiers, the resemblance between the two stories is just too close to ignore.

Valley of Death's subplot of conspiratorial sellout is also anticipated by *Apocalypse Now*. Soon after accepting his assignment to find and assassinate Kurtz, Willard heads up the Nung River toward Cambodia. As he reads the dossier on Kurtz given to him by his handlers, Willard's voice-over reveals to us that Kurtz had been at odds with his superiors over the conduct of the war since its earliest days. Kurtz had been in Vietnam when the war was still an off-the-books endeavor of the CIA. From what we are told, it's unclear whether Kurtz was a CIA agent or a military man on assignment to the CIA. But the file given Willard said Kurtz had been "groomed for a top position in the 'Corporation,'" an often-used code word for the CIA.[6] When Kurtz returned from Vietnam in 1964, we are told, "his report to President Johnson was rejected." That was the turning point in his career. He completed airborne training, joined the Special Forces, and returned to Vietnam.

Apocalypse Now is commonly understood to be an allegorical retelling of Joseph Conrad's novel *Heart of Darkness*, an exploration into the underside of the colonial psyche. But that literary reference veils the more political agenda of the film, which foretells some of the intrigue surrounding *Valley of Death*—the split between the CIA and the military over how the war would be fought and the paranoia of military people about control of their operations by the CIA, a secret civilian agency.[7] In the film, Kurtz is said to have gone insane, presumably driven mad by the horror of war. Washington wanted him assassinated because he was carrying out a maverick operation in Cambodia, using methods even more brutal than those employed by the Special Forces. But Willard wonders aloud "what they *really* had against Kurtz." "It wasn't just insanity and murder," he says; "there was enough of that to go around for everyone."[8] We never learn what it was that made Kurtz a target for Willard's hunter-killer mission or who the "they" was who had ordered the hit, silences that probably fueled the fantasies of viewers able to read the film's political subtext.

The idea that some GIs, whom the government publicly claimed to be MIA, were really defectors—another of *Valley of Death*'s subplots—is also introduced when Willard learns that a Capt. Richard Foley had previously been dispatched to kill Kurtz. Foley had not returned, and the

government had told his family he was MIA, although it knew he had
defected to Kurtz's unit. Again, the appearance of this story line in a film
that went into production in the mid-1970s, at a time when charges of
government lying about POWs and MIAs were first being made, points
to the intermingling of fact (there really were MIAs) and fiction that incubated *Valley of Death.*

The ambiguity of Kurtz's political identity, finally, allowed him to be
used as a prototype for the kind of paramilitary warrior drawn to the
militia movement in the postwar years. Prior to Willard killing Kurtz,
Kurtz tells him about the time he helped a Special Forces team to in-
oculate some Vietnamese children for polio. Later, some enemy soldiers had come and chopped off the inoculated arms and thrown them
into a pile. Kurtz was struck by the political brilliance of that act. "The
genius," he says. "The will to do that. Perfect. Genuine, complete,
crystalline, pure. Then I could understand that they were stronger
than we were. Because they could stand that." The enemy soldiers,
Kurtz said, "were not monsters but trained cadres who fought with
their hearts, who have families, who have children, who are filled
with love, men who are moral who at the same time are able to utilize
their primordial instincts to kill without feeling, without passion, without judgment."

A quarter-century later, it appears that the important subtext of
Apocalypse Now was not the dark side of the human heart so much as
the postwar political culture that was beginning to form. Kurtz had to
be assassinated not because he was crazy but because he had defected
from the softness of Washington liberalism and the feminization of
the nation's culture. He had made himself the enemy of an immoral
U.S. military culture that would send men to kill without knowing
why they were killing, or worse, knowing what the cause was and not
believing in it. Kurtz hadn't lost his morality, he had *found* it—in the
hearts of the people he had been sent to kill.[9]

Kurtz's embrace of horror as the ultimate expression of love for family and country seduced Willard into a similar mind-set. In retrospect,
the scene appears to have been an eerie harbinger of the political violence manifested by the American militia movement during the 1980s
and 1990s. If the film meant to suggest that Kurtz's will to kill lived on
in the personage of Willard, the likeness between Kurtz and an antigovernment militant like Timothy McVeigh is brought to mind. Indeed, the
coldly calculating and emotionally barricaded figure described by

McVeigh's biographers in *American Terrorist* could have been mentored in moral reasoning by Kurtz—or Willard.[10]

Winning two Academy Awards (Vittorio Storaro for cinematography and Walter Murch for sound), *Apocalypse Now* was surely the most widely viewed film of the hunter-killer genre, but it was not the last. In the mid-1980s there appeared a spate of films with defectors, most with a pursuing "hunter." *Final Mission* (1984) is set in Laos where Slater has defected to the enemy. Deacon hunts down Slater and brings him home, at which point the tables turn and Deacon is killed by the prey he had hunted. *Eye of the Eagle* (1987) could have been the screenplay version of *Valley of Death*. Its video jacket told the story: "The enemy is murdering U.S. soldiers. The enemy must be destroyed. The enemy . . . is American." The enemy, we learn from the film, is a unit of disgruntled AWOLs and deserters who have taken up arms against the regular army. *Night Wars* (1987) is a zombie film in which McGregor is a dissident GI who has gone over to the Viet Cong. In a POW camp he helps torture Trent and Jimmy who years later cross time and space in their dreams to return to Vietnam and avenge McGregor's treason. Finally, some of the specific imagery in Van Buskirk's Tailwind tale may have been sourced by *White Ghost* (1988). Steve Shepard, a former Green Beret, is being hunted in the Vietnamese jungle by a killer team of U.S. veterans years after the end of the war. White, blond, and looking for all the world like a surfer just off a stateside beach, Shepard eludes his captors at one point by diving down a spider hole.

And these are just the defector/hunter-killer films. By 1990, dozens of POW/MIA films of the Rambo-goes-to-the-rescue variety had American imaginations working overtime. It isn't possible to say for sure if one or another of the principals responsible for *Valley of Death* was influenced by these films—Robert Van Buskirk mentions having seen *Stone Killers* (1973)—but the resemblance between their content and what CNN telecast as Operation Tailwind provides a plausible alternative account of where the idea came from that there were defectors who were hunted down and killed.

SARIN SAYS IT ALL

How killing is done on the Big Screen is important. The technology of death is part of the attraction of war films. On the one hand, weaponry connected to the real-life experience of filmgoers—handguns, rifles, and knives—invites a visceral identity that bonds the viewer with the scene. Veterans, especially, can imagine themselves using such weapons, because they've had them in their hands. But can they imagine themselves killing with them? Most people, even veterans, have used those weapons only in training or, perhaps, for hunting. Hitting a target is very different from killing a person, and portrayals of killing that are too close to the real thing can shut down the emotions rather than excite them. As film critics often point out, most war films are surprisingly bloodless, a testament to the difficulty of marketing battlefield reality.[11]

Hollywood is about imagination and emotion. The power of the unknown to elicit awe, fear, or even mere interest is virtually unlimited. In film, the more esoteric the means of destruction the less personal the viewer's involvement becomes and the more freely the emotions are able to flow. Thus, in the Rambo series, the hero is portrayed with awesome-looking automatic weapons that most Vietnam veterans can't even identify, much less claim any hands-on relationship to. There is a sort of enchantment with things beyond our experience, beyond our comprehension even, that holds our attention. Extreme weaponry also delivers maximum sensual impact—loud noise, bright flashes, mushrooming fireballs—places in the script for the insertion of audio and visual special effects that have become hallmarks of contemporary film.

Nerve gas is an exotic weapon. Well beyond the experience level of all but the specialists who handle it, nerve gas can't be seen, heard, or smelled. Those qualities, plus the fact that it was first used in World War I, a war whose history has been mythologized nearly as much as that of Vietnam, have created an almost impenetrable mystique. In short, nerve gas in a story is a great tonic for the imagination. But how do you film nerve gas? As a silent and colorless weapon the victims of which die vomiting, nerve gas is a formidable challenge for the special-effects technicians, which means it is seldom the device *du jour* for war film directors.[12]

The first and maybe only instance of a chemical agent being used on human targets in a Vietnam War film was *Jacob's Ladder* in 1990. But who used it on whom? That question is the center of the plot. The film begins with a firefight during which something seems to go wrong. Jacob (Tim Robbins) is wounded in the fight, which is filmed to prompt questions: Are GIs fighting GIs? The scene of the conflict is kinda foggy—maybe it's smoke, or is it gas? Jacob dies in an evacuation hospital but not before we view the fantasies of his life that would have been, through a series of flash-forwards. By that device we learn that it *was* Americans battling Americans in the opening scene and that their own government had induced the fratricide by secretly giving an experimental drug to some of the troops. To cover its tracks, the government then denied that Jacob and the other dead soldiers had ever been in Vietnam.

Jacob's Ladder was a spice rack for right-wing imaginations. It portrayed an America at war with itself, a government that killed its own soldiers, and political officials who lied about the most essential of truths—where these young men died and why. But if the right fed off *Jacobs's Ladder*, its mythology was also reflected in the construction of the film's story line. As film critic Renny Christopher (1994) wrote, "This film probably wouldn't have made sense in 1980; the U.S. hadn't yet completed the laying of the ideology that makes the war about us, and only us." What Christopher meant was that because of the conservative social movements of the 1980s, stories about government betrayal of the military mission in Vietnam began to sound like common sense to many Americans. The government was lying about how many POWs had been left behind and what they had been doing when they were captured. Perhaps the government had even had some of the POWs killed—so why couldn't it be true that GIs had been used in a lethal drug experiment?

Jacob's Ladder's story of chemical weaponry being used against U.S. troops was made still more plausible by the historical context in which it was released. With Robbins in the lead role and a cast that included Danny Aiello and Macaulay Culkin, this widely viewed film hit movie theaters in the fall of 1990 just as the buildup of U.S. forces in the Persian Gulf was peaking. Fears that Iraq would unleash clouds of chemical agents against U.S. soldiers—fears stoked by the collaboration of the U.S. news media and the government—made the use of gas for warfare seem realistic in a way it hadn't since World War I. But the gas-in-the-Gulf hysteria had a twist—no sooner was American anxiety locked on to the Hussein-as-Hitler imagery than U.S. troops began returning home with mysterious ailments that came to be known as Gulf War Syndrome. In the absence of evidence that Iraq had used any chemical agents, speculation ran rampant that the United States had used its own troops, à la *Jacob's Ladder*, for some kind of drug experiment.

If it is true that *Jacob's Ladder*'s story line worked only because the Reagan years had prepped the political culture for it, it is no less true that CNN's *Valley of Death* worked—or its producers thought it would work—because the Gulf War and *Jacob's Ladder* had added to the public perception not only that the government might be involved in secret and sinister plots against its own military personnel but that it would resort to the "bad of the bad," as Robert Van Buskirk referred to nerve gas, to accomplish its aims.

The Persian Gulf War and *Jacob's Ladder* put chemical warfare, gas in particular, on the minds of the American people in a way that could not have been imagined after the universal denunciation of its use following World War I and the condemnation of Nazi genocide in the gas chambers of World War II. And it was kept on those minds when sarin nerve gas was used to attack the Tokyo subway system by the obscure Aum Shinrikyo religious sect. The illusiveness of the group's identity and the death of seven people in the attack added to the aura already associated with the possession and use of chemical agents. More importantly, going forward from the Tokyo attack, the dread associated with nerve gas could now be represented by a single word—sarin. Sarin became the one-word symbol of terror by exotic means. Few Americans understood the scientific fine print on the label or comprehended the whys and wherefores surrounding its use for political purposes, but to say "sarin" was to say it all: stealth, horror, death, and evil.

Valley of Death said "sarin," a word that Americans were cued up to respond to with revulsion. Except for mysterious Asian cults, Saddam Hussein, or maybe Hitler—which is to say, except for the anthropological "other"—*nobody* used sarin. To allege its use was a way of distinguishing "us" from "them," a way of disassociating ourselves from the alien, enemy "other." *Valley of Death's* claim that the government had used sarin was a rhetorical strategy to "otherize" our own government, a claim that *this* government was not *our* government. The invocation of sarin in this way carried the connotation that our government had been taken over by an outside power.

Taking the actual facts of Operation Tailwind at face value, there is plenty of ground for controversy over the type of weaponry deployed. Even veterans who, like John Singlaub, disassociate themselves from the sarin nerve-gas charge admit that a gas, possibly an illegal "incapacitating agent," was used on the mission. So why did the producers risk the credibility of their story with exaggeration? Why did they go with the over-the-top allegation that *sarin* had been used?

The only answer is that "sarin" had the conjuring power they wanted. Few members of the American public had even heard the word before the Persian Gulf War and the Tokyo subway attack four years later. In controversies during the Vietnam years surrounding the possible use of chemical weapons, moreover, the word "sarin" had not been not used. Its use in *Valley of Death,* therefore, was purely ideological in that it associated the U.S. government not just with the illegal use of a chemical weapon, but with the foreign likenesses of Aum Shinrikyo and Middle East tyrants. What the critics of *Valley of Death* missed in their examination of the sarin claim was that the use of the word in the story was an additional indication that the authors of *Valley of Death* hoped to convey a right-wing conspiratorial subtext.

There is no doubt, then, that feature films had pumped more than enough ideas and images into the American mainstream to account for why some veterans, journalists, and other citizens believed that nerve gas might have been used to kill defectors during the war in Vietnam. Indeed, we could wonder why the culture had not precipitated a *Valley of Death*–type story before 1998. The answer might be that, while all the ingredients were present in popular culture prior to the CNN broadcast, the chemistry between them needed to be activated by something. That "something," it turns out, came not from film but from Nelson Demille's novel, *Charm School,* and from Monika Jensen-Stevenson's pseudo-documentary, *Spite House.*

TALES OUT OF (CHARM) SCHOOL

The case for film being an influence on the creativity of *Valley of Death*'s producers is circumstantial but strong. Films like *Apocalypse Now* and *Deer Hunter* simply did not go unseen by members of the Vietnam generation. The America-at-war-with-itself narrative of those films, moreover, is so embedded in the nation's historical memory that it can assumed to be a background assumption of the society's cultural literacy.

The case of written fiction's influence on the CNN staffers is still stronger, however. One of the books that circulated among CNN's *Valley of Death* crew was *Charm School.* When I saw a reference to Demille's 1988 book in notes from an interview another writer did with one of the CNN journalists, I bought the book and waded in.[13]

Charm School is about Gregory Fisher's trip into the Soviet Union. Fisher has just gotten his MBA from Yale and a Pontiac Trans Am as a graduation gift from his parents. He ships the car across the Atlantic and, after touring Western Europe, gets the essential bureaucratic permissions to drive himself to Moscow. A hundred kilometers from his destination Fisher detours from his planned route to do some unauthorized sight-seeing and ends up lost on a forested and isolated dirt road after dark. Approaching a sign that reads "Government Property," Fisher, alone and afraid, gets out of his car to survey his situation. Out of the dark woods steps Jack Dodson.

Dodson is a U.S. Air Force major who has been a POW in the Soviet Union since being shot down over North Vietnam in 1973. He has escaped and asks Fisher to get the word to the air force attaché at the U.S. embassy that up to three hundred U.S. MIAs are alive at a camp called "Mrs. Ivanova's Charm School." Arriving at his hotel, Fisher calls the attaché, Sam Hollis. Hollis is also an Air Force officer. On his last mission over Haiphong, during the Christmas bombings of 1972, he had been shot down. As he swam to reach his injured radar officer, Ernie Simms, a North Vietnamese gunboat had snatched Simms away. Minutes later Hollis had been picked up by a Marine air-sea rescue helicopter, but the gunboat had not been pursued. Simms's name had never appeared on any list of MIAs, leaving Hollis to wonder what had happened to him.

Fisher's call to Hollis is tapped by the KGB and within hours the luckless tourist is dead. His message has gotten through, however, and when Hollis is told by the U.S. Department of Defense that there is no MIA named Jack Dodson, he is skeptical. Hollis's contacts in Moscow's political underground confirm that there really is an American named Jack Dodson and that he is alive—but not a POW. Shortly after being shot down and captured by the North Vietnamese, Dodson had traded military information to the Soviets in return for asylum in the Soviet Union. Dodson is a defector. Or is he?

The next six hundred pages of this Cold War thriller develop around Hollis's competition with the CIA's Moscow station chief, Seth Alevy, to pinpoint the location of the Charm School, find out what is going on there, and plan a course of action. Hollis and Alevy discover that the Charm School is a former Red Air Force base where captured American fliers had been brought to train Soviet pilots in U.S. flying tactics. Later, the base had been transformed into a kind of finishing school for spies, with the U.S. pilots teaching language, social mannerisms, and the nuances of American culture to young Russians who would be "placed" in the United States for espionage. The re-outfitted base now looks like Pleasantville, USA, with a 7-Eleven store, a VFW hall, and single-family homes with all the modern conveniences of late-twentieth-century America; its "students" would be able to make the transition to the American mainstream without a misstep. The erstwhile pilots, meanwhile, had taken Russian wives, raised families, and in most ways settled into a new and surreal life as Charm School faculty members.

Just like *Valley of Death*, the novel teases us with the ambiguity of the pilot-instructors' allegiances. Are these men prisoners or traitors? And had the U.S. government known of their existence as live POWs for years but kept it a secret in order to keep good relations with the Soviet Union? Have these men betrayed their country, or is it the other way around? The story heads toward its dramatic conclusion when Hollis is arrested by the Soviets and taken to the Charm School. Will he accept the offer to become an "instructor" or choose execution? Before we find out, Seth Alevy shows up with a helicopter-borne raiding party, just like in the Tailwind story.

But Alevy, it turns out, is not there to rescue the pilot/POWs nor even Hollis. With bullets flying and the chopper's rotors revving, Hollis learns that Alevy is there to capture the Charm School's sadistic headmaster, Colonel Burov, who will be taken to the States to administer the U.S. government's own variation on the Charm School. The government considers the pilots to be turncoats, Alevy tells Hollis, and their existence is to be forever denied—they can never come home. Alevy has planned a Tailwind-like exit, having dropped timed-release gas canisters around the landing zone on his way in, the canisters set to go off just in time to cover the getaway. The camp guards close in as Alevy and Hollis wrestle over the fine points of Cold War morality. When Hollis sees some of the enemy soldiers beginning to vomit, he knows that except for Burov, none of the Charm School's "residents" are leaving. "It wasn't sleeping gas you dropped from the helicopter, was it?" he asks Alevy. "No, it wasn't," Alevy replied. "Nerve gas?" "Yes, I used sarin."

While all the elements of *Valley of Death* are here in *Charm School*—MIAs from the Vietnam war, POW/defectors, tension between the CIA and the military, a daring helicopter raid to kill Americans, the use of sarin—it is the political issue subtly present in both stories that is their most extraordinary commonality. *Charm School*, like *Valley of Death*, raises a question about the identity of missing U.S. soldiers: are they POWs or defectors? Neither story answers the question definitively. Rather, both use the ambiguity to underwrite the subtext that is at the heart of both—if the pilots *did* defect, it is because their own government had abandoned them! By this device, the *anti*-government identity of the pilots-turned-instructors at the Charm School becomes an act of patriotism, their treachery redemptive. *Charm School* ends with Alevy being shot and Hollis getting a last-second pickup by the lifting helicopter. On his way home, Hollis pens a note to the U.S. ambassador to the Soviet Union who had helped plan the raid on the Charm School. Using words that *Hardball* host Chris Matthews might have borrowed to bait April Oliver and Jack Smith, Hollis renders the POW or defector question moot: "I demand you meet us personally in London four days from today. The people with me are surviving witnesses to the murder of nearly three hundred *Americans* by their own government."

Like no other work of fiction or nonfiction, *Charm School* combined the elements of POW/defectors, hunter-killers, and sarin in a way that is too close to *Valley of Death* to be circumstantial. *Charm School*, however, was purely fictional and could be dismissed as such. In order for the story line that became *Valley of Death* to be believed, it would have to be given at least a veneer of evidentiary legitimation. Monika Jensen-Stevenson's adoption of scholarly pretense to "document" the hunter-killer theme in her book *Spite House: The Last Secret of the War in Vietnam* filled the bill for some people.[14]

SPITE HOUSE: VIETNAM'S LAST SECRET OR LAST FAIRY TALE?

In some ways more central to the production of *Valley of Death* than *Charm School*, *Spite House* is based on the real-life case of Robert Garwood, a Marine Corps private who disappeared from his unit ten days short of coming home from Vietnam in 1965. When he resurfaced in 1979, Garwood was taken into custody by U.S. military authorities and court-martialed for collaboration with the enemy. Garwood, it seems, had indeed been captured by the Vietnamese and held a prisoner for about two years. At that time he may have begun cooperating with his guards, perhaps even bearing arms and helping to guard other U.S. soldiers.[15]

Garwood was one of only two U.S. soldiers ever charged with defection to the communist side of the war but his case faded from public attention after his conviction. Then, in 1984, Bill Paul, a *Wall Street Journal* reporter, published an article alleging that Garwood had told him that scores of POWs were still in Vietnam. With that, Garwood became a primary source for right-wing political groups trying to use MIA/POW issues to build their antigovernment movement. Garwood's eyewitness testimony proved, his champions claimed, that the government had been lying when it said there were no POWs left in Southeast Asia. Moreover, the government's conviction of Garwood for treason, they said, had been an attempt to erase the reality that he too had been an abandoned POW.

Jensen-Stevenson became interested in the story in 1985 while working on a piece about Garwood for the CBS program *60 Minutes*. She came to believe that he had been a POW, not a defector. In the course of her investigation, she learned about a failed 1981 raid on a prison camp in Laos where satellite pictures had revealed "longshadows," shadows too long to have been cast by Asians. The secret mission was led by Jarrold Daniels, who claimed to have seen American POWs on the mission but had been ordered at the last minute to abort the rescue effort. Shortly thereafter, Daniels died from exposure to some mysterious gas in Thailand; Jensen-Stevenson finds reason to believe he was murdered.[16]

Evidently, the U.S. government did not want the POWs brought home from Laos or their existence even acknowledged. Why? Jensen-Stevenson's answer, which is very similar to Mike Ruppert's, and which she claims to have pieced together from numerous "sources," is that the POWs in Laos were living proof that the United States had been conducting illegal and denied operations in that country. They were also witness to the CIA's involvement in the heroin trade that supported its unauthorized war.[17] Because of what they knew, the POWs were never going to be allowed to come home, even if it meant they had to be assassinated—as Scott Barnes, one of the commandos on the 1981 foray into Laos, said he had been ordered to do. Barnes, however, was a questionable source so it wasn't until Jensen-Stevenson met Tom McKenney, a retired Marine Corps colonel, that she had sufficient evidence that a plan to assassinate defectors had actually existed and been carried out.[18]

Jensen-Stevenson met Tom McKenney in 1991 and learned from him how the Marine Corps assigned specially trained teams to hunt down and kill defectors. McKenney headed the team that pursued Garwood, and it is his story that she tells in *Spite House*.[19] McKenney chased Garwood for over a year before being sent stateside, but until the end of the war, and even beyond, he obsessed about his prey and sought every detail of information available on his status and that of other suspected turncoats. During Garwood's court-martial, information came out that McKenney had not heard before, information that convinced him that Garwood had been a POW all along and, furthermore, that *the CIA knew it and had intentionally concealed the information*. McKenney was crushed with the realization that he had been deceived by his own government.

The poignancy of *Spite House* lies in its conversion narrative. McKenney was from Kentucky where he grew up in a family steeped in Civil War tradition. He idolized Confederate generals, admired the portrait of Jefferson Davis that still hung at West Point, and thought his own generation the last "to care about such things as honor, principle, and duty."[20] Old enough to have served in the last days of World War II, he left the Corps after the Korean War because he thought political skullduggery had cost the United States a victory there. McKenney remained in the Marine Corps Reserves, however, and returned to active duty in the late 1960s after being retrained for special operations. He volunteered for reconnaissance duty in Vietnam in 1968.

In his first days in Vietnam, McKenney suffered a traumatic experience that would haunt him for the rest of his life. As order-of-duty officer at a headquarters unit in Da Nang, McKenney eavesdropped on radio communications with a Navy pilot who had been shot down in the South China Sea near the Chinese island of Hainan. The pilot, who knew that help was on the way, was about the be plucked from the water when orders came from Washington to abort the rescue: civilian authorities did not want to provide the communist Chinese with geographic coordinates they could use to locate the incident. McKenney was the highest-ranking officer in the communications center at the time and could have ignored the orders from Washington and allowed the rescue to proceed. But he didn't, and the vision of the abandoned pilot bobbing helplessly in the ocean never let him rest.[21]

McKenney's response was to busy himself in his assigned duty, which was, he later told Jensen-Stevenson, "so highly classified it was never put on paper." Initially, he understood the assignment to involve the assassination of Vietnamese military and political leaders, but the job was soon expanded to include defectors. His own notion of military honor forbade shooting someone who was not expecting it, and he did not like the fact that the CIA often called the shots. However, McKenney's military background also gave him a special disdain for marine defectors, so when he learned that Garwood could actually be operating with NVA units, he didn't hesitate. Viewing him as "an enemy," McKenney sent instructions to every Marine First Force Recon patrol to "look for Bobby Garwood and kill him if they found him."[22]

As Jensen-Stevenson tells the story, it was the manipulation of McKenney's principles that made his reversal of fortune so devastating: first he stretched his sense of manliness enough to accommodate the government's order to take unsuspecting lives, and then he found out that he had been lied to about the character of his target. Over the years, McKenney gradually accepted that Garwood had been a POW all along. With great remorse, he eventually asked Jensen-Stevenson to tell Garwood, "I will crawl on my hands and knees to beg his forgiveness."

McKenney's conversion story is also important as a clue that there are deeper psychological forces at work in the construction and telling of stories like his. In the course of changing his mind about Garwood, McKenney became a fundamentalist Christian and, as Jensen-Stevenson put it, "a preacher, a missionary without pay." His self-defined "mission" was to counsel other veterans of the hunter-killer teams. According to Jensen-Stevenson, these were "men with troubled consciences [who] came to Colonel McKenney in a blind search for absolution from someone of stature within their own military culture who was also a man of God; at the very least they were looking for reassurance they had not damaged their souls by following orders to kill men who were American soldiers."[23]

One of those veterans was Bruce Womack, who had been referred to McKenney by a decorated Marine Corps captain, Wesley Keith, a Baptist preacher with his own informal congregation of Vietnam veterans. Womack described in detail his role in the assassination of Americans and some of those details led McKenney to suspect that Womack's targets had been POWs. Womack claimed to have killed thirty-two men on one mission and, overall, he estimated that as many as three hundred U.S. soldiers, defectors or POWs, could have been killed by hunter-killer teams. Womack was certain his operations had been under the control of the CIA but, like McKenney and the men of Operation Tailwind, he admitted that there were no written records to document his stories. On one of his missions, Womack had a religious epiphany and, like McKenney, was a convert to Christian fundamentalism by the time they met.[24] As Jensen-Stevenson tells it, Womack was important to McKenney because his testimony moved the colonel still closer to the realization that the hunter-killer operations had been systematic and that the hunt for Garwood had not been an isolated case. Womack was also important because his religious commitment strengthened McKenney's own belief that peace of mind could be found through Christianity. It was his faith, as Jensen-Stevenson writes, that moved McKenney to seek out Garwood personally.

Garwood was reluctant to meet McKenney. "In the ten years following his court martial," according to Jensen-Stevenson,

> a number of men claiming former assassination assignments had approached him, always secretly and sometimes anonymously, to tell him he had been their number-one target. . . . Most were from poor backgrounds not unlike Garwood's, and were patriotic and deeply religious in a fundamentalist way. Most had been troubled over the contradictions apparent in their assignment from the moment they had killed their first American. At least initially, they had all shared a particular similarity: an innocent and zealous belief that their government and the branch of service to which they were attached could do no wrong.[25]

In 1993 McKenney wrote to Garwood:

> I believed the lie about you and was part of the effort to kill you. I didn't just want you dead, I wanted the pleasure of killing you myself. . . . When I found out the truth about you and realized what it meant, it nearly finished me. I'm coming out of it now, doing better. I don't know about you this moment, but it is the Lord's job to square away all the wrong of it. . . . [O]nly He can heal us and He will if we will just ask Him. You're not alone, and there are still a few we can trust. Maybe we can finally get the truth out to the American people. . . . We need each other. There aren't many people I trust anymore, but you are one of them. I'm praying for you.
> Semper Fidelis.[26]

The ending of the Garwood-McKenney saga came with their emotional reunion at the 1994 annual meeting of the Upper Midwest National Alliance of Families, a POW/MIA activist organization. It was through the embrace of Garwood, the "enemy" who had defined the most emotionally intense period of his life, that McKenney found peace of mind and was able to become reconciled with his former self, the patriotic warrior committed to the principles of truth and loyalty. It was he *and* Garwood who had been betrayed by their government, a government no longer deserving of their support and from which *true* marines must defect. Like *Apocalypse Now* and *Charm School* before it, and *Valley of Death* after it, *Spite House* gave new meaning to Semper Fidelis.

THE ROAD TO REVELATION

If there was convincing documentable evidence that Operation Tailwind occurred the way the CNN broadcast claimed, one could dismiss as coincidental the similarity between its story lines and those found in film and novels. Or one could argue that authors and film makers had merely produced fictional accounts of history as it had actually happened. But the evidence for nerve gas having been used to subdue U.S. defectors in Laos is thin and of dubious quality. That being the case, it is easy to believe that films like *Apocalypse Now* and novels like *Charm School*, with their story lines so similar to *Valley of Death*, stimulated the imaginations of Americans to revise their own memories of the Vietnam War.

In an interview, Tom McKenney told me that he now believes the Caucasians killed on Tailwind could have been Russians, not American defectors. "I think the Russians learned perfect English," he said, "so they could impersonate Americans in order to demoralize other Americans." When I inquired how they could do that, he asked if I had heard of *Charm School* and proceeded to give me a summary; the 1983 film *Uncommon Valor* about commandos who defied U.S. government authority to return to Laos to rescue POWs that had been left behind is his favorite war film. Telling me about hunter-killer Bruce Womack, McKenney said Womack had killed two defector/POWs in hand-to-hand combat and that one of them had looked him in the eye and said, "I knew you would come"— words close to those spoken to Captain Willard by Colonel Kurtz as *Apocalypse Now* approached its end.[27]

The supposition that the line of influence ran from popular culture to public memory and onward to the work of journalists like April Oliver, who produced *Valley of Death*, raises other questions that need to be addressed.[28] For one thing, even with the recognition that popular culture is enormously influential in the reconstruction of public memory, there is still the question of where and how these stories ultimately originate. Do screenwriters and novelists just dream them up? And what predisposes some people more than others to believe the stories—enough, even, to retell them as true?

As it turns out, these are very hard questions to answer, but the sociology of why people believe what they do suggests that beliefs often function to serve social needs. The stories about the U.S. military killing GIs who were POWs and then claiming the targets to have been defectors are really stories about a government that has betrayed its own people. Clearly, those stories function in a political way to focus people's frustration with social conditions that are beyond their control. In a sense the stories are a form of scapegoating, whereby the government is made the goat onto which people angry about any number of things can discharge their feelings.

But what about the origin of the stories? They could, of course, have been consciously invented to serve the ends of the antigovernment paramilitary community within the political right. But if that were true, there should be an identifiable point of origin in time and place. That doesn't seem to be the case. Filmmakers, novelists, religious conservatives, and journalists, some of whom have little in common with each other, have all told variations of the same story. Rather, the stories seem to emerge out of America's post-Vietnam political culture. The similarity in the details of the stories, moreover, suggests that there is some sort of common denominator in the imaginative process giving rise to them. Some of the stories have a downed and missing pilot in them, many hint at the duplicity of the CIA, and several involve religious revelations as part of their plots. In these ways, *Valley of Death* and its look-alikes would seem to belong on the family tree of urban legend.

Yet one feature of the government-hunts-its-own stories distinguishes them from even the war-story variety of urban-legend fare, and that is the conversion narrative that accompanies them. The presence in the stories of men like Kurtz in *Apocalypse Now*, McKenney in *Spite House*, and of Van Buskirk, who attribute their spiritual awakening to experiences in Vietnam (Van Buskirk says he repressed his hunter-killer memories when he "had a vision of Christ" in 1974), narrows the etio-logical parameters. There is no single point of origin for the stories, but their popularity among born-again-Christian Vietnam veterans is an indication that their truth value rests on the persuasiveness of the irra-tional as much as of the rational. The veterans who testify to the verac-ity of the stories are all fundamentalist preachers who claim to have been hunter-killers, as were several other self-identified would-be as-sassins of Bobby Garwood who later sought him out for absolution.

So, unlike urban legends, whose origins are very diffuse, there is a cultural center of gravity to these stories located in the space where right-wing political culture and Christian fundamentalism overlap. That, plus the displacement of reason by revelation in the genesis of these sto-ries, suggests that myth has an even more prominent role in their mak-ing than it does in, say, the stories of spat-upon veterans. This suggestion gains support through a look at how similar stories have functioned in other times and places and through an analysis that locates the origin of the stories in the social climate of instability and uncertainty that per-vaded post-Vietnam America.

6

BEYOND REASON: REVELATION IN THE *VALLEY OF DEATH*

And locusts came out of the smoke onto the earth, and power was given to them to sting like the scorpions of the earth. . . . The shapes of the locusts were like horses prepared for battle; and on their heads were something like crowns of gold and their faces were like the faces of men. . . . They have breastplates, that seemed to be breastplates of iron; and the sound of their wings was like the sound of chariots of many horses running to battle. . . . They had tails like scorpions, and there were stingers in their tails; and their power was to hurt men five months. They had a king over them who is the angel of the bottomless pit.

—Revelation 9:3, 7, 9–11a

There are diverse opinions among Bible teachers as to whether these creatures are actually going to be a supernatural, mutant locust especially created for this judgment or whether they symbolize some modern device of warfare.

I have a Christian friend who was a Green Beret in Viet Nam. When he first read [Revelation] he said, "I know what those are. I've seen hundreds of them in Viet Nam. They're Cobra helicopters!"

That may just be conjecture . . . but a Cobra helicopter does fit the composite description very well. They also make the sound of "many chariots." My friend believes that the means of torment will be a kind of nerve gas sprayed from its tail.

—Hal Lindsey, *There's a New World Coming*[1]

Most critiques of CNN's *Valley of Death* program have focused on whether or not its producer, April Oliver, had sufficient evidence to support the claims made on the air that nerve gas had been used on Operation Tailwind to kill GIs who had defected to the North Vietnamese. While there is a range of opinion on how strong her case was and how carefully she used her sources, few critics have sought alternative explanations for where the story might have come from or inquired into the qualities that seem to make it so compelling.

As reported in the last chapter, a review of film and literature finds that all the central elements of the Tailwind story, including its conspiratorial metanarrative, were present in popular culture before Oliver did her interviews. That fact, coupled with the likelihood that people who worked on *Valley of Death* knew about a book like *Charm School* that told a story similar to *Valley of Death*'s suggests that the latter's true source can probably be located where the personal biographies of veterans and journalists intersect with popular culture.

Questions about the ultimate source of the story are different, however, from questions about why some people found the story believable and, like the CNN producers, chose to tell it again. Conventional approaches to why people believe what they do focus on matters of material evidence and reason. Philosophically speaking, those approaches are said to work within a rationalist epistemology where proof rests on logic and empirical verification. Applying that method for a critique of CNN's Tailwind report, most critics have sought some kind of material documentation for the nerve gas and defectors parts of the story as if to say, "It is believed *because it is true*."

But what if the real appeal of this story lies not in defectors and nerve gas per se but in the conspiratorial narrative encoded in the telling of Operation Tailwind when those elements are included? What if, when people are told the CNN-reported version of the raid, they "hear" another story, one that is only implicit in the report? If that subtext is what draws people into *Valley of Death*, we have to pursue a line of questioning that broaches the boundary between rationality and irrationality in order to understand why many people find the story believable.

Ultimately, the search for *Valley of Death*'s magnetism is an exploration into what needs it serves for the people who believe it. What this chapter seeks is the motivation for the story, what moves tellers to tell it and listeners to repeat it. There are several clues that the story springs from deep and powerful cultural forces that were agitated by the controversial nature of the war in Vietnam and that have never settled in the postwar years. Most important among those clues is the popularity of Tailwind-type stories among the fundamentalist Christian community, of which Robert Van Buskirk, one of April Oliver's sources, was a member.

FROM BEACHES TO BABYLON

"Early 20s, blond hair, looks like he's running off a beach in California, needs a haircut"—that is the way Robert Van Buskirk described the defector he chased into a spider hole at the site of the Tailwind raid. With no corroboration for this incident, it's hard to escape the conclusion that the veteran Green Beret imagined this scene as a way of representing the duplicity that he felt had compromised the U.S. mission in Southeast Asia.

If Van Buskirk's image of what was betraying the military mission in Vietnam was a conjured reflection of something cultural having "gone wrong" with American society, he had a lot of company. Critics of the social movements of the 1960s, of which the antiwar movement was the centerpiece, read them as signs of a breakdown in such traditional values as hard work, respect for authority, sexual abstinence, and male dominance.

The backlash culminated in the neoconservative movement that elected the Reagan-Bush presidencies of the 1980s and continued in the so-called culture wars that extended into the twenty-first century. As the new conservatives saw it, America's problem was essentially a moral one. The turmoil in the streets, the erosion of conventional gender roles, and challenges to the white Christian sense of order suggested that America had lost its moral compass and was in a state of decline as a result.[2]

Government became the lightning rod of the neoconservative reaction. The federal government, said its critics, had supplanted local authority, which meant that families, communities, and parishes were subject to social and legal forces that were beyond their control. Public schools and universities had fallen under the sway of radical philosophies that valued change over stability and individual freedom over community responsibility. The nation's involvement in international organizations like the United Nations and the World Bank exacerbated the problem, moving control still farther from local settings and opening the door for policy influences that were culturally and morally foreign to the core values of America.[3]

Prophecy in Ezekiel and Daniel

These expressions of gloom had particular resonance for fundamentalist Christians who understood America's place in history within the prophetic biblical tradition. In his book *When Time Shall Be No More*, Paul Boyer explains that prophecy belief is a manifestation of oppression that took an early literary form in the book of Ezekiel. After prophesying the sacking of Jerusalem by the Babylonian king Nebuchadnezzar, Ezekiel tells of a vision in which the Lord raises from the dead the people of Israel and restores them to their land. He forms them into an army to battle with Gog, the great enemy from the North. God's army defeats Gog and, in a fiery apocalypse that lasts for seven years, destroys the enemy's weapons of war. Ezekiel closes with the warning that God had put the Jews into captivity because of their iniquity and trespasses against Him.[4]

The book of Daniel retells the apocalypse but alters the details. In Daniel's dream, four beasts, representing a succession of kingdoms, arise from the sea. One is lionlike but with wings and human feet; another is like a bear with three ribs in its mouth; the third looks like a leopard with four wings and four heads; the fourth has ten horns, one of them a little horn with human eyes and "a mouth speaking great things." The little horn destroys three of the other ten before the fourth beast is destroyed by a mysterious figure who restores righteousness.

The Book of Revelation

The best-known story of the apocalypse is found in the Revelation of John, the last book of the Christian Bible. John is called to heaven where he is shown a book with seven seals which are broken by Christ to reveal the future. Within the first four seals are signs of war, famine, and death represented by the Four Horsemen of the Apocalypse. The fifth seal reveals slain martyrs, the sixth a series of terrifying natural disasters. The seventh seal promises eternal salvation to the faithful whom God has brought through the tribulations. Later, John describes a vision resembling Daniel's in which beasts appear from the sea. One of them, scarred from a previous wound, has authority from Satan to rule all nations for forty-two months. The Beast gains followers who persecute those who do not worship him. Then the Lamb appears; angels report the fall of Babylon and the punishment of those who followed the Beast. After another round of plagues, a "great whore" appears "with whom the kings of the earth have committed fornication." The whore rides on a seven-headed, ten-horned beast. The seven heads represent five kings who have fallen, one that reigns currently, and one that is still to come. After another description of the fall of Babylon in which the corruption of gold and silver and licentious living is spelled out, the final battle between Jesus Christ and Satan ensues. Christ and his army descend from heaven on white horses to cast the Beast's false prophets into a lake of fire. Satan is then sealed in a bottomless pit for a thousand years, the millennium, during which Christ reigns on earth with those martyred by the Beast.

Politics and Prophecy

The biblical tales of apocalypse are clearly political stories, and that is what makes them relevant to an understanding of why *Valley of Death*'s subtext about government corruption seems be particularly meaningful to fundamentalist Christians. Ezekiel, Daniel, and John leave no doubt that God will judge nations as well as individuals. It is *kingdoms*—nations and countries—and their leaders that transgress against the Lord, and God obligates his people to discern good from bad among pretenders to the seats of earthly power. Those who follow the Beast and his false prophets will be put to death on Judgment Day. Thus, in the present, it is incumbent on Christians to judge their government not just on the practical implications of its policies, but on its moral quality as well.

Biblical scholars also tell us that apocalyptic stories are the sighs of oppressed people. In their most basic form, they tell about "good nations" that have been conquered by "bad nations" and how God builds armies of avengers from those who have remained faithful to him. He

then returns to earth to defeat the oppressors and restore the good people to power. During their times of tribulations, revelations of the apocalypse give people hope that things will get better. Ezekiel, as noted, was
historically grounded in the Jews' defeat by Babylon, whereas Daniel's
story was told after Antiochus IV of Syria had captured Jerusalem, plun-
dered the temple, Hellenized some of the Jews, and tried to destroy Judaism. Judah (known as Maccabee) led a resistance movement that
retook the city. John's vision dates from A.D. 81–96, when Rome pressed
emperor worship on the Christians under its rule.

It is no surprise, then, that when apocalyptic beliefs are widely held
by poorer and politically marginalized people, and when such beliefs increase in popularity during hard times and periods of uncertainty, the
results can be highly volatile. In colonial America, for example, people
fleeing from religious persecution in Europe often interpreted their
newfound freedom and visions of hopeful futures using the framework
provided by Bible stories. Boyer recalls that Increase Mather of Boston
"speculated in 1676 about America's prophetic destiny as a forerunner,
or 'type,' of the New Jerusalem." Mather thought that King Philip's War
(1675–76), which pitted colonists against Indians, was foretold by the
Red Horse of the Apocalypse in the Revelation of John.[5] As the struggle
for independence loomed in late eighteenth century, patriotic prophecy
believers fit the events of the times into the biblical stories, casting
Great Britain as the Antichrist and the revolution as a chance to "begin
the world over again."[6]

By the middle of the nineteenth century the optimism of the revolutionary period had faded. The country had been through its first major
depression, and civil war was on the horizon. In 1859 an Irish preacher
named John Darby arrived with a dark and disturbing message for
America. According to his interpretation of prophecy, time was ordered
by a series of historical epochs, the ending of each of which was foretold
in the Bible. The last epoch had ended with Christ's crucifixion, the current one would end with the Rapture, when all believers would be
raised to join Him. America was not the New Jerusalem; terrible times
lay ahead. Darby scorned the state and rejected all organizational ties
beyond the local congregation—ideas that provided a religious rationale
for the laissez-faire ideology that was sweeping the nation.

The Civil War and the social and technological changes that followed
provided fertile soil for the most pessimistic readings of biblical
prophecy. Late nineteenth-century preachers like Dwight Moody re-

jected the Enlightenment idea that as science and government solved human and social problems, the world would evolve in a progressive direction. More likely, Moody taught, humankind would degenerate and earthly conditions would grow worse and worse as time passed. To the fundamentalist prophets, the promises of social reformers were false prophecy and the liberals who espoused a better world through policy were agents of the Antichrist.

Enter the Identity

This pessimistic strain of prophecy received reinforcements with the arrival of something called British-Israelism. British-Israelism grew out of an obscure belief that Anglo-Saxons were the tribe of one of Joseph's sons, Ephraim, and so one of the lost tribes of Israel. Some believers held that the British were, in fact, God's chosen people, whereas the Jews descended from the tribes in Judah who had mingled with Gentiles and could be redeemed only if they accepted Christ. Among British-Israelist extremists, Jews were said to be utter impostors who were responsible for revolutions, economic depressions, communism, and almost everything else that was wrong with the world. These "Demonic Jews" were the counterpart to the Antichrist of more mainstream prophetic tradition and they would be punished by God in some final cataclysmic event.

British-Israelism came to the Americas in the late nineteenth century with the addendum that the United States was another of the favored lost tribes, that led by Ephraim's brother Manasseh. The movement gained a powerful voice when William J. Cameron, a follower, became editor of the *Dearborn Independent*, the newspaper of Henry Ford's automotive dynasty outside Detroit. Between 1920 and 1922, Cameron published a series of articles titled "The International Jew." In those and subsequent articles Cameron introduced the myth of "The Protocols of the Elders of Zion," according to which the Jewish elite met once every hundred years to plot the overthrow of Christianity. The plot involved all the trends toward centralized government and decadence foretold in biblical prophecy, plus the role of Jews, who, masquerading as gentiles, infiltrated government and business organizations.[7]

The depression and rise of Nazism in Europe in the 1930s enlarged the audience for ideas that combined conspiracy with the scapegoating of Jews. In the United States, William Dudley Pellem founded the

Silver Legion, a.k.a. the Silver Shirts (a knockoff of Hitler's Brown Shirts); several political and media figures, including the radio commentator Fr. Charles Coughlin, rose to prominence with anti-Semitic messages. The success of the industrial union movement and the consolidation of Franklin D. Roosevelt's New Deal economic program fueled the fears of the political and religious right that the evils of centralization and government control were at hand.

The world wars of the twentieth century did little to brighten the spirits of those who use the apocalypse to interpret current events. In their minds, the advancements in the technology of war—gas in both wars, atom bombs in World War II—were signs that Moody was right after all. The Russian Revolution of 1917 made real the prediction that a great enemy, Gog, would arise in the North while the establishment of Israel in 1948 fulfilled the expectation that God would restore his chosen people to the promised land before the end of time. The creation of the European Common Market after the Second World War represented for some believers the new nation formed from the ten smashed toes of the statue dreamed by Daniel.

Post–World War II America was an ambiguous period with respect to belief in prophecy. On the one hand, the expanding economy and political stability that characterized the first twenty years permitted the country's white, middle-income citizenry to settle into a monogamous, nuclear-family lifestyle surrounded by picket fences and two-car garages. The millennial-like quiescence of the 1950s seemed so sure a sign of God's grace that the Pledge of Allegiance was revised to reflect the reality: "one nation *under God,* with liberty and justice for all."

On the other hand, the increasing affluence of Americans and the growth of government regulation—both attributable to the New Deal policies of the Roosevelt administrations of the 1930s and 1940s—portended trouble. The automobile, television, and recorded music brought new cultural influences into the home, changing basic values about sex, work, family, and religion. The growth of large corporations, the unionization of the workplace, the ecumenical church movement, the trend toward consolidated school districts, and the extension of wartime economic planning into the period of postwar peace diminished the sense that life on the local level really mattered. The internationalization of politics through the United Nations and the globalization of financial institutions at Bretton Woods on July 22, 1944, opened the door to foreign and non-Christian influences in America's affairs, all surely signs of the Antichrist's hand at work.[8]

The internationalism manifested in the United Nations, the World Bank, and the European Common Market foretold, in the words of Jack Van Impe in *11:59 and Counting*, a "World State, based on collectivism, the planned economy, the regimentation of the individual, and a political and religious dictatorship."[9] The Trilateral Commission begun by David Rockefeller and Zbigniew Brzezinski in 1972 was viewed as "the sanctum sanctorum of the shadowy network of groups seeking global control," part of a vast international conspiracy with the grand objective of changing the way we live. "[That] the world is moving toward a one-world government is no longer being disputed," wrote Hal Lindsey in his 1973 book *There's a New World Coming*. Lindsey repeated predictions of a complete and violent breakdown in civilization by the year 2000, foreseeing "the formation of an oligarchical and repressive world government run by technocratic elites who John referred to as 'the Beast.'"[10]

SETTING THE TABLE FOR TAILWIND

The war in Vietnam provided plenty of stimulus for end-of-time thinking. To begin with, the U.S. loss there made clear that the nation's place in the prophetic tradition was no longer that of the New Israel. America may have been God's favored nation but like the Israel of the Old Testament, its pursuit of worldly pleasures—long-haired men cavorting on California beaches during wartime, for example—and its disrespect for God's will were blasphemies that He had now punished through the defeat of its armies.[11]

The most interesting prophetic interpretations of the war, though, were those that saw U.S. aggression as an act of provocation by the Antichrist. Working through his false prophets in Washington, the Beast had pursued the war through losing methods in order to stir up trouble in the streets. The secular version of that view, held by the John Birch Society—with which April Oliver's source Adm. Thomas Moorer was associated—was that the government had been infiltrated by communists who then *posed* as anticommunists to carry on an unpopular and unwinnable war. Birchers felt that the subsequent breakdown in social order, alienation of youth, weakening of the economy, and other maladies produced by the war were all part of an international communist plot to destroy America.[12]

The lines between Christian fundamentalism, which expressed the more optimistic prophetic tradition, and the despairing Christian Identity believers became blurred as both streams of thought fed into the populist movement that grew rapidly in the Midwest and mountain states during the 1980s. The two branches disagreed about the role of Jews in Christian prophecy and about whether the United States was part of the problem or of the solution, but they shared a faith-based framework for the interpretation of current events, a framework that imbued the United States with biblical significance and saw the sinister hand of the Antichrist in government policy.

The Rise of The Religious Right

Events in the postwar years seemed to confirm the fears of some Americans that government and corporate power were spinning out of control. The release of the Pentagon Papers and the Watergate scandal that followed revealed lying and corruption at levels that most people had not even imagined. In the early 1970s, with dust of the nation's political crises still in the air, the Organization of Petroleum Exporting Countries (OPEC) raised its prices, driving the pump price of gasoline to three times what it had been. The increased cost of petroleum combined with depressed farm prices and rising interest rates to throw the U.S. agricultural economy into convulsions.

Farmers have always felt themselves to be at the mercy of powers beyond their reach and understanding. The weather, of course, tops that list, but banks and government follow close behind. The vicissitudes of farming breed uncertainty which begets a political culture that is basically conservative and fearful of "outside" interference. The insularity of farm politics can turn extremist in times of crisis, however, and, when it does, it often takes populist forms that bend to the right. Unable to affect the forces that are really responsible for their problems, some farmers fall prey to the rhetoric of scapegoating. So it was as right-wing groups like the Posse Comitatus plied the plains and intermountain states with its message that a secret conspiracy involving government planners and Jewish bankers was responsible for the crisis.[13]

The culture spawned by distress on the farms also contained a militarist thread. The spearhead of rural resistance to the government during the 1980s was the antitax movement ignited by Posse activities. Holding that the federal government has no right to tax, Posse Comitatus encouraged tax evasion and in the early 1980s it begin arming and training supporters in military tactics that could be deployed against authorities trying to foreclose on farms or arrest tax resisters. In February 1983, two federal marshals were killed while trying to arrest Posse member Gordon Kahl in Medina, North Dakota. Kahl escaped but months later was killed in another gunfight with federal officers.

Kahl was remembered as a martyr by his fellow radicals and his death added momentum to the growing paramilitary movement in rural America. That momentum would lead to more armed confrontations between government agents and right-wing militants, notably at Ruby Ridge, Idaho and Waco, Texas in the 1990s. But it was the Persian Gulf War of 1990–91 that particularly deepened the rightist paranoia about government secrecy and added the element of nerve gas to the conspiracy narrative implicit in CNN's Tailwind story.

The Persian Gulf War

In many ways, the Persian Gulf War was a continuation of the war in Vietnam; President George H. W. Bush said as much when he proclaimed that the "Vietnam Syndrome" would be exorcised in the Persian Gulf, a reference to the supposed reluctance the American people had for another war. Much of that "syndrome" derived from the nation's obsession with how "the boys" had been treated when they came home from Vietnam. The popular perception that Vietnam veterans had been neglected, even abused, was countered by a yellow-ribbon campaign to support the troops in the Gulf and parades to welcome them when they returned. But the ghosts of Vietnam were not so easily quieted.

Most Gulf War veterans had grown up in the post-Vietnam era and had only the experiences of Vietnam veterans to model their own coming-home after. The model, however, was mostly a product of popular culture that had constructed an image of veterans as victims of neglect and betrayal, the symptoms for which were bundled into post–traumatic stress disorder (PTSD). In a word, the culture that Gulf War veterans had been socialized into taught them to come home from war feeling betrayed and *sick*. Predictably, within weeks of their return home, the identity of Gulf War veterans was submerged in a newly created diagnostic category, Gulf War syndrome.[14]

Some symptoms of Gulf War syndrome closely resembled those of PTSD, but other reported symptoms—such as fluorescent vomit and semen that blistered the skin—seemed bizarre, and it was exactly that quality of the reports that aroused suspicions about "what really happened over there." Where medical science couldn't provide explanations for the sicknesses, inventiveness filled in the blanks. Nerve gas, secret drug experiments, nuclear weaponry, and deadly toxins spread by the Iraqis were alleged in some circles to be the culprits. Many of the stories contained more than a hint of conspiracy. Perhaps our own government was covering up its use of GIs as guinea pigs or hiding information it had about Iraqi chemical agents.[15]

It was the element of nerve gas in the Gulf War stories that presaged the construction of Tailwind as told by the CNN reporters. The near hysteria about gas in the Gulf made nerve gas synonymous with government-sponsored terrorism by the end of the war, and the concern was carried over in questions about what the government knew and wasn't telling people, not only about Iraqi nerve-gas capabilities but also about the kind of exotic weaponry the United States itself might have secretly deployed.

Had not the use of nerve gas been put on the minds of the American people by the Gulf War, the Tailwind story would not have had nearly the appeal the producers hoped it would. Indeed, the expectation that the nerve-gas component of Tailwind, as aired by CNN, would resonate with the viewing audience had to have been based on the presumption of anxiety about chemical warfare lingering from Gulf War news. The idea that government malfeasance might have gone beyond covering up information to the intentional use of U.S. troops as guinea pigs for chemical warfare experiments was shocking. Still, it was a war story, something that had happened under the extreme conditions of combat in a foreign country. Removed as it was from the reality of everyday civilian life, the upset over nerve gas in the Gulf War would probably have dissipated in a few years. But the government's 1993 raid on the Branch Davidian compound in Waco, Texas, would alter the time line.[16]

Waco: With a Segue through Ruby Ridge

On April 19, 1993, the FBI ended a fifty-one-day siege against an armed church group called the Branch Davidians by raiding its facility near Waco. The government's operation utilized heavy military weaponry, including gas, and left the compound burned to the ground. Seventy-four Davidians, including twenty-one children, were killed in the assault. For many Americans, the deaths in Waco represented gross overreaction to a minor problem, but for right-wing America, Waco was the government's counterattack in a war that had begun when a federal marshal was killed by Randy Weaver's family in a shoot-out at Ruby Ridge in Idaho nine months earlier.

Originally from Cedar Falls, Iowa, Weaver and his wife Vicki had adopted the Christian Identity religious ideas during the 1970s. Like other Identity followers, the Weavers believed that Christian citizens are obligated to obey only the Bible, the Bill of Rights, and the Articles of Confederation. They believed the income tax was unconstitutional and that the federal government was controlled by Jews who conspired to use the Internal Revenue Service and the Federal Reserve Board to manage the economy in their own interest and bring about an anti-Christian one-world government.[17] The Weavers were survivalists who believed the end of the world was near and that it was time to retreat to an isolated area and prepare for the final battle against the forces of evil. In 1983 the Weavers moved to Ruby Ridge, where they built a cabin with no running water or electricity, except from a generator. They home-schooled their children and stocked the cabin with guns.

In August 1992, a federal warrant was issued on Weaver for selling two sawed-off shotguns to an informant of the Bureau of Alcohol, Tobacco, and Firearms (BATF). When FBI agents and U.S. marshals cornered him at the family cabin, a gunfight ensued in which a marshal and Weaver's wife and thirteen-year-old son were killed. The killings began a ten-day standoff that brought scores of supporters of Weaver to Ruby Ridge, among them skinheads, white supremacists, and local anti-government activists.

On August 25, five days into the siege, the FBI was approached by James "Bo" Gritz who offered to mediate the crisis. By some reports, Gritz was the most decorated hero of the Vietnam War, the man on whom Hollywood's Rambo figure was based. According to his own story, published as *Called to Serve* with the financial backing of Christian Identity leader Pete Peters, Gritz had been a Green Beret lieutenant colonel in 1978, when he was approached by a private-sector group that included Ross Perot to resign from the military and to do what the government refused to do: lead a mission to Southeast Asia to rescue U.S. prisoners of war still being held there. Gritz duly resigned and eventually led several attempts to find and retrieve POWs, the most dramatic event of which was a month-long covert operation called "Lazarus" that was launched from Thailand into Laos in February 1983. According to his account, Gritz and his men were deep into communist-controlled territory when they received word that a former associate had betrayed them and that as a result the prisoners had been moved. Gritz's team came under attack by the communist Pathet Lao. The commandos fought their way out of Laos and barely escaped back to Thailand without the POWs.[18]

Gritz was frequently in the news for his POW activities during the 1980s, appearing once on the cover of *Parade*, the Sunday supplement magazine, as the "American warrior." By the time he came to Ruby Ridge, he had also established his credentials as a political figure on the far right. Gritz's forays into Southeast Asia had convinced him that POWs were still being held there and that the U.S. government was conspiring not only to keep that fact from the American people but actually to sabotage efforts like his own to find and rescue them. The reason: highly placed officials in the government were implicated in the drug trade that was bringing heroin into the United States from Southeast Asia. If they admitted now that they had been lying about the existence of POWs, the rest of the plot would be unveiled.[19]

Gritz's conspiracist views put him in league with the John Birch Society and the Posse Comitatus, and in 1988 he briefly joined the presidential campaign of former Ku Klux Klansman David Duke as Duke's running mate on the anti-Semitic Populist Party ticket. Gritz resigned from the ticket to run in the Republican Party's Nevada primary, but pledged himself to campaign on the Populist Party platform.[20]

According to Michael Novick, who wrote about Gritz in his 1995 book *White Lies, White Power*, Gritz was drawn to the crisis at Ruby Ridge because he had known Weaver as a Green Beret and thought that Weaver had been targeted by the government for what he knew from his military experience. The raid on Ruby Ridge, in other words, was an assassination mission. Gritz arrived carrying a letter to Randy

Weaver written by Pete Peters. In part, the letter read, "Five hundred Christian Israelites from 40 states . . . are now praying for you and the Gideon situation you face." The letter asked Weaver to cooperate with Gritz and end the standoff. Three days later, on August 31, Weaver, his wife and son dead, surrendered to face charges for the death of federal agent William Degan.

Gritz's involvement at Ruby Ridge gave that conflict public visibility it might not otherwise have had. In addition, his persona bundled right-wing emotions emanating from issues left over from the Vietnam War, such as the government's supposed abandonment/assassination of POWs, with issues of current concern, such as governmental attack on the constitutional rights of citizens to bear arms and practice religion freely. As told by the far right, Ruby Ridge was a story about the government having turned against the people—indeed, a story about governmental authority having been usurped by anti-American individuals and groups. It was Ruby Ridge's story of subversion and betrayal that made elements of Tailwind sound familiar a few years later.

If there were any holes in the tapestry of right-wing imagination that unified unsettled sentiments of Vietnam, frustrations surrounding taxes and racial issues, and apprehensions about constitutional rights, the holes were filled in Waco when on February 28, 1993, the Bureau of Alcohol, Tobacco, and Firearms raided a religious center called Mount Carmel. Since 1955 the center had been occupied by an offshoot of the Seventh-Day Adventist church known as the Branch Davidians who believed the end of the world, as prophesied in the Bible's book of Revelation, was at hand. The raid began in early morning when BATF agents approached the compound, where they were met by the Davidians' leader, thirty-three-year-old David Koresh.[21]

Who fired the first rounds is still a matter of controversy, but for the next three hours the Davidians and the BATF traded shots that left four agents and six Davidians dead, and twenty federal agents and four church members wounded. Quickly, Waco became a kind of Alamo for a paramilitary movement that was already experiencing rapid growth in many states. Writing in their own publications, like Klan leader Louis Beam's *Jubilee,* and speaking to a broader audience through press conferences, the rightist movement used the siege at Waco as an opportunity to spread its warning: "There are individuals in this world, within the country, and in our own government who would like to rule the world. . . . [They] are working on sabotaging our freedom by destroying the Constitution of the United States, in order to establish the New World Order. To bring about this New World Order and ultimately the single World Government, . . . the American people must be disarmed."[22]

From inside the compound, Koresh held the attention of the news-viewing public with the release of homemade video tapes that explained the Davidians' apocalyptic views: the U.S. government was the "seat of modern Babylon," a government so spiritually corrupt that God would bring it down in the second coming of His son, Jesus Christ. In the aftermath of Waco, Davidian Charles Pace explained that the group believed that the fulfillment of the prophecy had begun with the BATF raid on Mount Carmel on February 28 and that Koresh was the servant who would initiate the government's downfall. In secular terms, Pace said, this was all "talking about the One-World Order."[23]

On April 19 the government launched the final assault. M-60 tanks outfitted with giant wrecking booms rolled up to the compound and began smashing holes in the roof and walls of the wood-frame structures. Gas canisters were then discharged into the building from the booms. Around noon a fire started; it grew to an inferno that quickly consumed the buildings and the seventy-nine people, including twenty-five children, inside. At one point the fire set off a gigantic explosion, producing a mushroom-like fireball that network newscasts made into the icon of the Waco tragedy.

Many Americans thought Waco represented an egregious example of government overreaction to a minor problem, but for the political right Waco bore out their prognostications—the U.S. government was at war with the American people. The absence of definitive answers to such basic questions as who was responsible for the last assault, what happened on that last fiery day, what kind of gas had been fired into the compound, and who started the fire left a lot of blank space to be filled in by creative minds.

Right-wing supporters of the Davidians claimed that some of the fire victims had died of rifle fire from Special Forces troops accompanying the FBI assault team and that the fire had been started by incendiary devices contained in the gas canisters. The gas itself was identified—in a story written for the *Boston Phoenix* by a former Davidian—as nerve gas.[24] The government, on the other hand, claimed that the gas had been a nonlethal tear gas, that there had been no military involvement in the operation, that no shots had been fired by its agents, and that the Davidians had set the fire themselves to create a self-fulfillment of their own prophesied doom.

RELIGION'S IMPRINT ON *VALLEY OF DEATH*

It's a long road from Daniel Ellsberg's liberation of the Pentagon Papers to the government's attack on the apocalyptic, gun-toting religionists at Waco, and in the minds of most Americans it is a discontinuous road through unrelated events. But in the conspiricist mind of the far right and those who are attracted to its views, the Pentagon Papers, the farm crisis, the Persian Gulf War, and Waco add up to a whole that is greater than the sum of its parts, and that *whole* is a story about the nation's subjugation to conspiracies that betray the trust of the American people and use the power of government against their sovereign will. Fear of big government and of intellectual elites is deeply rooted in American populist traditions; in the climate of disappointment and economic restructuring that followed the U.S. defeat in Vietnam, talk-show hosts like Rush Limbaugh and conservative politicians like Pat Buchanan assisted the right in spinning these events in ways that amplified legitimate concern beyond reason. In a phrase, it was the "fear of the unknown" that united thousands of otherwise disparate Americans in a culture of suspicion about the role of government.

Fear of the unknown is the purview of religion and, when the fears are about government, Christians of the prophetic stripe answer the call. When Peter Arnett introduced Robert Van Buskirk on the *Valley of Death* program, he made a passing reference to Van Buskirk's being a "born-again Christian" with a jailhouse ministry. Jim Cathey, one of the two other Tailwind veterans who testified on camera about having seen "longshadows" in the camp that had been attacked by the commandos, was introduced to CNN viewers while he was reading aloud from the Bible. Peter Arnett's voice-over identified him for viewers as a Baptist preacher.[25]

In retrospect, the fact that two out of the three men claiming actually to have seen defectors (or POWs) in the camp were connected to conservative religious organizations should have struck me as a significant overrepresentation of an occupational category. But it didn't. It wasn't until reading *Spite House* and learning that many of the men claiming to have been assigned to hunter-killer missions in Vietnam were today fundamentalist preachers that I thought religious belief might have played an important role in the origins of the Tailwind story.

Van Buskirk in particular fit the profile that was emerging for me. He was clearly April Oliver's main source among the six veterans shown on camera, and he was the only one who testified to the veracity of both the defector and nerve-gas parts of the story. (Jay Graves also confirmed those points but he was later discredited as not having been at the site.) I noted that Van Buskirk's book *Tailwind,* about his role in the raid and his subsequent religious conversion, had been published by Acclaimed Books in Dallas, Texas and distributed by International Prison Ministry.

Writing to Acclaimed, I acquired the list of materials it sells. Besides *Tailwind,* it offers a video, *Without a Parade,* featuring Van Buskirk's message about the need for incarcerated Vietnam veterans to accept Christ. Also on the list was *When Hell Was in Session,* written by Vietnam veteran and former POW Jeremiah Denton. I ordered the video and Denton's book; when they arrived I was surprised to find in the package a copy of a small book I had *not* ordered, *World War III and the United States,* by W. S. McBirnie. The book had a foreword written by "Chaplain Ray," who appears to be the leading figure in the International Prison Ministry with which Van Buskirk is associated, as well as the "host" of the video with Van Buskirk. The book identifies McBirnie as a Bible scholar, radio commentator, and minister of the United Community Church in California.[26]

World War III and the United States presents a synopsis of the biblical visions of the apocalypse and interprets them literally to be foretellings of war between the Soviet Union and the United States. McBirnie predicts that Europe will unite under the threat of U.S. and Soviet imperialism and that "the leader of this new Europe is known in the Bible as the Antichrist." The Antichrist, says McBirnie, will use "war, peace, deceit, and his own tremendous personality to bring about World Government."

The trail leading to *Valley of Death* is littered with evidence that it is a story cooked in the caldron of prophetic fundamentalist Christian culture. McBirnie's sense that someone interested in Van Buskirk's book *Tailwind* would also be interested in his tract on the coming of world government and the apocalypse more or less seals the case that, in the minds of Christians like him and Van Buskirk, the Tailwind tale told by CNN is a kind of parable to be read as a sign that the end of time is near.

What isn't so clear, though, is why April Oliver and other journalists found this story which had emanated from such an zealous subculture to be so compelling. By looking more closely at two of Oliver's prime sources, Adm. Thomas Moorer and John Singlaub, we can pick up a different trail, one pointing toward political ideology and personal experience as factors motivating her interest.

7

CONSIDER THE SOURCE(S): THOMAS MOORER AND JOHN SINGLAUB

I grew up in a small town in northwest Iowa during the 1950s. Chitchat between residents was common but it seldom became personal, and secondhand stories about one's neighbors were particularly unwelcome. When told that the source of the information was the "town gossip," a listener might abruptly end the conversation, saying, "Yeah, well, consider the source."

Most criticism of the CNN program *Valley of Death* has focused on the credibility of Oliver's sources and whether or not she used the information told her in a fair and honest manner. The credibility matter has been construed very narrowly, however. Critics have mainly sought to determine if a source really was involved with the Tailwind raid in the way he claimed to have been. In the case of Jay Graves, for example, doubts raised about his relationship to the operation led to his admission that he had not been at the scene. And Robert Van Buskirk, while he appears actually to have been involved in the assault, claimed after the airing of *Valley of Death* that he suffered from post–traumatic stress disorder and that his memory of Operation Tailwind had been "recovered" only when Oliver prompted him.

What was said in the interviews versus what was told to viewers is, of course, critical to the assessment of the CNN program, but there is another dimension to the issue of credibility, one that critics have not ventured into. A deeper look into the backgrounds of Oliver's key informants raises real possibilities that their organizational involvements and ideological beliefs may have biased what they told her.[1]

Thomas Moorer and John Singlaub, two of Oliver's main sources, both have extensive ties to the "hard right" segment of conservative politics in the United States. As characterized by Chip Berlet at Political Research Associates, an institution that monitors extreme right-wing organizations, the hard right believes that secret elites control the government and banks as part of an international conspiracy to force the United States into global collectivism. The hard right is militantly anti-communist and tends to be anti-Semitic. The affinity of Moorer and Singlaub for these sentiments is very significant in light of the fact that the Tailwind story reported by CNN contained suggestions of government conspiracy and coverup involving the military's mission in Vietnam and the well-being of American POWs in Southeast Asia.[2]

The light shed on Moorer and Singlaub in this chapter won't make any clearer whether the story Oliver produced for CNN was true. But with their full resumés brought into view, we have to wonder why no one said to Oliver, "Yeah, well, consider the source(s)," and thereby ended her ill-fated pursuit of the story. So suspect are Moorer and Singlaub that even those who are inclined to believe that she managed to get some things right are left to ask why she believed *them*.

THOMAS MOORER

Moorer was Oliver's trump card. As the former chairman of the Joint Chiefs of Staff, he was the most senior source she could have had for a story on the Vietnam War. His rank, plus his age, eighty-six at the time of the interview, seemed to be an unassailable combination. Who would dare question the veracity of an elderly gentleman with his experience and credentials?

As it turned out, Moorer was the joker in Oliver's deck. Following the June 7, 1998, broadcast of *Valley of Death*, the Reuters news service double-checked Oliver's sources and reported that Moorer refused to confirm that he told her that nerve gas had been used in Southeast Asia. Subsequent inquiries raised questions about how Oliver had used Moorer's testimony and whether he was too old to be a reliable source. While these were appropriate questions, they avoided more important issues, such as Moorer's record of involvement in Washington's Watergate-era political cabals and his connections to extremist organizations with histories of fabricating conspiratorial tales like those making up the subtext of *Valley of Death.*

Moorer: A "Plumber" Before His Time

Moorer spent most of the Vietnam War years in Washington. As chief of naval operations and a member of the National Security Council (NSC) in 1969, he helped develop a secret plan to escalate the war in Vietnam. Code-named Duck Hook, the plan grew out of Richard Nixon's and Henry Kissinger's fears that with the war going badly and domestic opposition to the administration's Vietnam policy escalating, a knockout punch had to be delivered to North Vietnam by the end of the year. The plan called for the massive bombing of cities and of the dike system that irrigated the rice fields, a ground invasion of the North, and the destruction of the Ho Chi Minh Trail, possibly with nuclear devices. According to Seymour Hersh, Duck Hook was hatched in Moorer's office, using what was called "the military liaison office" to shuttle information between the Pentagon and the White House bypassing the office of Secretary of Defense Melvin Laird, who held moderate views on the use of military force in Southeast Asia.[3]

The fear that their actions could not stand the light of public scrutiny led to a virtual paranoia among the plotters that sensitive information might be leaked to the press. Laird was a target of suspicion because he was viewed as soft on the war; hard-liners feared that he might pass secrets to the press in order to ingratiate himself with reporters as a secret dove. Laird was so distrusted that Nixon treated him "as a sort of foreign government out to get him." This obsession with secrecy led Nixon, Kissinger, and Moorer to construct a catacomb of back-channel communication paths cutting out civilian authorities like Laird.[4]

In addition to the military liaison office, the Digital Information Relay Center (DIRC) circumvented Laird and the State Department by connecting the White House and Moorer directly to field commanders in Vietnam. DIRC was exposed in 1971 when Stephen W. Linger, a disaffected enlisted man working in the center, began leaking information to newspaper columnist Jack Anderson. One of those leaks led to Anderson's March 24, 1971, column that revealed U.S. contingency plans for bombing the North and mining Haiphong Harbor. In his book on

Henry Kissinger, *Price of Power*, Seymour Hersh said the story "threw the White House and Admiral Moorer's office into a panic" that led to intensive internal investigations and interrogations. Linger also leaked information about Tailwind-type operations being run into Laos and Cambodia.

Yeoman Radford's Spy Ring

Moorer became chairman of the Joint Chiefs of Staff on July 1, 1970, just in time to assume the management of one of the most controversial and secretive covert operations of the entire war—the raid on Son Tay in North Vietnam where it was thought that as many as seventy U.S. prisoners of war were being held.

When Moorer took over, Son Tay had been under aerial surveillance for several weeks; planning for a POW rescue mission was already under way. The plan called for about fifty Special Forces troops to launch by helicopter from a site in Thailand, fly over Laos, and land inside the prison compound. Simple though it sounded, the operation was actually highly complex, involving in-flight refueling of several helicopters and their support aircraft over enemy territory, coordination of fighter-bombers providing covering fire for the raiders, and a massive sea-launched bombing raid on the Hanoi area to divert attention from the attack on Son Tay, twenty-three miles to the west. Training for the mission took place over several months at Eglin Air Force Base in Florida. The military spent millions of dollars for the construction of a mock prison site that was used for repeated rehearsals of the raid, and for thousands of rounds of ammunition expended in the practice runs. The raiding party itself was made up of some of the war's most decorated soldiers, including the legendary Green Berets Bull Simons and Dick Meadows.[5]

North Vietnam had always been publicly off limits for U.S. military personnel, although the whole purpose of SOG, as outlined in chapter 2, was to conduct operations into so-called denied areas, including North Vietnam, using Vietnamese or indigenous troops. For the United States to use its own men in a major action just miles from Hanoi, therefore, was a major political and diplomatic risk. At home, the raid would be viewed by Nixon's opponents as an expansion of the war, while abroad it could undermine the administration's efforts to rally international opinion around U.S. positions at the Paris peace talks. The situation called for the highest levels of secrecy and covert maneuvering between the Pentagon and the White House, activities at which Moorer was already adept.

The raid was launched on the night of November 20, and it was a failure with Keystone Kops coloration. One chopper crash-landed after hitting a tree; Bull Simons's team of twenty-two men landed in the wrong place, at a secondary school a quarter-mile south of the target; and, to top it all, there were no POWs in the supposed prison compound. Son Tay was empty.[6]

In the aftermath, paranoia ran rampant. Moorer, though he had conspired with Kissinger's office to end-run Secretary Laird, didn't fully trust Kissinger, so he enlisted a navy yeoman, Charles Radford, to spy on him. Radford was a secretary to Adm. Rembrandt Robinson, then to Adm. Robert Welander, Kissinger's liaison with the Joint Chiefs of Staff; his official job was to copy and shuttle documents between Kissinger's staff in the Executive Office Building and the White House. Since his boss was part of Kissinger's staff, Radford was duty bound to keep confidential anything he saw or heard in the secretary of state's office. But Radford purloined as many as five thousand documents during his fifteen-month stint in the position. He copied memoranda from Kissinger to Nixon, lifted classified documents from the "burn bags" that included drafts of foreign policy statements, and snatched secret information from the Paris peace talks. Using a technique that Seymour Hersh says may have come from Moorer, Radford would cut off from a document any markings, such as a letterhead, and copy the rest of it against a backing of plain white paper. When he accompanied Kissinger on trips abroad, such as his secret trip to Peking in July 1971, Radford would rifle Kissinger's luggage and briefcases for sensitive documents. At one point his own suitcases were so overloaded with pilfered papers that he used the U.S. embassy in New Delhi to ship three large manila envelopes back to Washington. Moorer maintained a special safe where he kept the stolen material.[7]

Radford grew to dislike Welander and turned to columnist Jack Anderson to release sensitive information that Anderson then used in his columns. When Radford was confronted by Nixon's own network of spies, later dubbed the "plumbers," he confessed to leaking information to Anderson and to being a spy for Moorer. Kissinger fired Welander and demanded that Nixon fire Moorer. Nixon refused because Moorer had been a team player in the conspiracy against Laird, and now, with the guilt of the spy ring hanging over him, Moorer was even more compromised and beholden to the White House. The incident left Moorer, in the words of White House aide John Ehrlichman, "preshrunk."[8]

Moorer, however, had his own insulation from White House recriminations. A native of Alabama, Moorer was a good friend of George Wallace, who was campaigning to be the Democratic Party's 1972 nominee for the presidency. In his biography of Kissinger, Seymour Hersh speculates that Nixon was reluctant to fire Moorer lest Wallace make an issue of his dismissal in the campaign. Wallace, of course, was the staunch segregationist who, as governor of Alabama, had resisted the integration of the state's university in 1963, prompting President John F. Kennedy to dispatch federal troops to Little Rock, Arkansas. The Wallace campaign was cut short on May 15, 1972, when he was shot by Arthur H. Bremer at a campaign stop in Laurel, Maryland.

With the assassination attempt, the political triangle formed by Wallace, Moorer, and Nixon was broken up and the Admiral's spy ring never became a campaign issue. Nor did Nixon pursue the prosecution of Yeoman Radford, claiming the proceedings would have brought too many state secrets to light. Hersh, however, concluded that Nixon was really afraid that the prosecution of Radford would the reveal the existence of the plumbers, who a few months earlier had broken into the office of Daniel Ellsberg's psychiatrist.[9]

Moorer: The John Birch Society and More

After his retirement from the military, Moorer's political involvements became unabashedly right-wing. In 1979 he became a board member of the Western Goals Foundation, formed by John P. McDonald, chairman of the John Birch Society.[10] Described by Scott and Jon Lee Anderson as an organization of "rightists who lamented the passing of domestic surveillance of 'subversives,'" Western Goals sought to raise money for the collection of information on individuals and organizations deemed "communist" by its leaders. Joining Moorer on the board were John Singlaub and the notorious McCarthy-era red-hunter, lawyer Roy Cohn. Moorer was also a co-chair of the American Security Council (ASC). Begun in 1955, the ASC set up "a dossier system modeled after the FBI's, which was intended to weed out employees and prospective employees deemed disloyal to the free enterprise concept." As described by Russ Bellant in his book *Old Nazis, the New Right, and the Republican Party*, the founders of ASC had political histories "going back to the racialist and anti-Semitic groups in the 1930s that were working in concert with Hitler's war aims." One of those individuals was John B. Trevor, secretary of the American Coalition of Patriotic Societies (ACPS), an ASC affiliate. The ACPS had been formed by his father (John Trevor) who had been actively involved in pro-Nazi, anti-Semitic, and anticommunist work during the 1930s and 1940s. In 1985, the ACPS and the ASC shared the same address.[11]

The ASC also spearheaded Ronald Reagan's campaign to unseat Democratic president Jimmy Carter in the 1980 election. Having honed their liberals-are-soft-on-communism rhetoric against Richard Nixon's opponents ten years earlier, the ASC formed the Coalition for Peace Through Strength in August 1978 to oppose the SALT II nuclear weapons treaty which Carter supported. The coalition produced a film called *The SALT Syndrome* which warned that Carter would unilaterally disarm the United States. ASC members stumped for Reagan's election and raised money for the campaign through the coalition's affiliated bodies. One of those groups was the National Confederation of American Ethnic Groups, which Bellant described as "an organization forum for, and dominated by, Nazi collaborationists, emigré fascists, and anti-Semites."[12]

Throughout the 1980s, the ASC continued to raise money for right-wing political candidates, red-baited antinuclear proponents as Soviet dupes, and produced films like *Attack on the Americas,* which drummed exaggerated messages about the communist threat in Central America. Positioned as it was—with connections to the upper echelons of the Reagan administration on the one side and, on the other, to the ultra-right paramilitary organizations that carried out the administration's off-the-books Contra war against the Sandinista government of Nicaragua—the ASC was a major player in both formulating and executing Reagan's Central America strategy.

Moorer's intimacy with the hard right continued through the time when April Oliver was using him as a source for her story. In June 1999 Moorer became a board member of NewsMax.com, an avowedly ultra-rightist Internet news portal. From that position, Moorer broadcast the John Birch Society's warning that the pending turnover of the Panama Canal to Panama in 2000 would open the way for communist China to gain influence in the Americas. In February 2000, Moorer was joined on the board by former New York congressman John LeBoutillier who

NewsMax.com said at the time "currently runs Sky Hook II, dedicated to recovering living American POWs in Southeast Asia." In a January 2001 editorial on NewsMax.com, LeBoutillier wrote that 1,200 U.S. POWs "have been relegated to serving as slaves to Hanoi and sacrificial lambs for the preservation of political careers back here in Washington." He went on to say, "America as a nation and as a people will not be whole until we go back to Vietnam and bring each and every surviving POW home—no matter the financial cost."[13]

From his early connection to George Wallace and his involvement in Yeoman Radford's spy ring, through years of organizational involvements with the John Birch Society, collaboration with Nazi groups, and a collegial relationship with John LeBoutillier, Moorer's biography intertwines again and again with the most paranoid and conspiratorial elements in American politics. While that background might not necessarily disqualify him as a source for some stories on Vietnam, the consistency between the particular conspiratorial elements of *Valley of Death*—such as the speculation that the Americans killed by the commandos were really POWs, not defectors—and Moorer's affinity for the very community that nurtures fantasies of that sort, constituted an ideological conflict of interest that compromised his testimony.

Did Oliver not know about Moorer's long history in what many people consider to be the lunatic fringe of American politics? Not likely. His shenanigans as a Pentagon plotter were exposed in a widely read biography of Henry Kissinger written by Seymour Hersh, himself one of the heroes of investigative journalism, Oliver's own trade. Nor could she have been oblivious to Moorer's role as a leading anticommunist figure during the Reagan years. Oliver had reported on the Contra war from Central America for Public Television's *McNeil/Lehrer NewsHour* and rubbed elbows with the very people that Moorer was mobilizing through the American Security Council.[14]

To make the opposite assumption, that Oliver *did* know the details of Moorer's background, reasserts the question that piqued my own interest in the subject: why? Why did April Oliver believe this story considering who told it to her? The assumption that she knew raises additional questions about what, then, she must have assumed about the gullibility of her audience were Moorer's background to become public knowledge. Did she really think that millions of viewers would find someone with his resumé credible? The poignancy of these questions only becomes sharper when we turn the spotlight on her other big-name source, John (Jack) Singlaub.

JOHN SINGLAUB

Singlaub did not appear in the *Valley of Death* broadcast and was not originally cited as a source by Oliver. Independent investigator Floyd Abrams reported that Oliver had used three confidential sources for her story and that one of those was "a former high ranking officer intimately familiar with SOG."[15] Singlaub emerged as that source when shortly after the program aired he announced plans to sue Oliver for defamation. In response, Oliver charged that by going public Singlaub broke their confidentiality agreement for which she countersued him.

Singlaub is a bona fide warrior whose combat service includes World War II, Korea, and Vietnam. He instructed the Chinese in guerrilla operations against the Japanese, helped establish the Ranger Training Center at Fort Benning, Georgia, and was CIA deputy chief in South Korea during the Korean War. In Vietnam, Singlaub was the third chief of MACVSOG, the command center for covert operations.

General Singlaub vs. President Carter over Korea

In 1977 Singlaub was an army major general and chief of staff of U.S. forces in South Korea. In May of that year, a dispute erupted between him and the newly elected president of the United States, Jimmy Carter. Carter had announced plans to withdraw forty-two thousand troops from South Korea over a four or five year period. Singlaub criticized that plan, saying it would encourage communist North Korea to attack. The withdrawal would "lead to war," the *Washington Post* quoted Singlaub as saying. In response, President Carter ordered Singlaub home from his assignment in Korea. Calling Singlaub's public remarks "inflammatory" and wanting to signal to the rest of his officer corps that he would not tolerate insubordination, Carter relieved Singlaub of his command on May 21. A week later, Singlaub was reassigned as chief of staff of army forces at Fort McPherson, Georgia, a move the Carter administration described as "lateral," not a demotion.

Military leaders viewed what happened to Singlaub differently. Many thought that Singlaub's analysis of the Korean situation was correct, and they read Carter's rebuke as intended to embarrass and humiliate the general. In their anger at Carter they were joined by conservative politicians like South Carolina Republican Strom Thurmond, who said he thought Singlaub had spoken out "for the best of reasons." Barry Goldwater, Republican senator from Arizona, said he was "disturbed" by the treatment handed Singlaub and "puzzled" by the administration's Korea policy.[16]

Nor was Singlaub sanguine about the turn of events. He defended his view on Korea before the House Armed Services Committee, charging that he had been "sandbagged" by the *Washington Post* reporter who, he said, had misrepresented his intentions. Apologizing only for his "naiveness about press relations," Singlaub took his punishment and assumed his new post at Fort McPherson on July 6 as ordered.[17] Nine months later, in April 1978, Singlaub resigned from the military after still another publicly aired policy disagreement with Carter, this time over the president's intention to relinquish control of the Panama Canal and his decision not to produce the neutron bomb.[18]

Out of the Service and Into the Shadows

When Singlaub spoke out against President Carter's Korea policy in 1977, his peers expressed surprise. "Jack Singlaub is not given to shooting his mouth off," a fellow officer told the *New York Times*. "He's not the kind of officer who thinks he's leading a crusade," a Pentagon source said, "he's apolitical." The image of Singlaub as a neutral professional uninterested in policy may have been public relations spin or perhaps he was leading a double life that escaped the attention of his colleagues and reporters on the military beat. The reality, in any case, was that beneath Singlaub's Clark Kent demeanor was a political zealot with decades-old ties to an international network of right-wing paramilitary groups.

On one level, this should have been understood. Singlaub was a covert-operations specialist whose career had begun during World War II. As the war against fascism ended, the U.S. intelligence forces began a clandestine war against their erstwhile allies on the political left. Fascists and Nazi sympathizers were recruited to the U.S. side for the value of their intelligence networks and for their technical skill in conducting undercover activities behind enemy lines. Klaus Barbie,

the infamous "Butcher of Lyon," was one of the more high-ranking recruits to the U.S. Cold War cause, but the infusion of Nazi talent was
accomplished at ground level as well.[19]

One of SOG's most legendary figures was Maj. Larry A. Thorne.
Born in Finland, Thorne had joined the German-aligned Finnish military in 1938 and achieved fame as a commando, carrying out behind-
the-lines operations against antifascist forces. He completed the
German School for Sabotage and Guerrilla Warfare in January 1945
and then joined a renegade unit of German marines who continued a
campaign against the Soviet Union after Germany's surrender in the
spring of that year.[20]

Thorne was eventually captured and imprisoned by Allied forces
but he escaped and made his way to the United States where he became a citizen and enlisted in the army. By 1963 he was commanding Special Forces units in Vietnam. When SOG was outfitted for
cross-border operations in 1965, he was selected as operations officer for its recon teams' launch site at Kham Duc, ten miles from
Laos. In October 1965, Thorne's helicopter disappeared on an insertion mission along the border; neither he nor his chopper were ever
found.

The mystery surrounding Thorne's disappearance added to the
aura of his legend. For years there circulated rumors that he had been
taken captive and was being held in the Soviet Union—rumors that
should not be discounted for the part they played in stimulating the
imaginations that created *Valley of Death* thirty-three years later. It is
precisely the link between military heroism, covert operations, and
the inconclusiveness of his disappearance, on one hand, and the paranoid culture of Nazism of which Thorne and his admirers were part,
on the other, that is the nexus of the story told by CNN's *Valley of
Death*.[21]

More important for our understanding of April Oliver's relationship to
the story she produced, however, is the fact that her source, John
Singlaub, *lived* for years in a shadowy netherworld inhabited by characters like Larry Thorne, a cultural space defined by distrust, violence, secrecy, and mythology. As Singlaub disappeared from public view with
his resignation from the army in 1978, he began immediately to establish himself as a leader in the underground world of paramilitary covert
operations. Ten years later he would reemerge from the shadows as a
major player in the Iran-Contra scandal.

Singlaub and the World Anti-Communist League

Singlaub's ignominious departure from the military echoed that of Gen. Douglas MacArthur, fired by President Harry Truman during the Korean War. MacArthur had wanted to press the war across the Chinese border and refused to obey Truman's order to clear policy statements through the Defense Department. His firing rallied conservative opinion that weak-kneed liberals in charge of U.S. foreign policy were putting the nation at risk to the rising tide of international communism. In Singlaub, the ultra-right saw a new martyr to Washington's insidious softness on communism, a symbol who could give their cause new legitimacy; in the rightists, Singlaub saw a constituency with organizational assets he could mobilize for a private war against communism at home and abroad. Within a few years, Singlaub was as well connected to the organized right as Moorer, joining the admiral as a prominent leader of Western Goals and the American Security Council.

Seizing on his popularity with the right, Singlaub convened a meeting of ultra-right-wing leaders in November 1981 to form a U.S. chapter of an organization already in existence, the World Anti-Communist League (WACL). The league had been formed in 1966 out of the remnants of European and Asian fascism that included the Croatian Ustashi, the Chinese Kuomintang, and the Unification Church, headed by the South Korean Sun Myung Moon. Ray Cline, an intelligence officer during World War II and CIA station chief in Taiwan from 1958 to 1962, was the conduit through which U.S. influence and money flowed to help found the league. Singlaub and Cline had been friends since the 1940s when they served with the Office of Strategic Services (OSS) in China. Cline was also involved in starting the Political Warfare Academy, a training facility in Taiwan that teaches covert operations to counterrevolutionary organizations in Asia. According to Scott and Jon Lee Anderson, who wrote about WACL in their book *Inside the League*, the expertise of the academy was transferred to right-wing terrorist organizations in Central America in the 1980s. One of the academy's trainees was the Salvadoran Roberto D'Aubuisson.[22]

Although the U.S. government had assisted the formation of the league, many of the league members harbored suspicions that the American commitment to the cause of anticommunism had been compromised for decades by inside communist influence. The Romanian Iron Guard and other Eastern European fascists, for example, believed that the United States had fought on the wrong side of World War II and should have joined the Nazis in their campaign against Soviet communism. The Asians charged that the Americans had been too timid in Korea and Vietnam; the Latin Americans and Cuban exiles thought that successive U.S. administrations had sold out to Fidel Castro. Then there were, as Anderson and Anderson write, the American and Western European neo-Nazis who were convinced that the United States was in the pocket of the Zionists who were using their control of international finance to subsidize the spread of communism.

In the late 1970s, the administration of Jimmy Carter became a lightning rod for the ultra-right's paranoia about Washington's weak commitment to the anticommunist cause. Carter's recognition of the People's Republic of China had enraged the league's Asian affiliates, his call for the end of apartheid in South Africa and Rhodesia had evoked the enmity of its racist leaders, and his support for the pursuit and prosecution of World War II–era Nazi collaborators sent chills through the European Nazi factions of the league.[23]

Some league members thought the Carter administration was hopelessly naïve, while others spoke openly of "Carter communism." A few weeks after Mario Sandoval Alarcon, then vice president of Guatemala, accused Carter's Inter-American Commission on Human Rights of being a "Marxist instrument," the league-leaning Paraguayan newspaper *Hoy* called Carter's ambassador to Paraguay, Robert White, a "Bostonian with Marxist feelings." The failure of the United States to confront communism more forthrightly was attributed by the League to democracy. Hernan Landivar Flores, of the Bolivian league chapter, said in 1974 that he was "convinced that Freemasonry, Judaism, and Communism act together to subjugate the world," and that the "so-called democracy" through which the United States acts is "no other than the anti-room to immorality and Communism."[24]

Singlaub began building ties to the Central American branches of the league within a year after he left the army. On a December 1979 trip to Guatemala, Singlaub met with Alarcon and other rightists to whom he promised support from a new administration if Jimmy Carter could be turned out of office in the 1980 election. Singlaub's networking paid off as money from the Guatemalan oligarchy flowed into the Reagan campaign.[25] Alarcon was rewarded with an invitation to Reagan's inaugural ball, even though he headed Guatemala's National

Liberation Movement (MLN), known to be the political party behind the death squad called La Mano Blanca (The White Hand).[26]

With the license provided by Alarcon's connections to the White House, the Guatemalan right initiated the most gruesome period of death-squad activity in the country's history. As bodies piled up from the reign of terror against individuals and organization deemed subversive, Alarcon used the league to spread his murderous campaign to neighboring El Salvador where his protégé was Roberto D'Aubuisson. Modeled after Alarcon's MLN, D'Aubuisson's Nationalist Republican Alliance (ARENA) party set its own bloody records for murder and mayhem, while Singlaub used WACL channels to mobilize support for the Nicaraguan Contras operating out of Honduras.

Meanwhile, Singlaub had also gotten his U.S. league chapter up and running. With financial help from Taiwan and staging provided by the Liberty Lobby, the new organization was born as the "United States Council for World Freedom (USCWF)" on November 22, 1981. On its board were retired military men like Gen. Lewis Walt and prominent conservatives like Anthony Kubek and Fred Schlafly, who were in turn connected directly and indirectly to what Anderson and Anderson have called "the anti-Semitic, fascist, and neo-Nazi elements that populated the World Anti-Communist League."[27]

Bridging the boundary of mainstream U.S. conservatism and the international fascist right as it did, the USCWF gave the league credibility in policy circles that it had never had. By 1983, Singlaub was the chairman of the International League; through its U.S. chapter and its affiliated new right organizations the league had the ear of the Reagan administration and the role it wanted in linking the U.S. military with the ultra-rightists in Central America and elsewhere. After aid to the Nicaraguan contras was cut off by Congress in 1984, Singlaub collaborated with Oliver North and other officials on the National Security Council to subvert Congress by raising money for the war from private donors. The illegal nature of that enterprise and the terrorist war it supported were publicly unveiled by the Iran-Contra hearings.[28]

What is troubling about Oliver's reliance upon Moorer and Singlaub isn't just that their political commitments place them beyond the pale of respectability, but that the particulars of those involvements implicate them in the very subtext of CNN's production of *Valley of Death*. The core of that subtext is a conspiratorial narrative about the subversion of

the United States through the infiltration of its government by alien political and ideological forces. The touchstone of Moorer and Singlaub's
identity with that subtext is formed explicitly, in Moorer's case, through
his intimacy with the John Birch Society, the country's premier propo-
nent of conspiracy views; Singlaub's fellowship with WACL members
who publicly expressed fears that Marxists had taken over the Carter
government places him in the same ideological constellation. Moorer
and Singlaub are such large figures in the subculture that incubated *Valley of Death* that Oliver's use of them as sources mocks journalistic standards of objectivity and presses to the fore, again, the question of what
preconditioned her to believe them.

8

WHAT WAS SHE THINKING? APRIL OLIVER'S WILLING SUSPENSION OF DISBELIEF

A con man I once knew told me that, "It takes two people to run a con. Somebody like me and somebody who wants it to happen. I'm the realist; he's the dreamer."

—Bruce Jackson

Bruce Jackson is a folklorist who conducted a series of interviews with Jim Bennett for a film he was making about Vietnam veterans. Bennett was a decorated Special Forces veteran and a munitions expert who had been wounded while on an assassination mission that was so secret that all his records were classified. On one occasion, Bennett introduced Jackson to Gen. William Westmoreland, the retired former commander of U.S. forces in Vietnam. Jackson's relationship with Bennett became collaborative when they began working together on film and writing projects.

As their relationship intensified, Jackson noticed that Bennett did not always deliver on his promises. Bennet would say that he had contacts that could help fund their film project, but they never materialized; he said he had a night scope like the one he had used in Vietnam and kept telling Jackson he would loan it to him, but the scope never appeared; when Bennett was hospitalized, some friends came to visit him and with Jackson in the room they asked him to return the Vietnam service medals they had loaned him. Eventually, Jackson was led to the realization that he had been conned: Bennett wasn't the Vietnam veteran he claimed to be.

Jackson "felt like a fool," but he resolved to bring something constructive out of the experience by writing about how such deceptions can take place. Working through what had happened, Jackson began to understand "that Jim fit perfectly the kind of narrator I wanted to hear at that time." Bennett's stories were rich with detail and visual imagery and reconnected the professor with his own distant past, including years spent in the military. "All stories are coauthored," Jackson concluded, "[by] teller and listener, writer and reader, actor and watcher, each a necessary participant in the creation of the space in which the utterance takes life."[1]

What is remarkable about Bruce Jackson's story of being taken in by Jim Bennett is that Jackson was a skilled researcher, professionally trained to identify the elements of legend and lore in a story. Yet he was fooled precisely because his own life course had predisposed him to believe things that were not true. Bennett's story had served the needs of his listener as much as his own. What happened to Professor Jackson could happen to anyone, and it did happen to April Oliver.

HOW THE EMPEROR GOT DRESSED

If Bruce Jackson's Achilles's heel was his yearning to reconnect with his youthful military identity, what made April Oliver vulnerable to tales spun by the likes of Robert Van Buskirk, John Plaster, and Thomas Moorer? The study of why people believe what they do, known as phenomenology, is a strange one, because those who undertake it presume that the individuals studied, the believers, don't always know why they believe what they do. Believers, moreover, are often defensive about attempts to probe the whys and wherefores of their certainties. Thus, simply asking the believer why he or she thinks something is true won't suffice.

In my sociology classes I use the fable of the "Emperor's New Clothes" to make the point that people sometimes believe lies about themselves and others because some self-interest is served by the belief. In the version of the fable I use, the King and his retinue have been tricked into believing that if they don't see the King's fine clothes they will be disinherited. It is a black slave boy with no stake in the inheritance system, and thus no stake in the lie, who is able to see the naked truth.

In the real world, matters are rarely so clear. For one thing, self-interest goes beyond material necessities. People have emotional needs, including needs to maintain personal identities, that are served by what they believe to be true. As with Bruce Jackson, an individual seeking to integrate different periods of his life might be led to accept as truth certain details of someone else's biography because those "facts" enhance the consistency of his own story. In most respects, the personal interest served in that way is a necessary part of maintaining a healthy sense of self across one's life course; when it interferes with professional judgment, on the other hand, it can be embarrassing, as it was for Professor Jackson, or even career ending, as it was for April Oliver.

While scholars interested in empirical questions will end their studies when satisfied that the King is indeed unclothed, phenomenologists are interested in how the minds of the King's loyalists have dressed him. Applied to CNN's *Valley of Death*, phenomenology asks how April Oliver came to confer truth upon the stories told her by her sources. Unlike Bruce Jackson, though, April Oliver will not admit that she was conned, much less reflect for the record on what made her vulnerable to the appeal of her sources. So, just as the narrator of the story about the birthday-suited King explains to us that it is the class structure of the kingdom that has blinded His Majesty to his true sartorial state, an account of Oliver's commitment to the veracity of *Valley of Death* has to spring from an analysis that puts her in a social and historical relationship to Vietnam—so that we can see, à la the King and his faux fashion, how she constructed the truth she sees.[2]

SIGHTINGS

It is clear that Oliver was inclined to believe stories of a certain type from tale tellers with certain characteristics. Fundamentally, she seemed be drawn to ordinary war stories, the kind with which veterans have regaled young listeners since the beginning of time. Her reliance on John Plaster and his book *SOG* is "Exhibit A" as evidence of her gullibility. Plaster's book reads like a fiction/nonfiction crossover, the type of volume shelved at the train station between war novels and memoirs, written by men with sketchy credentials but exact recollections of how they single-handedly won the battle for Guadalcanal. Plaster's writing is the kind of stuff that shows up in sensationalist male adventure magazines like *Soldier of Fortune,* so it's no surprise that his account of Operation Tailwind appeared as an excerpt in that publication's November 1998 issue.

Stories about the betrayal of the military by civilian conspiracies seem to have had a special appeal to Oliver. As noted in previous chapters, the way the Tailwind story was packaged so as to suggest that it may have been POWs, not defectors, who were killed, as well as Oliver's collaboration with Chris Matthews's conspiracy-baiting on his July 7, 1998, *Hardball* program, constitute something of an indictment of her on this point. Of course, Oliver's role in shaping the provocative subtext of *Valley of Death* and her participation in Matthews's histrionics may have been mere reflections of telejournalism's pursuit of ratings at any cost rather than of her own belief in conspiracies. But her performance on the conspiratorial Jeff Rense radio program six months later suggests otherwise.

The title of Rense's website is *Sightings,* a reference to sightings of unidentified flying objects (UFOs). Belief in UFOs is most commonly associated with speculation that extraterrestrial beings periodically visit Earth, giving us occasional glimpses of their saucer-shaped vehicles. But there is a larger following of people who believe that the mysterious objects in the sky are actually military craft on secret operations being conducted by the U.S. government. On the outer edge of the small population who have seen UFOs are those who believe the craft belong to the military forces of a foreign power that has already taken control of the nation. Known as the "black helicopter crowd," these conspiracists are sometimes associated with anti-Semitic organizations who believe that, unbeknownst to the people of the United States, the nation is already under the thumb of the Zionist Occupation Government (ZOG).[3]

Oliver was a guest on Rense's radio show on December 30, 1998. With her was Michael Ruppert, the editor of *From the Wilderness*, a newsletter in which he had published his own "POWs, CIA, Drugs & Sarin Gas" the previous July. As explained in chapter 3, Ruppert's article laid out the thesis that the Americans supposedly killed during Operation Tailwind had really been POWs. On the air, Ruppert mentioned having met Oliver in person a couple months earlier and reiterated his theory on the Tailwind story. When he finished, Oliver offered her endorsement of his position in an exchange that went as follows:

RUPPERT
One of the things I brought out in my article, is my strong belief, based on a combination with April's excellent work with other existing stuff, Monika Jensen-Stevenson in *Kiss the Boys Goodbye*, and other sources I have, is that the sarin was intended to kill not only defectors but prisoners of war because we never ever wanted the POWs to come home. And, of course, the second point I make is that Shackley, Secord, Atterholt . . . all of the guys—the Shakleys, the Secords . . . who were there in the CIA, in the operational theater at the time, the guys who were involved in CIA drug running. The same guys had their hands on both the POWs and the drugs.

OLIVER
That's really interesting, Michael. And I've read that article, and that's a *good* article that you laid out there with a lot of very provocative points. . . .

After Ruppert made some endearing personal comments about Oliver, there was this:

OLIVER
One of the books I've been reading in trying to get myself organized to write my own book is Fletcher Prouty's *Secret Team* . . .

RENSE
Fletcher's been on the program many times, what a man, yeah . . .

RUPPERT
I think I can sum up the whole point of the last twenty minutes, in my opinion, by saying I don't think the Third Reich lost the Second World War. I think it just changed venues. We brought a lot of those guys over here.

OLIVER
You know, again, it's not just the Nazis the U.S. brought over here but the astonishing revelation . . . is the Japanese had a huge germ warfare program and we apparently cut a secret deal with the Japanese who were conducting experiments on live POWs with these terrible weapons. And so all these Japanese were interrogated for the information and left off easy and weren't prosecuted for war crimes. Instead the U.S. got all the secrets.

It's true, of course, that the U.S. government helped German Nazis relocate to universities, corporations, and government agencies in this country after World War II, but the idea that Hitler's Third Reich was able to continue its war by means of infiltrating operatives into the United States with the help of traitorous Washington "insiders" is not true.[4] Oliver's improvisation on the theme, attempting to create a linkage between supposed U.S. acceptance of POWs being used by the Japanese for biological experiments and her belief that sarin nerve gas was used against POWs on Operation Tailwind, is an even greater stretch.

What's more interesting, though, is Oliver's reference to Fletcher Prouty as someone who could, as she put it, help organize her thoughts for writing her own book. Prouty is a former air force officer who worked with the CIA during Vietnam and who, undoubtedly, as Jeff Rense said, had been on his show many times. His book *Secret Team: The CIA and Its Allies in Control of the United States and the World*, is the fountainhead for ideas about a CIA/Jewish conspiracy to establish a one-world government. Originally published in 1973, with no overt anti-Semitic themes, *Secret Team* was later republished by the Institute for Historical Review, the anti-Semitic organization that leads the field of Holocaust-denial studies.[5]

Taken together—Ruppert's theory of an American Reich, Ruppert's and Rense's endorsement of Prouty (despite his conciliation with anti-Semitic conspiracism), and Oliver's apparent affinity for grandiose conspiracy theories—the ideas expressed on Rense's show don't exactly add up to a coherent whole. What is Oliver doing on a show where a guest, Ruppert, says he believes Hitlerism may have been reincarnated within the United States, while the host, Rense, thinks it ominous that Prouty might be right about an Israeli/CIA consortium— but would rather search for space aliens? Oliver, meanwhile, seems to be oblivious to the incongruity of the Rense and Ruppert positions but content with the notion that some sort of conspiracy of alien ideologies is at work within the United States.

Michael Ruppert and Jeff Rense are minor figures in the right-wing conspiricist community, so Oliver's pairing with them on a single radio show might be excused on the grounds that she did not know the company she was keeping. But she *did* know—she acknowledged that she had read *and liked* Ruppert's piece interpreting Operation Tailwind as an assassination mission with POWs as targets and sarin nerve gas as the weapon.[6] And any experienced political journalist working at the top of the news industry would certainly know who and what the Institute for Historical Review is. Rense ended the program, moreover, with a reference to Oliver and Ruppert as friends.[7]

The "didn't know" excuse would be even less viable regarding Prouty. He is, first of all, very well known to journalists and scholars interested in government intelligence operations. That Oliver, with her background in investigative reporting and ties to the Council on Foreign Relations, could have known enough to pick up Prouty's book without being aware of his reputation for over-the-top conspiracy views is unimaginable.[8]

Oliver's public embrace of hard-core, right-wing conspiracy views within months after *Valley of Death* collapsed merely sets in relief what it was that made her so gullible with respect to the Tailwind tales she swallowed while producing the program. To have bitten so heartily she had to have carried into her investigation a proclivity for conspiracist views—which in turn are probably more characteristic of American political thought than is commonly believed.

PARANOIA AMERICAN STYLE

In his 1965 essay "The Paranoid Style in American Politics," historian Richard Hofstadter described a mode of political expression that tends to be over-suspicious, apocalyptic, and preoccupied with "the existence of a vast, insidious, preternaturally effective international conspiratorial network designed to perpetrate fiendish acts." It was a paranoid style, he said, that emerged after the arrival in nineteenth-century New England of fundamentalist Christian beliefs that certain secular intellectual movements were actually manifestations of the Antichrist.[9]

Following the Civil War, paranoia ran rampant in the South. The vanquished Confederates blamed northern radicals for having incited the conflict and sought among southern whites traitors to the cause of slavery. In the postwar period of Reconstruction, veterans of the defeated Gray army regrouped into local militias to terrorize suspected collaborators in their communities and drive out the northern carpetbagging "outsiders." Federal troops sent to keep order were viewed as a foreign occupying army controlled from a distant center of power, Washington, D.C. The resentment of absentee authority and suspicion of centralized power seethed in the South for over a century, making the region a breeding ground for right-wing populist causes, states' rights movements, and assorted racist and paramilitary organizations. The South's xenophobia translated easily into the rubric of twentieth-century anticommunist propaganda, with the result that, as W. J. Cash notes in *The Mind of the South*, hysteria over "'Red perils' and 'alien menaces' nowhere found more receptive soil than in Dixie."[10]

Nostalgia for the Old South lingered into the twenty-first century as well. The battle flag of the Confederacy still flew over some state capitols or had been incorporated into state flags at the turn of the millennium. Attempts to purge the "Stars and Bars," as the flag is affectionately known by those who fly it, met staunch resistance in several southern states in 2000. After months of wrangling, the South Carolina legislature voted in April 2000 to move its symbol of "old times not forgotten" to a statue on the statehouse lawn. The statue honored Wade Hampton, one of the South's largest slaveholders before emancipation who was also a revered Confederate general and South Carolina's first post-Reconstruction governor. Wade Hampton is also April Oliver's great-great-grandfather.

APRIL OLIVER'S LANDSCAPE

The philosopher Ortega y Gasset once wrote, "Tell me the landscape in which you live, and I will tell you who you are." Ortega y Gasset was using the word "landscape" in a metaphorical sense, the way sociologists use the term "social position" to refer to our relationships to other people and the groups to which we are affiliated. We live our lives in a matrix of social coordinates that exert powerful influences over what we know and how we see and understand the world. Those coordinates can be described in cultural, political, and economic terms that together constitute a social position. By knowing our social position we can better know ourselves and, as Ortega y Gasset suggests, by locating others in their landscape we can know them.[11]

Where's April Oliver?

As CNN's *Valley of Death* story disintegrated, critics became increasingly interested in the person who had produced it. We quickly learned that Oliver was an experienced reporter who had begun working in public television in 1985 as an associate producer for a PBS documentary hosted by the former aide to President Jimmy Carter, Hodding Carter. From 1986 to 1988 she worked as a producer for ABC News and Mac-Neil/Productions, specializing in interview-format programming. Between 1989 and 1994 she produced interviews for the *MacNeil/Lehrer NewsHour*. Sandinista leader Daniel Ortega, Salvadoran President Alfredo Christiani, and Nicaraguan President Violeta Chamorro were among the Central American leaders she interviewed. In the Middle East she interviewed Israeli Prime Minister Yitzhak Rabin, Jordan's King Hussein, and Palestinian leader Yasser Arafat. In the four years at CNN prior to *Valley of Death*, Oliver had reported for and produced several programs, including *Newsmaker Saturday, Evans and Novak, Late Edition,* and *Inside Politics Weekend.*[12]

Giving us little more than these details from her resumé, however, critics left the impression that Oliver was an accomplished television journalist who had either tripped over her own ambitions by overreaching her sources or was being scapegoated by CNN bureaucrats trying to save their own behinds. In other words, the conclusion seemed to be that wrong though she was, she had believed what she reported because it is what her sources told her. While that conclusion was never satisfying to those who had been skeptical of *Valley of Death* to begin with, it became even less tenable as investigations into her reporting revealed her pattern of manipulating sources, and the sources began to disassociate themselves from the program she had produced. By the fall of 1998, it was apparent that *Valley of Death* was as much a product of Oliver's imagination as of her research. But what would have prompted conspiratorial imaginings so powerful that she made the facts fit her fancy?

To have believed the Tailwind tale she told, Oliver had to have a deep appreciation for the integrity of war veterans and an inherent, if latent, skepticism of government. Those characteristics could have come from early immersion in a culture steeped in military tradition and suspicion of centralized political authority—a socialization that would have been hard to avoid growing up in a Hampton household.[13]

Oliver's great-great-grandfather, General Hampton, was the third generation of Wade Hamptons to inherit what Manly Wade Wellman calls in his biography of the general "a far-flung private empire." The family homestead, "Millwood," on the Congaree River east of Columbia, South Carolina, housed hundreds of Negroes in two villages of cabins. The Hampton empire also included other large plantations in South Carolina, cotton land in Mississippi, a sugar plantation in Louisiana, and thousands more slaves.[14]

As a South Carolina state senator before the Civil War, Hampton opposed the "extremists" in the North who aimed to abolish slavery, though he rejected the reinstitution of the slave trade with Africa, which had been banned since 1807. Hampton thought the importation of new slaves would cheapen the value of the human stock he already owned and "infect" the existing slave population with "evil influences." His greatest fear, though, was that the renewal of the slave trade would give northern abolitionists an issue with which to precipitate a war. For Hampton, the *only* issue was "the union of the South for the preservation of the South."[15]

Hampton opposed secession, but when it came for South Carolina on December 20, 1860, he committed himself and his wealth to the cause of the Confederacy. Following the shelling of Fort Sumter on April 12, 1861, he accepted a colonel's commission and set about raising his own thousand-man "legion." He mortgaged land to buy rifles for his troops, pledging his mules, crops, and equipment to the war effort. He distinguished himself on July 21 at "Bloody Manassas," where he was wounded while leading his men in a rout of Union forces.[16]

Hampton was promoted to general before the end of the war, but his personal and financial losses outweighed the honor. He had been wounded several more times; his son Wade had been wounded; his brother Frank and his son Preston had been killed. More importantly, the war—and with it the South that Hampton loved so dearly—had been lost. As his biographer wrote in the next century:

> Hampton knew little but sorrow. He had no source of income, he mourned the loss of kinsmen and friends. Three thousand Negroes who had once called him master were now lost among the throngs of freedmen who questioned, begged and sometimes rioted. His Confederate money and his lieutenant general's commission were alike valueless bits of paper. Home from the wars he had brought memories of defeated toil and struggle, a gray uniform which he was forbidden to wear, and the scars of five wounds. That was all.[17]

Remnants of the Old South, Hampton among them, chafed under Washington-managed Reconstruction. A hearing in Washington heard charges that on February 17, 1865, Hampton had strewn thousands of bales of cotton in the streets of Charleston and then torched them as Gen. William Tecumseh Sherman advanced on the city. The hearing was inconclusive on the case, leaving responsibility for the city's incineration a matter for historians to debate.[18] When ex-Confederate soldiers formed into militias affiliated with the newly organized Ku Klux Klan, Hampton opposed federal efforts to disarm them, advising the use of northern lawyers to "defend our Ku Klux cases."[19]

Hampton's first election to South Carolina's postwar governorship was thrown out because of fraud. In 1876 Hampton rallied reactionary Democratic Party forces for another run at the governorship. His Republican opponent, incumbent Daniel Chamberlain, had won four years earlier with the support of Reconstructionists and free blacks. Hampton baited Chamberlain as a radical and carpetbagger and exploited his own former slaves for his campaign. Democratic Party "rifle and saber clubs" mustered as full-blown military units in anticipation of federal intervention in the election.[20]

By the end of the campaign, Hampton had remilitarized South Carolina. Outfitted with red shirts, his units "rode like the cavalry of Hampton's old brigades."[21] On election day, federal troops occupied county seats, protecting black voters from Hampton's Red Shirts. When the ballots were cast, Hampton appeared to have eked out a thousand-vote victory, but troops, Blue and Red, patrolled the state for weeks as charges of fraud and intimidation were investigated.[22] On November 26 President U. S. Grant declared South Carolina to be in a state of rebellion and ordered federal troops to defend the state's Republican administration. An armed showdown between Grant's soldiers and Hampton's paramilitary rebels at the state capitol signaled to all that war was imminent.

The vote count in South Carolina would determine not only who would govern the state but the outcome of the Rutherford B. Hayes–Samuel J. Tilden contest for the U.S. presidency as well. Ultimately, a series of rulings that went to the U.S. Supreme Court decided the vote, but it wasn't until March 1877 that Hayes won the White House. A month later federal troops vacated the South Carolina statehouse, and Hampton took office.[23]

The century between Wade Hampton's protofascist rise to power in 1877 and April Oliver's coming of age in the 1970s may have produced differing interpretations of the general's place in history and left a mixed legacy for his descendants. What there isn't doubt about is that one strand of the family history preserved reverence for what became known as "The Lost Cause." At the time of Klan resurgence in the 1920s, Hampton's daughter Daisy Hampton Tucker endorsed a paean to the Red Shirts by journalist Alfred Williams; when the South Carolina legislature proposed moving the Confederate flag to the General Hampton statue in 2000, Wade Hampton Oliver—April Oliver's father and the only direct descendent of the old slave master—told the Associated Press he would be "very, very pleased to have the flag there," because of what his great-grandfather had done to rebuild the state's economy after the war.[24]

Not Far from the Tree

Coming, as she did, from a family steeped in the paranoia of the Confederate tradition, it was not surprising to find that Oliver took a year off from Princeton in 1980 to work for Lee Atwater in Ronald Reagan's first presidential campaign. Atwater was from Columbia, South Carolina, and a protegé of archconservative Strom Thurmond. By the 1970s Atwater was already known for his Watergate-style dirty campaign tricks. He planted rumors against opponents and Jew-gay-and-liberal-baited their staff workers. After he won South Carolina for Reagan in the 1980 primaries, Atwater was promoted to regional director for the Southeast; when Reagan won the White House, Strom Thurmond got him a job as the president's deputy assistant for political affairs.[25]

It is hard to say what April Oliver's role was on Atwater's staff. Atwater died of cancer in 1991 and left no papers that I've been able to find. My attempts to use the campaign records at the Reagan library were rebuffed. Nor do we know how she got the job with Atwater, although journalist Arthur Allen interviewed her at length for a major story in the *Washington Post* and later surmised that family connections had landed her the position. In any case, Oliver's involvement with the paranoid-style Thurmond/Atwater/Reagan stream of American politics was consistent with her family background and anticipated her receptivity to the conspiratorial subtext of the Tailwind tale sixteen years later.

During her months on Atwater's campaign staff, Oliver could well have come in contact with military or CIA-connected people who stimulated her imagination about government conspiracies and the betrayal of the U.S. mission in Vietnam. One of Atwater's first campaign gigs, after all, had been General Westmoreland's failed 1974 run for the South Carolina statehouse. Westmoreland had been the commander of U.S. forces in Vietnam from 1964 to 1968, so there is no doubt that the network of Atwater political operatives that Oliver stepped into when she enlisted in the Reagan campaign was laced with militarism.[26]

It may have been experiences or conversations during the Reagan campaign that primed Oliver for the Tailwind stories, but that wasn't the only preparation she had. In 1982 she went to Pakistan to tour Afghan refugee camps and collect information for her senior thesis at Princeton. Exploiting what she called "influential personal contacts," Oliver was able to visit a dozen refugee camps over a six-week period; there she observed the training of the mujahideen troops—"freedom fighters," as she called them—who would later support the establishment of a radical Islamist state in Afghanistan.[27] The training in those camps was largely under the tutelage of U.S. special operations forces and the CIA. When Marc Fisher interviewed her for an article about how she had become interested in the cloak-and-dagger stuff that led her to *Valley of Death,* she recalled her time in Pakistan as "her first exposure to the covert world of intrigue." With her tour of the camps, wrote Fisher in the *Princeton Alumni Weekly,* "Oliver was hooked."[28]

DON'T KNOW MUCH ABOUT HISTORY

In 1983, the academic journal *NACLA: Report on the Americas* did a special issue on war and the news media. The editors wrote that reporters frequently lack a sense of history with which to assess the quality of their sources. The editors used as an example stories about a new minister of defense in El Salvador that had appeared in the *New York Times* and the *Dallas Times-Herald.* Written by Lydia Chavez, who had relied on "official sources" because she had little familiarity with the situation in El Salvador, the *Times* story portrayed Gen. Carlos Eugenio Vides Casanova as an honest reformer who had helped bring to justice the guardsmen who murdered four church workers in 1980. The *Times-Herald* piece, on the other hand, was written by the more experienced Bob Rivard who worked into his story historical details and information from informed but unofficial sources in order to implicate Vides Casanova in the cover-up of those killings.[29]

Even more than Chavez's in the *NACLA* report, Oliver's mistakes in producing *Valley of Death* make her a poster figure for journalists with no sense of history. With better historical grounding in the war, she would have known that there has never been any reason to believe that there were more than isolated defections of individual American soldiers during the war. Familiarity with the history and culture of the antiwar movement, moreover, would have told her that even people on the political left who might have *wanted* to believe that GIs would have joined the communist forces never trafficked in rumors about actual defections. She would also have known that the use of sarin nerve gas to kill defectors (or POWs) would have made no political or tactical sense.

Just as important as what she would have known with a grounding in the history of the war is what she would *not* have known. April Oliver was as much victimized by the falsified images that had been written *into* history as by what had been written out. The whole Tailwind tale that Oliver came to believe was full of Hollywood imagery—the swashbuckling "special ops" guys, the exotic technology of helicopters and obscure weaponry, Americans in search of Americans, multiple levels of betrayal, and a war fought "over the fence" on the Ho Chi Minh trail. So much of it was right out of the movies.

Oliver came to political maturity during the late 1970s and early 1980s when, as we've seen, the war in Vietnam was being heavily mythologized in popular culture. She hasn't cooperated with attempts to document her formal educational experience, so I can't say what courses she may have taken at Princeton or what books she may have read about the war. Assuming the best about the quality of her course work and reading habits, however, there is no gainsaying that powerful cultural forces leave their stamps on the generations exposed to them, and that for the 1980s cohort of young intellectuals of which Oliver was a part there was no more defining political theme than the Ramboesque mission to shake America's Vietnam syndrome by continuing the war. In her most impressionable years, America's movie theaters were stuffed with films with MIA/POW themes, like *Missing in Action* (1984), and films with hunter-killer plots, like *Eye of the Eagle* (1987). Those films' story lines began leaching into the nation's political culture when President Ronald Reagan alluded to *First Blood* in a 1985 speech about the hostage situation in Beirut; soon other political leaders were aping Rambo's lines.[30]

Educators who teach the history of the war in Vietnam have known for several decades that most of what post-Vietnam generations know (or think they know) about the war is derived from popular culture, and there is no reason to think that April Oliver would have been an exception. In fact, given the similarity between what Hollywood put on the screen in the 1980s and what Oliver aired for CNN in the 1990s, we have every reason to doubt that she was sufficiently reflective to ask why what she was hearing from her sources sounded right to her.

The Perils of Oral History

Oliver's methodology also betrayed her and, again, her mistake grew out of assumptions that had been spawned by the war itself and that by the 1990s had received the imprimatur of mainstream academic and journalistic practice. Oliver was overly reliant on oral history, the recollections of first-hand participants in the events she was interested in. As a method, oral history became popular during the 1970s as a counterweight to the more traditional use as sources of leaders of organizations and of documents generated by private and public institutions. It was largely the skepticism of "official sources" for information on the war that led reporters and scholars to seek alternative points of view, and the alternative they found for the Vietnam War to the view from "the top," such as spokesmen for the Pentagon or State Department, was the grunt-level view of GIs. The formation of Vietnam Veterans against the War, with its own network of antiwar newspapers, speaker bureaus, and guerilla theater events, provided an organized link between the in-service dissent that was rampant by the late 1960s and the civilian press corps. By the end of the war, reporters like Michael Herr who had gotten into the field and spent time with the troops had the greatest credibility with the American audience.[31]

In the academic world, there were parallel methodological developments. Historians pioneering what became known as "history from the bottom up" were expressing exuberance for oral, as opposed to written, accounts of history. It was a technique, said its advocates, that privileged the voices of those with limited literacy or access to the means of making written records. Historians were particularly interested in the oral histories of rank-and-file workers and people who had been socially marginalized by their race or gender identities. The same approach was eventually adopted by sociologists who extended the deference afforded "different voices" to all victims of social violence.

The Tailwind topic that Oliver dived into in 1997 was right at the convergence of methodological revisionisms flowing out of journalism and academia. More than for any other war in history, the history of Vietnam was being mediated by the memories of the men who fought it, and the more victimized the veteran, the more credible his voice. The voice of the victim-veteran was amplified when in 1980 the Veterans Memorial Wall in Washington, D.C., was unveiled. The Wall, as Marita Sturken tells us in her book *Tangled Memories*, had the effect of screening out everything else that was important (such as the three million Vietnamese dead and U.S. government policies that got us into the conflict), leaving us to contemplate solely the American victims of the war. At about the same time, the psychiatric profession canonized post–traumatic stress disorder (PTSD) as a diagnostic category for troubled Vietnam veterans. Central to the notion of PTSD was the claim that veterans had been greeted with hostility upon their return from war, adding to the trauma of their wartime experience. By the 1980s the influence of the Wall, the legitimation of PTSD, and the establishment of the whacked-out veteran as the stock Hollywood image of Vietnam veterans were all working in harmony, and the cachet of the victim-veteran voice soared. Television documentaries were loaded with veterans telling war-is-hell-but-coming-home-is-worse stories, and public schools began to teach the history of the war (if at all) by having local veterans tell their stories in school assemblies.[32]

In some ways, then, the centrality of Robert Van Buskirk to April Oliver's research caricaturizes her blindness to the pitfalls in her approach—reliance on twenty-five-year-old memories of a veteran who claimed to suffer from PTSD and told warrior stories that should have been immediately suspect. As proof that she really had bought into all the fallacious assumptions implicit in her method, Oliver countered her critics with guilt-tripping innuendo, implying that the voice of veterans should be beyond reproach and that Van Buskirk's PTSD gave him immunity from criticism.[33]

FITTING THE PROFILE

Marc Fisher's description of Oliver as "hooked" on the intrigue of covert operations was a damning charge to make against a journalist. It implied that Oliver had lost a sense of objectivity on the subjects she was supposed to be investigating and was incapable of making professional judgments about the logic of the story she had produced and the quality of her sources.

Oliver's response to critics only lengthened Fisher's indictment. A year after her sacking by CNN she told a group of young journalists at the National Press Club that she was the victim of a disinformation campaign that ran from Special Forces veterans trying to protect their own reputations through CNN managers trying to protect their careers and the company's assets, to former Nixon advisor Henry Kissinger and secretary-of-state-in-waiting Colin Powell.[34] When Richard Shultz, author of *The Secret War against Hanoi*, began talking to Oliver about her research for *Valley of Death*, he found her cooperative, but as his skepticism about her methods grew, her attitude changed. In October 2000, he told me, Oliver would not talk to him any more, saying "She thinks there is a conspiracy against her and that I'm part of it."

If one had to profile a person who would buy into political conspiracy theory and believe a story like *Valley of Death*, Oliver would be easily identified in the lineup of suspects: too young to know the war in Vietnam except through movies and novels, politically conservative, and steeped in a culture of betrayal. In short, April Oliver is the Bruce Jackson in this story; for reasons having far more to do with her background than with her character, she was pulled into the conspiratorial subtext of the Tailwind tale and felt a compulsion to produce it for her audience. Like Bruce Jackson, she had as much need to believe the stories told to her as the tellers had to tell them.

Oliver, of course, was not flying solo on her production of *Valley of Death*. Jack Smith was a coproducer, and the contents of the show were vetted through CNN's legal department and then by high levels of management. The fact that *Valley of Death* could sound right to so many well informed and otherwise responsible people suggests that there is something even more important at the root of the Tailwind affair than one reporter's predisposition to believe. As the next chapter will show, April Oliver's willingness to believe the unbelievable was not an occurrence unique to her profession, nor was it particularly associated with stories related to the war in Vietnam. The loss of the war, however, contributed to the pervasive climate of fear felt by Americans in the last years of the twentieth century.

9

THE CNN-TAILWIND AFFAIR: JOURNALISM IN A FEARFUL AMERICA

Oliver and Smith fell in love with their story.

—Rick Kaplan, Chairman CNN/USA

The only love affair was Rick Kaplan's love affair with his big-time job. He likes the power, money, and being boss just a little too much.

—Jack Smith, CNN Producer (fired by Rick Kaplan)

CNN had fallen in love with the prospect of a hot, newsmaking, ratings-building story as a curtain-raiser for its new series.

—*Columbia Journalism Review*[1]

The finger-pointing for the fiasco of *Valley of Death* began soon after the story was retracted, and students of American journalism could have predicted who would blame whom for what. The issue of journalist bias was embedded in the affair from the outset. Oliver's passionate commitment to the story was implicit in her courage to pursue it, despite knowing that she was swimming against some powerful political currents, and in the aggressiveness she exhibited in her interviews. When questions were raised about the veracity of her report, it was not surprising that critics zeroed in on her objectivity.

Oliver, perhaps on the advice of Smith, had made sure, however, that she had plenty of organizational support for the story she took to market. Rick Kaplan was the chairman of her division at CNN, and he had read the script before the broadcast. Walter Isaacson, managing editor at Time, Inc., thought the *Time* version of the story, authored by Oliver and Peter Arnett, was sufficiently sourced and gave the go-ahead to run it. Other higher-ups at CNN, such as President Tom Johnson and Pam Hill, had access to Oliver's research and raised no objections to it prior to air time. With good reason to think the CNN and Time, Inc., organizations covered their backs, Oliver and Smith were understandably upset to find themselves gunned down by the very people they looked to for cover. The ultimate responsibility for the story lay with Oliver and Smith, something they never denied, but Kaplan's isolation of their mistakes from the organizational and societal contexts within which they were made—which his crack about "falling in love with their story" surely did—was an exercise in scapegoating.

Smith's countercharge that *Valley of Death*'s troubles stemmed from managerial faux pas was likewise off the mark. Intra-organization dynamics have long been recognized as an important factor in what gets produced as news and how the job gets done. News organizations operate on tight deadlines and budgets, realities that sometimes conflict with the obligation that journalists and reporters feel to produce high-quality news measuring up to the standards of their profession. For investigative journalists working on something historical like Operation Tailwind, however, the production time lines are not as short as they are for the daily news reporters. Nor, from anything I've seen, did disagreements over the budget for *Valley of Death* become an issue. The amount of air time allotted to the broadcast—eighteen minutes is what Oliver and Smith got—was an issue, and it might be true that to save air time editors cut material that could have made *Valley of Death* a little stronger. But the postmortem on the broadcast revealed flaws that a longer segment would not have repaired. Indeed, one might suppose that, given the course Oliver and Smith were on with their production, they might have used the additional time to dig themselves into a deepening hole.[2]

In any case, Smith's charge that Kaplan was too interested in Kaplan pertained to the postbroadcast brouhaha, not to what had gone wrong in the production of the story and management's prebroadcast approval of it. Undoubtedly, the chairman of CNN/USA was protecting his own job and his managerial reputation with his finger-pointing, but Smith's effort to meet Kaplan's personal attack with an assault of his own on the boss's integrity evaded his and Oliver's responsibility for a shoddy piece of journalism.

The *Columbia Journalism Review*'s instinct to look beyond Smith and Kaplan's personal impugnations is constructive. Writing in its September/October 1998 edition, *CJR*'s editor-at-large Neil Hickey said overzealous producers (Oliver and Smith) and insufficient supervision of production (by management) had both played a role in the affair but added that those mistakes had occurred in a pressurized climate as CNN strove to reverse falling ratings. *NewsStand*, of which *Valley of Death* was the first edition, was a joint *Time* and CNN venture designed to buff CNN's credibility as a news organization, while the regular televising of the *Time* logo was intended to increase the magazine's visibility in the electronic marketplace. What Hickey was hinting at was that the drive to make a profit had pushed *Time* and CNN into lowering their journalistic standards and that the planned journalistic synergy created by their merger had been overrun on the road to a higher bottom line.[3]

Hickey, however, was just scratching the surface. The social, economic, and political environment within which the story had been produced, broadcast, and then trashed was indeed important, but there was much more to that story, too. To begin with, a cloud of government, specifically Pentagon, censorship hung low over *Valley of Death* from beginning to end, while the manner in which commercial culture played into the affair was really quite different from what Hickey's approach suggested.

FROM ORWELL TO HUXLEY

The nation's concern that its press be free from governmental restraint is embedded in the constitution, and during the twentieth century that freedom provided a marker by which Americans measured the distance between the quality of their own society and that of others. "Freedom of the press" achieved near-shibboleth status, designating what the United States stood for, its absence sufficient to condemn a rival power as a totalitarian dictatorship. Little more was needed in those years to rally public support for military intervention than the assertion that the would-be enemy did not allow freedom of the press.

Freedom from the dominance of government was at the root of the twentieth century's great wars, and freedom of the press was at the top of the list of the freedoms worth fighting for. The Kaiser, Hitler, Stalin, and Castro were personifications of centralized authority, political dictatorships that spied on their own people and then used their control of the press to mislead the masses about the true state of affairs. For most Americans, the dependence of a foreign people on "state-owned media" was a sure sign of enslavement, while their own consumption of news from "independent," privately owned media companies testified to the "openness" of life in the United States.

But for people working in the press establishment, freedom from governmental control seemed limited and tenuous, its boundaries less an established "right" than a point of conflict and negotiation between government agencies and journalists. Those conflicts intensified during the Vietnam War as the government tried to restrict press access to the battle zones and systematically misled Americans about the real nature of the war. When the government tried to stop the *New York Times* from publishing a collection of secret documents on the war, known as the Pentagon Papers, lines between the news professionals and the administration of Richard Nixon hardened. The papers revealed, when the Supreme Court allowed their printing, that the Pentagon had been lying about the war—a fact that, coupled with the government's attempt to keep the papers secret, seemed to confirm for many Americans in and out of the news business its Orwellian nature.

The Tailwind affair was colored with the same issues almost from the outset. Recall that even in the original broadcast of *Valley of Death,* the reporters excused the absence of documentation by reference to "missing records," information intentionally "left out" of battlefield reports, and the Pentagon's slowness to respond to requests for information. Given the covert nature of military operations "over the fence" in Laos and the degree of secrecy that surrounded the real Operation Tailwind, the sparseness of the historical record was no surprise. Then, in the postbroadcast scuffle, Oliver alleged that CNN had "caved" to pressure from the Pentagon to kill the story. In her mind, the subtext of the affair was Big Brother—the government was guilty of covering up its misdeeds in Laos in 1970s and now of threatening to cut off CNN's access to Pentagon information sources if it did not retract *Valley of Death*. Between the lines, Smith's accusation that Kaplan had sacrificed him and Oliver to save his job was really an accusation that Kaplan had canned them to save CNN's privileged access to Pentagon sources.

Smith and Oliver's counterspin on the aftermath of the Tailwind affair was not unreasonable and, in fact, caught the ear of media critics like *Nation* magazine columnist Alex Cockburn. Nonetheless, however true it might turn out to be that CNN dumped the producers in order to preserve its legitimacy with the Pentagon, the reasons that the network aired it at all have less to do with governmental restraint than with freedom *from* it.

During the last quarter of the twentieth century, concern among Americans about the concentration and control of information by the government shifted to alarm that private-sector corporations were gobbling up the media companies responsible for gathering the news and distributing it to the public. Beginning with changes brought by the Reagan administration in 1984, newspaper companies were allowed to merge with radio and television companies, thus narrowing the range of choices that Americans had for news sources. Subsequently, corporate interests unrelated to media began to take over the news companies.[4]

The mergers of corporate interests with news organizations became major news stories themselves when manufacturing companies like General Electric and Westinghouse began buying media firms in the 1980s and 1990s. Owning, respectively, NBC and CBS, these producers of electrical appliances, nuclear power plants, and military equipment gained the power to use the media to shape consumer behavior and public opinion about government policy bearing on their products. The concern about those combinations was not only that the drive to make money would muscle aside the mandate to report the news, but that the integrity of the news side might be compromised by the business interests of the parent corporations. Some of those fears were proven to be well founded when critics pointed out that NBC squelched stories about GE's nuclear plants and faulty aircraft engines.[5]

But there is another dimension to the problem of corporate interlocks that probably was a bigger factor in the Tailwind fiasco, and it is one that the *Columbia Journalism Review* and other critics have overlooked: the impact on political consciousness of the combination of news and entertainment organizations. The concern that the needs of the bottom line would drive the news production was recognized by *CJR*'s Neil Hickey, but there is a difference between NBC flacking for GE's nuclear power plants and a news organization creating "infotainment," news with content chosen for its entertainment quality *and* for its potential to stimulate the market for other entertainment products sold by the parent company. As culture critic Neil Postman put it in his book *Amusing Ourselves to Death*, the danger of a public misinformed by government or corporate propaganda might now be surpassed by the nightmare of a populace that can't distinguish between truth and lies—and doesn't care.

The fusion of ABC with Disney in 1996 put major news programs such as *World News Tonight* with Peter Jennings, *Nightline*, and *20/20* under the control of the world's largest entertainment corporation. When Australian Rupert Murdock's news empire purchased the U.S. moviemaker Twentieth-Century Fox, there was little doubt that the brave new world described by Aldous Huxley—its denizens destroyed by what they loved—was at hand. Neil Hickey may have been right that CNN's managers and *Time*'s editors couldn't see *Valley of Death*'s journalistic shortcomings because they were blinded by the dollar signs they thought its titillating content could generate, but it's just as possible that it was the story's come-hither qualities—period—that seduced them. News organization though CNN was, it was competing in a market where entertainment more than information was becoming the lure for audiences.

In other words, the reason *Valley of Death* was accepted so uncritically by those who should have pulled the plug on Oliver's work long before air time may have had less to do with what the editors couldn't see and didn't know than with what they thought they saw and knew. Writing in the same issue of *CJR* as Hickey, *Time* editor-in-chief Norman Pearlstine said that in retrospect he did not think the story belonged on the air or in *Time*. He faulted himself, he said, because when the story came in, "I didn't fully appreciate that it was a controversial piece." He might just as well have said that the story was so close to common sense for him that he saw no reason to question its plausibility. Pearlstine went on that he "probably should have been smarter about that."[6]

But "smart" might not have been the right criterion; the issue posed by Pearlstine's decision to publish the piece is less the quality of his judgment than how he had arrived at his "common sense" about the war in Vietnam. As with Oliver, Pearlstine's lack of a basic sense of history seems to have been a factor in the decisions he made. He told writers Mary Murphy and Dennis McDougal for their four-part *TV Guide* series on the CNN-Tailwind episode that the biggest failure of those involved was not to "comprehend the enduring sensitivities, the unhealed wounds, of Vietnam. . . . There is still so much emotion about the war," Pearlstine said, with a palpable "golly gee."[7]

Furthermore, by the time Pearlstine was rethinking his own role in the Tailwind disaster, the world of U.S. journalism had already been rocked by a decade-long series of scandals involving phony vets using the news to promote their needs. Recall, for example, that Joseph Yandle had been released from prison after *60 Minutes* was suckered into airing his phony PTSD story, and John Plummer had used ABC's *Nightline* to legitimate his false claim of involvement in the napalming of Trang Bang. One can only wonder where Pearlstine, Kaplan, and others in the *Time*-CNN hierarchy spent the 1990s while these and many other stories like them swirled through the news industry. For them to say they didn't know seems disingenuous and raises still more interesting questions about relationship between journalists and the cultural environment in which they work.[8]

"ONE LEG AT A TIME . . . "

I was once on a basketball team that didn't win many games. The coach would try to narrow the confidence gap between our team and the opponents by assuring us that we were as good as they were. "They put their pants on the same way you do, one leg at a time," he would say. Notwithstanding the awe in which we may have regarded the other team, the coach's words emboldened us to try again.

I often think of the coach's motivational ditty when I consider what sociologist Herbert Gans had to say about how journalists decide what goes into the newspaper. In his 1980 book *Deciding What's News*, Gans observed that "journalists practice an expertise that is not and cannot be purely professional." Even though they sometimes perceive themselves to be "outsiders," journalists are members of the society they report on, which means, said Gans, that "they react to the news with the same attitudes and values as some, if not all, members of their audience."[9] In other words, when it comes to deciding what should be reported as news, reporters and editors, so to speak, put their pants on the same way the rest of us do.

Gans wrote that journalists mainly "express, and often subscribe to, the economic, political and social values which are dominant in America." He identified a set of "enduring values" that he said characterize American culture. Among those values were altruistic democracy, responsible capitalism, small-town pastoralism, individualism, moderatism, social order, and national leadership. In annotated form, that meant that a large portion of the American people believed that politics should be based on service to the public interest, as provided for in the Constitution; the small, family-owned firm is the ideal form for business, whereas monopoly corporations are undesirable; rural and small-town environments are preferable to cities, as is simple technology over complex; individualism is a bulwark against the conformity demanded by mass society; political extremists and ideologues are suspect; predictability in social institutions is desirable, and events and behaviors that upset the expected order of things are newsworthy (as are attempts to restore order); social process is shaped by the society's leaders and, therefore, the opinions and activities of leaders should be privileged in news reports. Gans found that journalists made choices about which stories to develop and which sources to use through a mostly unconscious application of these enduring values. Moreover, since writers and editors came from what Gans considered to be mainstreet America, their sense of what was important and who was credible was more or less in line with what their readers and viewers thought. Indeed, so indistinguishable in his study were the social ideals of the journalists from those of the news-consuming public that Gans said his book was as much about the dominant culture in America as about the journalists themselves.[10]

Gans's study is a classic in the fields of journalism and sociology, but what it tells us about the CNN/Tailwind affair is not so clear. At first blush, his approach might seem to support a kind of "disconnect" thesis on what went wrong: the journalists—Oliver and Smith in particular— were so out of touch with the reality of American political life that the version of the story they produced didn't resonate with a large portion of Americans. When the people responsible for the economics of the CNN-*Time* organization came to their senses, they retracted the story in order to salvage the longer-term credibility of their companies. A different conclusion that Gans's work might point to is that the country itself had changed, that the values he identified had not endured, and that Oliver, Smith, and the higher-ups who approved the story the first time around were in sync with characteristics of American culture that simply hadn't existed when Gans did his research. This conclusion would hold open the possibility that the story was subsequently killed not for reasons of the market but due to pressure from the Pentagon and its civilian boosters.

History being what it is, though, neither of these two conclusions singularly captures the complexity of what had transpired between 1970, when Gans wrote, and the late 1990s, when *Valley of Death* germinated. While there was a gap between what the news people responsible for *Valley of Death* were thinking and the way a majority of Americans view the world, it wasn't a total disconnect. Moreover, whatever social and cultural changes there were, their importance was eclipsed by other developments of a more structural nature: the rural and small-town environments that Gans said were the spawning grounds of middle-class values and of the middle-class journalists he studied were fast disappearing. Those material changes meant that the organic *gemeinschaft* he identified as the nation's dominant culture was being supplanted by a popular culture emanating from sources far from Main Street.

Stated differently, what had changed since Gans wrote was not so much the values that middle-Americans held near and dear but their sense that those values were no longer dominant. Events beginning at the end of the Vietnam War undermined public confidence in the idea that government by, for, and of the people was the reality; that small businesses were playing on a level field; and that the moguls of popular culture in New York and Los Angeles had any respect for the small-town way of life widely held to be the backbone of the nation. What we saw in the reprise of those postwar events in chapter 6 was that they also ginned a middle-class backlash that leaned to the political right and reached for simple explanations to complicated problems. Following the pattern wrought powerless by past instances, the movements of the 1980s and 1990s took the values that Gans had characterized as "progressive" and twisted them into a vengeful, reactionary populism.[11]

THE MIDDLE CRUMBLES, JOURNALISM STUMBLES

Gans's theory predicts that journalists would have followed the drift of their constituency away from the center, thus anticipating the entanglement of some of them in a Tailwind-like mess twenty-five years later. Demographically, the population that sustained the enduring values that defined the commonsense world of journalists was decimated by the farm crisis of the 1980s. Farmers epitomized individualism and moderatism, the survival of their farms providing living testimony to the enduring viability of small, family-owned enterprises. When those homesteads were shuttered, the faith that *anything* could endure was challenged.

The damage was not limited to the farms. The "small-town pastoralism" that Gans wrote about could as well be called "farm-town" America. The little shops that give such places their identity were mostly service centers for the surrounding farms: implement dealers, grain exchanges, gas stations, barber shops, hardware and grocery stores, and bars. As their organic link to the agricultural economy was dissolved, the towns were colonized by the giants of agribusiness, which used some of the local infrastructure and the roads and rail lines that passed through it to extract produce and labor—and abandoned the rest. The towns that survived into the twenty-first century did so by appending themselves to tract-housing developments that crept out from larger cities. This suburbanization of rural America also created the environment in which redneck anger still boiling from the farm crisis mixed with the white-flight sentiment spilling out of the cities. By the late 1990s, the venues that Gans credited for progressivism were centers of anything but.[12]

Other events and trends during the late 1980s and 1990s also provided context for public receptivity to a story like *Valley of Death*. The government raids on Ruby Ridge and Waco raised questions about the judgment of federal authorities who ordered those actions, while during the same years Hollywood studios stepped up their production of conspiracy-themed films.[13] Growing public unease with central government could have been offset by the interventions of a progressive pro–public sector press, but the mishandling of the media by the government during the Gulf War and suspicions that military authorities lied about their conduct of operations opened the mainstream press to the spin coming in from the right.

Even before the 1991 war against Iraq ended, the stated reasons for the U.S. intervention were attacked by critics. There were also questions about the conduct of operations, and the way the military handled the press only raised the eyebrows higher. To begin with, military authorities placed severe restrictions on reporters' mobility in the war zone and their access to information. Using a system devised during the U.S. invasion of Grenada in 1983, selected reporters were assigned to a pool from which individuals would be chosen to cover certain events. It was an arrangement that government and military leaders hoped would preclude public scrutiny of the kind they felt had handcuffed operations in Vietnam. On the flip side, however, the rules merely fueled press suspicion that the military was doing things in secret that were illegal or unethical, suspicions that were borne out in the weeks following the war when it was revealed that U.S. troops had killed defenseless prisoners.[14]

The press corps's lingering discomfort from the military's chafing restrictions on coverage of the war was met empathetically by post–Gulf War sentiment rising from the political right. Ultra-rightist organizations like the John Birch Society had opposed the war, viewing it as a trial balloon run up by the George H. W. Bush administration to see how receptive the American people would be to a new global political economy. The Birchers' protests that Bush's wrapping the U.S. initiative in the flag of the United Nations and his rhetoric about "the world against Saddam Hussein" might compromise U.S. sovereignty found receptive ears in the conservative mainstream. When the president adopted "A New World Order" as the slogan for his postwar vision, the far right heard "One-World Government," and alarm bells went off.

FUSION PARANOIA

In a 1995 *New Yorker* article, Michael Kelly wrote about what he called "fusion paranoia," the post-Vietnam phenomenon of liberal and right-wing suspicions of the government coming together. Kelly acknowledged that the kind of extreme political paranoia manifested in the actions of paramilitary warriors like Timothy McVeigh were still exceptional but argued that the ethos of distrust in government (of the type historian Richard Hofstadter had written about forty years ago) was now deeply ingrained in American culture. Even moderate conservatives, he found, see "an implicit conspiracy" between liberals in government, academia, the press, and Hollywood, while liberals see conspiracy in government, corporations, and the networks of social conservatism. "The paranoid view of government and of government's allies," Kelly wrote, "has become received wisdom for many millions of Americans."

Journalists, as Gans told us, are *of* those millions, which means that trying to understand what happened with CNN's *Valley of Death* broadcast as matters of individual failure (April Oliver's unbridled careerism) or organizational imperatives (CNN's pursuit of profit) miss most of what is important and interesting. In the same sense that Gans found news people to be a cultural window on America, the individuals who bought into the Tailwind tale are most important for what their work tells us about the United States at the turn of the millennium.

But journalists, because they tend to be ideologically liberal, also form the informational and cultural synapses connecting the right to the rest of the country. The right's courtship of middle America, as media critic Chip Berlet has characterized it, cast reporters and editors in the role of Cupid—and in Oliver and Smith they found eager matchmakers.[15] The dangers inherent in their flirtation with fascist fantasies faded as millennial anxieties waned and the economy recovered in the months after the broadcast. When 2001 began, *Valley of Death* remained an important piece of journalism history, an event that for a time threatened to destroy one of the world's largest news organizations, and in itself a story with elements of human tragedy worthy of Shakespeare. By the end of 2001, the apocalyptic subtext of the Tailwind tale had taken form, sending the country into a frenzy of conspiracism that gave its paranoid political style a whole new look.

SEPTEMBER 11 AND THAT "PARANOID STYLE"

In early April 2002, I received an e-mail message with a link to a website claiming that the U.S. government had "played some role" in the attacks on the World Trade Center and Pentagon on September 11, 2001. On one level, I wasn't surprised. As I watched the burning towers on that day, I had known it was only a matter of time before groups and individuals associated with the hard right would be speculating about who was "really" behind the attacks.

I was, nevertheless, caught off guard by this particular message. It came from an acquaintance who added his own endorsement of the idea that "powerful Americans," possibly the CIA, may have actually planned the attacks. The source of his information, to which his message e-linked me and others, was an "independent journalist" whom he described as "credible." The journalist, it turned out, was Mike Ruppert.

What Ruppert had done was compose a time line of about fifty items that began around 1990 and extended into the weeks following September 11. The sequence of the assembled events supposedly established a logic for why certain U.S. economic interests would have benefited from the attacks. Most of the items on the list were things I was familiar with and knew to be true. The problem was in how Ruppert had combined them into a whole that was less true than the sum of the parts themselves. Moreover, the subtext of Ruppert's report, as with the Tailwind tale, was that still more sinister (but unnamed) forces, burrowed into the Washington woodwork, were the real culprits. For those who couldn't decode the text, Ruppert was more than ready to translate. His website, www.copvcia.com, led his readers, again, to Jeff Rense, who was promulgating the theory that the airliners that hit the World Trade Center and Pentagon had been electronically hijacked by Chinese or Israeli AWACS-type aircraft flying off the coast of the United States.[16]

The message troubled me also because the person sending it had been very involved in progressive movements for peace and social justice such as Ralph Nader's 2000 campaign for president. He was not naïve. Yet without knowing anything about Ruppert, he was willing to publicly declare Ruppert to be credible. It struck me immediately as another case of someone accepting something as plausibly true just because it resonated with his "common sense." It was, moreover, "common sense" about the same kind of conspiratorial story that had sunk April Oliver and, judging by the other addresses to which he had sent the message, he presumed that people of a liberal-left persuasion would generally accept Ruppert as a valid source. My real concern was that my friend might be right; just as CNN and Chris Matthews had guessed that the conspiratorial subtext of the Operation Tailwind story would find a broad-based audience in the media market, so too I thought no small number of people, some of them on the left end of the political spectrum, might entertain the idea that the attacks of September 11 could be traced to the highest levels of power within the U.S. government.

CATNIP WITH NINE LIVES

Conspiracy theories allowed to live are certain to reemerge in new forms that can confuse even the most mindful observers. The episode of conspiricism most widely experienced by the public immediately prior to September 2001 was CNN's 1998 broadcast of *Valley of Death*. But rather than see its conspiracism for what it was, media critics, whom we should have been able to count on to debunk it, actually legitimated the story's paranoid subtext by taking it seriously.

In its August 24/31, 1998, edition, *Nation* columnist Alex Cockburn took up Oliver and Smith's cudgel that CNN management was the CIA's flunky in abetting a cover-up of the agency's 1970 murderous misadventure in Laos. A short time later, *The Nation* contracted with investigative journalist Steven Weinberg to do a special report that would vindicate April Oliver. Weinberg finished his work just before September 11, 2001, and its printing in the magazine was pending when the planes struck.[17]

It isn't clear when and why *The Nation* decided to scrap Weinberg's defense of Oliver but, at some point after the September attacks, the magazine began to work the other side of the conspiricism street. The May 30, 2002, issue of *The Nation* carried a piece by David Corn entitled "The September 11 X-Files." In it, Corn effectively debunked Mike Ruppert's claims about a CIA role in the attacks by showing that the primary source for key parts of his time line, Delmart "Mike" Vreeland, is nothing more than a small-time con artist. Valuable though Corn's piece was, it showed no recognition that the September 11 Ruppert was the same as Tailwind-tale Ruppert who, along with April Oliver, stood to be exonerated by research his magazine had paid for! Moreover, Corn did nothing to penetrate the culture that gestates conspiratorial theories; much less did he provide a reflexive critique, as Bruce Jackson might have done (see chapter 8), that would help us learn from the experience.[18]

Vulnerable though left-of-center intellectuals might be to the siren of conspiracism, the political paranoia that generates conspiracist tales emanates from other ideological quarters. Conspiracy theories spring from the middle-class American anxiety that is given voice by the right and kept in play by the mainstream media.[19] Rather than put a dagger into these ideas, the news business, itself unsettled by political economic instability and paranoid rumors, uses their emotional magnetism to draw viewers and readers. The *New York Times*, for example, weirdly seems to give credibility to conspiracy themes while simultaneously disassociating itself from them. Its "Week in Review" section on Sunday, June 16, 2002, featured a cover-page story headlined "The Evil That Lurks in the Enemy Within." The story is accompanied by a half-page red, white, and blue poster from 1917 warning a slumbering America to "WAKE UP!" to the dangers of internal subversion; the glaring presentation would win the story any picture-worth-a-thousand-words contest. Yet the article, by Richard Gid Powers, parodied the Bush administration's string of "chicken little" warnings in the months following the attacks of September 11 that terrorists were about to strike again. The particular target of Powers's barbs was the government's detention the previous week of Jose Padilla, an American citizen who authorities alleged was plotting to explode a radioactive "dirty bomb" in the United States. Powers likened the administration's fear-mongering to the Palmer Raids and McCarthyism, two periods of political hysteria that swept the country during the twentieth century.

If the mixed signals sent by the juxtaposition of this piece's text and visuals didn't create enough confusion, its continuation on the inside pages was accompanied by a large multicolored sidebar containing a pseudoscientific explanation of X-rays, gamma rays, and other technology associated with "dirty bombs." Serious stuff, indeed. Still not confused? On page 1, front section, of the same edition of the *Times* a major news story by David Johnson treated the developments lampooned by Powers with utmost earnestness. The Johnson article, which opened to another full page on the inside, called the arrest of Padilla "a foiled terrorist plot" and fit the event into a chronology of "global terror" that had begun with September 11.[20]

The synergy between the news and entertainment functions of large media organizations has intensified since September 11, 2001, making it still more likely that the "commonsense" judgments of news people that Herbert Gans said were once shaped by the enduring values grown in the soil of community life are now contrived by creative geniuses keying scripts, staging sets, and cutting tapes—themselves caught in the feedback loops of conspiracy-laced movies and television docudramas. In the weeks just before the Padilla/dirty-bomber story broke, the entertainment world was buzzing with news about the soon-to-be-released *Sum of All Fears* starring Ben Affleck. On the serious talk shows like Charlie Rose (and in the *New York Times*), we learned that the U.S. military had provided unprecedented infrastructural support for the film's production, and that its basic story was about a terrorist plot to explode a nuclear device near an East Coast population center.[21] The bomb had been produced in the United States and apparently stolen by the CIA and illegally sold to the Israelis (à la Iran-Contra) before ending up in the hands of Russian separatists. When we see the on-screen explosion, it's clear that this is not a Hiroshima-scale nuclear event but something more like a "dirty" bomb spreading radioactive havoc. The film opened in theaters concurrently with the arrest of Padilla, making it impossible to not wonder whether his arrest seemed more legitimate to some news people (and lots of news consumers) because of their preconditioning by *Sum of All Fears*.[22]

THE PROBLEM WITH CONSPIRACISM

The problem with conspiracist interpretations isn't that conspiracies don't exist. In fact, there are real conspiracies. There are laws, for example, against companies conspiring to fix prices and the courts occasionally find corporate executives guilty of conspiracy to violate those laws. As this book went to press, former company heads of Enron, WorldCom, Arthur Anderson, and ImClone were under scrutiny for conspiratorial practices, as was housewares maven Martha Stewart, suspected of profiting from inside information on ImClone stock trades. There are also political conspiracies, such as Watergate, in which government leaders colluded to cover up lawbreaking, and Iran-Contra, in which they secretly and illegally sold arms to Iran, using some of the money illegally to fund the Nicaraguan Contras (while lining their pockets with the rest), and then perjuring themselves to hide their misdeeds.

The word "conspiracy," however, is sometimes misused. Careful planning among business and political leaders is commonplace and much of that planning is done in secret. Indeed, much of what is meant by "private" in the idea of private enterprise involves the privacy of information and planning; what goes on in corporate board rooms is nobody's business—it's secret, it's legal, and it's not a conspiracy, at least not in the sense in which the term is used in the phrase "conspiracy theory."

Used to refer to a theory or explanation for social or political events, conspiracy purports to be the cause of something—an event happened *because* of the conspiracy. Moreover, unlike the identifiable business leaders who periodically gather at, say, the World Trade Organization, the participants in conspiracies are unknown. Indeed, part of the *theory* of a good conspiracy theory is that bad things are happening because the individuals or groups at work are *unknown*. The unknown, in other words, becomes an agent of causation in its own right. Unlike the research approach known as "elite theory" or "power structure research," which illuminates the identity of powerful decision makers and the ways they do their work, thereby narrowing the parameters of what we need to know and don't, conspiracy theory actually injects unknowns into the analysis, which broadens the field of what we don't and *can't* know.

Conspiracy claims lead to an overemphasis on bad people being the source of the danger. Such claims stem from a need for moral accountability that is hard to fix without individual persons to hold responsible; when the alleged culprits are admittedly unknown, the claims lead almost inevitably to witch hunts that jeopardize everyone's constitutional rights to freedom of speech and assembly. Conveniently for government leaders who are afraid that their misbehavior might be uncovered, conspiratorial beliefs that the real enemy is "within the gates" establishes a climate wherein legitimate criticism can be discouraged and opponents repressed. The search for bad people also lets flawed institutions and bad policy go unexamined, and it totally neglects the structural dimensions of the far-flung American empire. Far more important for the safety and security of Americans than divining motives for a supposed CIA attack on the World Trade Center is a deepened awareness of the war against the two-thirds of the world's people living on a dollar a day—a war that was being waged from, among other sites, the twin towers themselves—and how that institutional violence is complicit in the horror of September 11.

Conspiracy theories also raise havoc with practical politics by distracting us from what we need to be thinking about. The exploitation of the world's resources and people by U.S. corporations and the death and destruction that the American military has visited upon defenseless people over the last half-century is explanation enough for why millions of people around the globe apparently applauded the attacks of September 11. The American people are put at risk far more directly by the legal and very visible policies of their own institutions than by either the ill-defined strategies and tactics of foreign "terrorist" organizations or the alleged secret planning by unidentified CIA "insiders" supposedly pursuing the destruction of the United States. Serious thought needs to be given to how we remove from positions of political power the dangerous people we *can* see and foil the plans for war that we *do* know about if the world is to be made safer.

Conspiracy theories also discredit legitimate claims that private and public-sector leaders plan economic and military campaigns to increase control of whole global regions. The so-called war against terrorism that was launched within days of the September 11, 2001, attacks is best understood as a strategical move on the part of the United States to extend its political, economic, and cultural hegemony over southwestern Asia and the Middle East. Plans for that campaign were in place long before the attacks—as evidenced by the published reports that U.S. Special Forces were working in the former Soviet republics bordering Afghanistan for months prior to 9/11—but that is a claim vastly different from the conspiracist one that someone inside the government, therefore, caused the attacks to happen. Because the conspiracist claims are present in the political culture, however, many Americans are afraid to speak out about the real danger and immorality of actual U.S. policies, lest they be labeled "conspiracy nuts."

The ironic reality is that the preoccupation with phantom subversives created by conspiracism makes it easier for Washington to discredit reasoned dissent and forestall the abatement of its corporate-sponsored global mayhem. In the end, Oliver, Smith, and others at CNN and *Time* who may have thought they were striking a blow against conspiratorial government "insiders" by airing *Valley of Death* actually created a more intimidating climate for investigative reporting and widened the playing field for the conspiratorial right.

AFTERWORD

The CNN-Tailwind fiasco is out of the news but it will be in the text-books for a long time. To begin with, the real Operation Tailwind has a lot to tell us about the U.S. war in Vietnam. As one of the largest operations of its kind, designed to penetrate deeper into Laos than most crossborder actions, Tailwind had its claim to uniqueness even though its value as a case study probably lies still more in the ways it typified the use of covert operations in Southeast Asia at the time.

Tailwind was a single covert mission, but for Americans who know so little about that facet of military strategy in Vietnam, it opens a large window on the history of America's secret war against the North. Through Tailwind we get a glimpse of the huge amount of resources put into covert operations against the government in Hanoi—recall that over a hundred soldiers constituted Operation Tailwind alone when its only purpose was diversionary, a fact that underscores just how committed U.S. policy makers were to the mistaken idea that the war was being prolonged due to the "outside" aggression from the North rather than popular resistance to the Saigon regime. Tailwind also enlightens us about the practice of denied operations and how they were carried out through, for example, the outfitting of personnel with identity-neutral clothing—"going in sterile" was the terminology for it. We also learn how U.S. special forces used terror tactics

like planting faulty weapons to be picked up for use by the Vietnamese who would be injured or killed when the device malfunc-
tioned.

The real Operation Tailwind also debunks the Hollywood images of
what special forces troops were all about and how they did their work.
Far from seeking to engage the enemy in open combat upon every
occasion, the typical Green Beret mission involved reconnaissance, psychological operations, and the propagandizing and training of indigenous people. What we learn from the accounts like Tailwind is that for
commandos, doing their jobs right meant avoiding combat or at least organizing someone else to do the fighting and dying. Indeed, had April
Oliver really wanted to kick a hornet's nest, she might have asked why
only Montagnard mercenaries died on the mission and opened thereby
a new line of investigation and historical study on the U.S. practice of
exploiting tribal people for its own military ends.

Knowing about Tailwind and similar SOG operations also enhances
our ability to see through the guises of current U.S. involvements
abroad. When news leaked during the first days of the so-called war
against terrorism after September 11, 2001, that special forces, not conventional troops, might be used against the Taliban regime in
Afghanistan, anyone familiar with Tailwind knew that that was code for
a strategy that would use one tribal group against another, with Green
Berets and other special operations personnel staying in the background. When the Afghan "Northern Alliance" appeared out of
nowhere a few weeks later, those who knew their history of the war in
Vietnam recognized it immediately as a front cobbled together by special operations people who had been working in the region for months
prior to September 11.

The Tailwind tale will also go into the books as a case study in
American culture at the turn of the twenty-first century. The most
important dimension of that culture is the crisis of collective identity
wrought by the loss of the war in Vietnam. American identity is
linked to the nation's position in the global order in ways that are un-
characteristic of most other countries. That linkage was forged in the
aftermath of World War II when the United States enjoyed the pres-
tige of having fought and won "the good fight" against fascism and
then reaped the political and economic spoils of victory for two
decades. Few pillars in the American identity stood taller during

those years than the claim, "We're Number One!"; so overpowering was it that the perceived need for some other way to think about who we were and what we stood for receded to the back of people's minds. The defeat by the Vietnamese, then, was huge, felt not only as a loss of whatever material advantages derived from U.S. dominance in that part of the world—indeed, most Americans were oblivious to the connection between military might and the cheap prices they pay for consumer goods—but as loss of sense of self on collective and personal levels. The need to recover that identity, if not preserve what was left of it, led to a search for alternative explanations for why the war had been lost and for new opportunities to prove the American mettle.

The idea that the United States lost the war in Vietnam because of betrayal at home had become the dominant American narrative at the turn of the twenty-first century, and it is that narrative that constructed both poles of attraction that comprised the CNN-Tailwind affair—the story that was told and the audience that listened. The "reading" of "the great American betrayal" will go on for decades, and it is through the study of stories like the Tailwind tale that the components of the narrative can be animated: heroic masculinity, conspiracy, political assassinations, esoteric technology, and the threat to the collective good represented by drugs and the "insiders" who traffic in them.

Most importantly, the knowledge of Tailwind's subtext assists our understanding of the social movements that are driving American politics in the early years of the new century. The far-right paramilitary militia movements that stepped out the shadows and onto the front pages during the 1980s and '90s were overtly motivated by revenge, the need to recover something they believed to have been lost in Vietnam. Their search for the organizational and cultural forces they held responsible for the "stab in the back" of the military directed them toward traditional racial and ethnic targets to scapegoat, as well as new targets like the antiwar movement and later the federal government—wherein, they allege, the ultimate traitors reside.

Occluded by the end-of-time hysteria that surrounded the turn of the millennium and then the conspiracist frenzy that followed the attacks on the Pentagon and World Trade Center, the ultrarightist movements are currently out of view, but the politics of betrayal that they manifest are very present. Republican party politics since the first Reagan campaign, which

April Oliver worked in, have been motivated by the legacy of Vietnam. The neoconservative politics that propelled the "Reagan Revolution" were energized by a feeling that the culture of permissiveness that permeated the 1960s also eroded the moral fiber of the nation and softened the nation's will to win in Vietnam. Republicans have been running for office, quite successfully, on the fumes of that sentiment since 1980, and there is no reason to think the tank is empty.

Interpreting Van Buskirk's fantasy of chasing a beach-bum defector down a spider hole as an expression of his own anxiety about American values helps ground our understanding of what is at stake in the culture wars that rage on into the new century and how deeply that angst runs in the American psyche; that Van Buskirk and others find resonance for their feelings in ancient biblical fables testifies to the depth of the cultural well that they draw from and the breadth of the audience that hears what they are saying. For a single window on something as vast and multifaceted as American culture, it would be hard to surpass the view that the Tailwind tale affords us.

The Tailwind tale, finally, will be a staple for journalism schools for years. For talking points about the commercial pressures on writers, producers, and editors and the standard topics about the tensions between professionals, managers, owners, it is a mother lode of material. Beyond that basic syllabus lie the still more interesting (Neil) Postmanesque issues about the influence of entertainment values on the culture of news production that are inherent when news and entertainment organizations interpenetrate one another. But even that is only the beginning.

Oliver tripped on two large obstacles that others in journalism would fail to recognize at their peril. One is the culture of supposed objectivity in which the profession is steeped. The standard explanation for Oliver's failing is that she "fell in love with her story," which is to say she lost her objectivity. Accepting the terms of the criticism, Oliver herself responded with the standard journalism defense that she had retained her objectivity throughout and "only let the facts speak for themselves." The problem with that tête-à-tête is that both sides accept the false premise that political realities can exist, objectlike, independent from journalists or others who observe and interpret them.

The spirit of critical thinking that is basic to the contemporary liberal arts curriculum has, for the most part, moved beyond teaching the importance of identifying one's values and preferences and then bracketing those "biases" so they can't contaminate the consideration of "facts." That kind of positivism, which journalists still want to pretend is a viable practice in their workaday world, is viewed today as naïve and self-deluding by social critics. Far better that schools of journalism incorporate the principles of social constructionism into their curriculum, sharpening students' sensibilities to their own political and cultural values and leading them into engagement with the history and sociology of the issues they want to report on. Students need to learn, as C. Wright Mills taught, to locate themselves within the social milieu of their work and community lives, and be shown how to incorporate that positioning into their observations rather than denying its influence.

The largest stumbling block in Oliver's path was her lack of grounding in the history of her subject, the war in Vietnam. At points too numerous to reiterate here, Oliver reached conclusions that stunned knowledgeable minds—how could she have believed *that?!* Dangerous though it is to reduce a disaster with as many dimensions as *Valley of Death*'s to a single cause, it is tempting to say that, with a better sense of history, Oliver might still be a star at CNN.

Journalists, as the cliché goes, write the first drafts of history. There is good reason for the saying because so much of what historians produce is reliant upon newspaper accounts as a form of primary documentation. This places an enormous burden on journalists to get that first "draft" right because what they write, mistakes and all, is subject to endless reproduction by scholars in the future. Still, there are checks and balances, of a kind, in the process as a whole in that journalists are not historians and their first drafts are ostensibly only the raw material that historians integrate with information from other sources to create the record that we come to know collectively as our history.

However, if that image of a world so neatly compartmentalized that journalists could once work in an institutional setting isolated from academics, and vice versa, was ever accurate, it is surely naïve in the twenty-first century. The power of the electronic media (television and film in particular) to shape what we know about our past and think about our present overwhelms whatever role is left for academicians to play. The concentration of resources in the mass communication industries has also collapsed the institutional boundaries separating news production, book publishing, filmmaking, and television

programming. With that institutional implosion has come the conflation of the roles that once defined the separate professions of journalists, book authors, and screenwriters. Consider what Joseph Galloway
did. As a reporter in 1965 he wrote the first draft of the history of the
battle for Ia Drang Valley in the Central Highlands of South Vietnam.
Thirty years later, as a historian, he coauthored *When We Were Soldiers Once . . . and Young* with Gen. Harold Moorer who led the U.S.
troops in that fight. Not finished, Galloway then wrote the screenplay
for a popular movie that featured his own role as the reporter from Ia
Drang!

The concentration of media power is a fact of life and the availability
of talented journalists with the boldness to play gatekeepers to public
memory is not a bad thing. But journalists *qua* journalists are schooled to
report news and, in small ways, to adjudicate between sources and make
interpretations about the meaning of the events they cover. They're able
to do those broader tasks competently to the extent they have good backgrounds in history, social science, and cultural studies, but the lesson
from *Valley of Death* is that not all of them are up to the task.

In practice, journalism has moved far beyond the time when the facts
could be allowed to speak for themselves, and the schooling of journalists needs to rise to the occasion. Studies of epistemology and phenomenology, which may heretofore have been relegated to Ph.D. programs
in mass communication departments, need to be mainstreamed in the
curriculum for students aspiring to write for public consumption. Incorporated into that curriculum, the CNN-Tailwind affair can teach
about the need for journalists to acknowledge their own political and
cultural backgrounds and accept that those parts of themselves are going to influence their work. Tailwind can also underscore how the interaction of experience and popular culture produces a dynamic element
in the construction of the memories of journalists' sources. Used creatively, the Tailwind tale offers studies in memory and the fallacy of
eyewitness testimony, subjects already popular in psychology and law
school classes.

There is, finally, the importance of history. In the past, it may have
been adequate for journalists to come into their profession with good
liberal arts backgrounds in history, but those days too are gone. History
isn't just some*thing* that today's journalists need to know so much as a
craft they need to practice. The reexamination of how Oliver arrived at

infamy is something that journalism schools should not avoid; it can generate a whole curriculum specific to the historical dimensions of the work journalists do. Done creatively, that exercise can give us a new cohort of journalists able to both recognize and debunk the dangerous mythologies embedded in the nation's collective memory. Using the power that the communication industry has amassed for their disposal, journalists who have learned the lessons of the *Valley of Death* debacle can play a role in neutralizing the reactionary political forces that prey on people's insecurities and reconnect the American consciousness with the heritage of an informed citizenry on which our future rests.

FILMOGRAPHY

Alice's Restaurant. 1969. Regional Films. Color, 85 mins.
Apocalypse Now. 1979. USA. United Artists–Zoetrope. Color, 93 mins.
Black Six. 1974. USA. Cinemation. Color, 84 mins.
Brotherhood of Death. 1976. Omni Capital Films. Color, 85 mins.
Bus Riley's Back in Town. 1965. USA. Universal. Color, 93 mins.
Coming Home. 1978. USA. United Artists. Color, 128 mins.
The Deer Hunter. 1978. USA. Universal. Color, 183 mins.
Eye of The Eagle. 1987. Concorde. Color, 82 mins.
Final Mission. 1984. USA. Motion Pictures Distributors. Color, 101 mins.
Getting Straight. 1970. USA. Columbia. Color, 125 mins.
Green Berets. 1968. USA. Warner Brothers–Seven Arts. Color, 141 mins.
Hail Hero. 1969. USA. Cinema Center Films. Color, 97 mins.
Jacob's Ladder. 1990. USA. Tri-Star/Carolco. Color, 120 mins.
JFK. 1991. USA. Warner Bros. Color, 188 mins.
Jud. 1971. Duque Films/Maron Films. Color, 80 mins.
The Lively Set. 1964. USA. Universal. Color, 95 mins.
The Lost Battalion. 1984. A&E. Color, 100 mins.
Missing in Action. 1984. USA. Cannon. Color, 101 mins.
Motor Psycho. 1965. USA. Eve Productions. Black and white, 73 mins.

Night Wars. 1987. USA. Warner Bros. Color, 89 mins.

Satan's Sadists. 1969. USA. Kennis-Frazer Films. Color, 86 mins.

Saving Private Ryan. 1998. USA. Dream Works/Paramount. Color, 170 mins.

Stanley. 1972. USA. Crown. Color, 108 mins.

The Stone Killer. 1973. USA. Columbia. Color, 96 mins.

Sum of All Fears. 2002. USA. Paramount. Color, 118 mins.

Taxi Driver. 1976. USA. Columbia. Color, 113 mins.

Usual Suspects. 1995. USA. PolyGram. Color, 106 mins.

Waco: A New Revelation. 1999. MGA Films. Color, 50 mins.

White Ghost. 1988. USA. Gibraltar Films. Color, 95 mins.

Without a Parade. n.d. USA. International Prison Ministry. Color, 30 mins.

NOTES

Preface

1. The details about the CNN program and the investigations into it are presented in chapter 1. The history of the real Operation Tailwind is the subject of chapter 2.

Chapter I

1. CNN would not make copies of the tape and transcript available for research. Laura Hogan, my student assistant, acquired a copy of the tape from another source, enabling me to excerpt the program.

2. The term "roundeyes" was commonly used in Vietnam to distinguish Americans and other Caucasians from Asians. Similarly, "longshadows" refers to the greater height of Americans—the shadows they cast were longer than those of Asians.

3. This account of how *Valley of Death* came to be produced is drawn from Mary Murphy and Dennis McDougal, "Tailwind: Behind the TV Story of the Year," part 1, *TV Guide*, December 26, 1998.

4. See Jim Wolf, "Vietnam-Era Nerve Gas Report to Be Checked," *Boston Globe*, June 9, 1998, A2.

5. Murphy and McDougal, "Tailwind: Behind the TV Story of the Year," part 3, January 9–15, 1999, 52–54. Graves confirmed to me in an October 22, 2002, interview that he had not been on the Tailwind mission.

6. This and the following paragraphs on the Abrams Report are taken from the report itself.

7. This source was probably John Singlaub. The triangle of exchanges between the producers, him, and Admiral Moore is examined below.

8. In an August 5, 2002, phone conversation with me, McCarley maintained his position that no nerve gas had been used and defectors were not the target of Operation Tailwind or any other SOG missions that he was aware of. He still felt that he had been misused by April Oliver.

9. Graves told me (interview, October 22, 2002) that he had told Oliver and Smith about a different raid he had been involved in and that they had spliced his videotaped testimony into the program in a way that implied that he was talking about Operation Tailwind. He said he told Jack Smith the night before the program aired that he had not been on Operation Tailwind. Graves, however, talks in a dissembling style that makes it difficult to tell what he means to say or intends the listener to believe.

10. See Evan Thomas, "What's the Truth about Tailwind?" *Newsweek*, June 22, 1998, 32; and Joe Sharkey, "Memories of Wars Never Fought," *New York Times*, June 28, 1998, WK 6. Van Buskirk did not respond to any of my requests to interview him left on his answering machine.

11. Arnett and CNN parted company in April 1999.

12. Research leading to *Valley of Death* began twelve months earlier, but some of that work went into another CNN broadcast about SOG in September 1997.

13. There are many small but telling items in the volumes of transcripts and briefs related to *Valley of Death*. One of those relevant here is Oliver's and Smith's claim that Singlaub had told them it might be safer to kill a defector than their Vietnamese or Russian captors. *Russian?* The idea that there were Russians lurking in the jungles of Southeast Asia is a long-standing right-wing political fantasy, and, for reasons that will become more apparent in later chapters, it is not unlikely that Singlaub really said it. For now, it is only necessary to note the Russian reference as a signpost pointing to the political culture from which *Valley of Death* was carved.

14. In some ways, knowing that Graves was not even involved in the Tailwind raid makes this a moot point. But it is clear that even within the context of their rebuttal—when it was becoming clear to everyone that Graves was not the eyewitness source they had presented him as—they continued to manipulate the truth about how they had used him in the story.

Chapter 2

1. John L. Plaster, *SOG: The Secret Wars of America's Commandos in Vietnam* (New York: Onyx/Simon and Schuster, 1997), 275–83. There are different accounts of Operation Tailwind, with different details. Plaster says there were

110 mercenaries (versus 140 according to the CNN broadcast) and "as many as 60 killed." Note that the proper name of the NVA was the People's Army of North Vietnam.

2. The development of that post-Vietnam culture is detailed in later chapters.

3. Richard H. Shultz, Jr., *The Secret War against Hanoi: Kennedy's and Johnson's Use of Spies, Saboteurs, and Covert Warriors in North Vietnam* (New York: HarperCollins, 1999), 28. Others argue persuasively that the real purpose of the U.S. military mission in Vietnam was to secure the region for capitalist economic expansion; the justification offered to the American public by their government has always been that the purpose of the war was to stop communism. The thought that the support of southerners for national independence and communism may have been consistent with their values and long-term interests and therefore the basis for authentic support for the Viet Minh seems either to have never entered the minds of U.S. policy makers or to have been simply hidden from the American people.

4. I've relied on Shultz, *The Secret War against Hanoi*, for the history of SOG. According to him (pp. 2, 17) the idea for SOG originated in the "Basic Counterinsurgency Plan for Vietnam" drafted by the U.S. Military Assistance Advisory Group in Vietnam and forwarded to Washington by the U.S. embassy in Saigon. Plaster, *SOG*, 22, seems to give more credit to Colby, while Shultz (p. 19) implies that Colby was hesitant about the possibility of successful covert action.

5. See Shultz, *The Secret War against Hanoi*, 82.

6. I've relied on Shultz's rather thin documentation on the North's double cross. His method is basically to describe a classic case of double cross involving German agents being run back by England during World War II, and then to imply that the North Vietnamese were doing the same. Some of what he says warrants skepticism. In one case, for which he provides no documentation, a double agent code named Ares called for more air strikes against the North. According to Shultz (p. 92), this seemingly contradictory act "fit perfectly into Hanoi's international propaganda campaign of portraying the United States as a bloodthirsty aggressor."

7. See Shultz, *The Secret War against Hanoi*, 114.

8. Shultz, *The Secret War against Hanoi*, 129.

9. The CIA turned special operations over to the military in 1964 at which time it was given the name Studies and Observation Group, or SOG. The CIA continued to be involved in planning operations and supplying SOG with items like the enemy's own weaponry.

10. Shultz, *The Secret War against Hanoi*, 174–83.

11. This description of NAD's mission is from Shultz, 183.

12. These details of the Tonkin Gulf Incident are drawn from Stanley Karnow, *Vietnam: A History* (New York: Viking Press, 1983), 365–72.

13. See Shultz, *The Secret War against Hanoi,* 147. Shultz says that their variations on the Paradise Island routine sometimes involved training captured fishermen as SSPL intelligence agents before sending them back. Others were trained to organize defections to the South. Any of the fishermen who themselves wanted to defect were assisted in doing so.

14. Shining Brass became Prairie Fire in 1967.

15. If SOG operations had the limited geographical scope that Shultz says, other U.S. military activities may have penetrated more deeply into Laos. Fred Branfman, *Voices from the Plain of Jars: Life under an Air War* (New York: Harper and Row, 1972), page 16, says the Americans manned a radar site in Sam Neua Province west of Hanoi from which bombing runs on the North were guided. Another site at Phou Pha Thi was overrun in March 1968; twenty Americans were killed.

16. For Robert S. McNamara, the secretary of defense.

17. Shultz relies on the recollections of SOG veteran Charlie Norton for this.

18. See Shultz, *The Secret War against Hanoi,* 256.

19. Despite its sensationalist quality, Plaster's book is recognized by SOG veterans and some scholars as a good source. His account of Tailwind is the most thorough we have.

20. Where Oliver got those elements is a story to be told in a later chapter. For a brief account of the Bertrand Russell war crimes tribunal see David Dellinger, *From Yale to Jail: The Life Story of a Moral Dissenter* (New York: Pantheon, 1993), 244.

Chapter 3

1. Michael Ruppert, "The POWs, CIA, and Drugs: Uglier Truths behind the Sarin Gas Stories," *From the Wilderness* (July 1998), uses the example of the CIA's Site 85 on a hilltop in Laos, surrounded by poppy fields. Allegedly, the CIA flew heroin out of Site 85 in return for the support of local growers. When Site 85 was overrun by the Pathet Lao in 1968, eleven Americans were captured, according to Ruppert. The government feared that if these Americans ever returned home they might reveal the CIA's involvement in the "secret war," paid for through the drug trade. Better to kill them.

2. The best source on the CIA and the drug trade is Alfred W. McCoy, *The Politics of Heroin in Southeast Asia* (New York: Lawrence Hill, 1972). Judging from the content of Ruppert's newsletters, he seems to have carved out a specific niche within the spectrum of the far right. His criticisms are focused on the CIA. He aligns himself with Fletcher Prouty, whose book *The Secret Team* is a virtual bible for right-wing critics of the agency. Ruppert appears, however, to reject the racism of many right-wing groups and denies that he is left- or right-wing, presenting himself rather as an investigative reporter.

3. In a later chapter, Oliver will be tied more closely to Ruppert.

4. When it was founded in 1982, the *Washington Times* received endorsements from the Moral Majority's leader, Jerry Falwell, and conservative political leaders Jesse Helms, Paul Laxalt, and Orrin Hatch. Scott Anderson and Jon Lee Anderson, *Inside the League: The Shocking Expose of How Terrorists, Nazis, and Latin American Death Squads Have Infiltrated the World Anti-Communist League* (New York: Dodd, Mead), 1986.

5. See Eleanor Randolph and Michael Isikoff, "*Washington Times* Gets New Editor," *Washington Post*, March 20, 1985, D1; and Edwin McDowell, "Behind the Best Sellers Arnaud de Borchgrave and Robert Moss," *New York Times*, June 22, 1980.

6. Chapter 7 provides a more detailed look at these organizations.

7. See chapter 10 of Scott and Jon Lee Anderson's *Inside the League* for an extended discussion of the *Washington Times* and other Moon organizations.

8. See Eleanor Randolph, "*Washington Times* Editor's NPC Bid Draws Opposition," *Washington Post*, November 22, 1988, E3; William P. Cheshire, "Letter to the Editor: The Independence of the Times." *Washington Times*, June 4, 1991; Associated Press, "De Borchgrave Named UPI President and CEO," December 19, 1998; and NewsMax.com 1999.

9. De Borchgrave's role on the program was truly odd. He only spoke once, near the end of the program, and then seemingly to discredit the conspiratorial subtext of *Valley of Death*. That anomaly, combined with the fact that the *Washington Times* embraced the story initially only to back away from it, suggests an ambivalence about it in certain far-right circles.

10. The authenticity of such patches is a matter of controversy. In my unit in Vietnam, any outerwear other than officially issued items was strictly forbidden. Researcher Regina King learned from librarian John Baky at LaSalle University, however, that some units may have been more lenient. At the library, Baky heads a special collection of Vietnam war artifacts such as patches.

11. The correspondence between Oliver and Paddock came to light in January 1999, when Paddock sent the letters to the *Washington Post*. See Arthur Allen, "April Oliver's War: How a Single-Minded Journalist Tripped over the Ghosts of Vietnam," *Washington Post Magazine*, November 29, 1998, for one of the best critiques of *Valley of Death*.

Chapter 4

1. Charles J. Reid began his defense of *Valley of Death* saying, "People forget, but by any measure, the Vietnam War was a criminal war. . . . So when CNN & Time reported . . . that the U.S. had used nerve gas in 1970 in the Laotian theater[,] . . . few familiar with the war's history were surprised."

2. "The Great Gas Flap," *Newsweek*, April 2, 1965, 20.

3. The most straightforward claim that an actual nerve agent was used in the region came in a 1972 article by Gerard Van der Leun in *Earth* magazine. Van der Leun wrote, "In late June or July of 1968 the U.S. Air Force dropped two fifty-pound canisters of Type VX nerve gas" on a North Vietnamese equipment recovery station in northeast Cambodia. The article has no citations, no sources, no indication of any sort where the author got the information. Daniel Brandt, at Public Information Research, Inc., in San Antonio, has made extensive efforts to corroborate Van Der Leun's claim but to no avail. My own efforts to follow up on the story led me to David Harris, who did some writing for *Earth* at the time. He recalled some controversy over the subject but nothing more.

4. Mindful that one cannot prove that sarin or some other nerve agent was *not* used in Southeast Asia during the war, it is nevertheless true that researchers who have devoted their lives to uncovering the truth about U.S. chemical and biological warfare in the region had never heard reports of sarin's use prior to the CNN broadcast. Fred Branfman, author of *Voices from the Plain of Jars,* about the secret U.S. air war over Laos, had heard one story of Lao children getting sick from picking up pieces of paper dropped from the air but nothing that would support a Tailwind-type claim. Interview, November 12, 2002.

5. One of the sources for the continuing suspicion that nerve gas was used in Vietnam is Carol Brightman's article "The 'Weed Killers'" in *Viet-Report,* June/July 1966. In the introduction to the article Brightman wrote, "At least one 'nerve gas,' BZ, has been used in Vietnam." But Brightman seems to be hedging. She always put quotes around nerve gas and in a table constructed to provide technical details she gave the chemical name for BZ and then wrote, "A nerve gas?" She does not refer to sarin in the article, and the information provided in the article does not provide strong evidence that even BZ was used. One of Brightman's footnotes is to a May 10, 1966, *New York Times* article, "Tear Gas Dropped on Vietcong Base," which mentions a charge by the North Vietnamese, denied by the United States, that the United States had used "toxic gas." The article made no mention of sarin, nerve gas, or BZ. Brightman also footnoted an article by Pierre Darcourt in *L'Express* (March 14–20 [*sic*], 1966), which I was unable to locate. Brightman does document that the United States was heavily involved in the development of chemical and biological agents in the 1960s. In May 2002 the Pentagon released documents about experiments done in the Pacific during the 1960s using sarin. See Thom Shanker and William J. Broad, "Sailors Sprayed with Nerve Gas in Cold War Test, Pentagon Says," *New York Times,* May 24, 2002, A1, and Matt Kelley, "Military Used Nerve Gas in '60s," Associated Press, May 24, 2002.

6. Descriptions of the gases can found in Jack Raymond, "Gas as Weapon: Pro and Con," *New York Times,* March 28, 1965, and "The Truth about 'Gas

Warfare' in Vietnam," *U.S. News and World Report*, April 5, 1965. Robert Harris and Jeremy Paxman, *A Higher Form of Killing: The Secret Story of Chemical and Biological Warfare* (New York: Hill and Wang, 1982), provides a history of chemical and biological warfare. *Newsweek*, April 5, 1965, citing a military spokesman, wrote, "The gas employed in Vietnam—actually a mixture of souped-up tear gas and a peppery chemical called adamsite which causes weeping and nausea—does not result in permanent injury."

Sarin's chemical name is isopropyl methylphosphonofluoridate. It was discovered by Dr. Gerhard Schrader, who worked for I. G. Farben chemical company during the Nazi period. The title "sarin" is an acronym of letters from the names of four individuals involved in its first production in 1938: Schrader, Otto Ambros, Colonel Rüdriger, and van der Linde. Rüdriger was head of the German army's poison gas installation at Spandau; Ambros was an associate of Hitler's who helped build and run the Nazi war gas plants (Harris and Paxman, 54–55).

7. In court documents released in Oliver's defense against John Singlaub's lawsuit against her, she made available the notes from her interview with Singlaub. In one place, her notes read as follows:

JS
Of course, we trained with CS.

AO
But CS is a mild tear gas, quite different from GB. It does little to deter an enemy. . . . We have talked to a lot of chemical experts including a career chemical researcher at Aberdeen named Bill Dee. . . . And he points out that you would have to be in a sealed chamber with extraordinarily high levels of CS to get the kind of vomiting and convulsions and diarrhea that you get with GB. . . . Early on in this story, some people were trying to get me to believe that it was just CS out there but I am way beyond that, sir, I really am.

8. See Richard Moser, *The New Winter Soldiers: GI and Veteran Dissent during the Vietnam Era* (New Brunswick, N.J.: Rutgers University Press, 1996), 74–77, for a fuller account of rebellion in military prisons.

9. See Moser (77–79) for more detailed numbers on AWOLs and desertions. David Curry, *Sunshine Patriots: Punishment and the Vietnam Offender* (Notre Dame, Ind.: University of Notre Dame Press, 1985), has a good discussion of discipline problems and desertion rates. In 1944 there were forty-four desertions per thousand active-duty troops. Korean War desertions peaked at twenty-two per thousand in 1952 and 1953. Vietnam-era rates rose from sixteen in 1965 to seventy-three per thousand in 1971.

10. The most insupportable part of *Valley of Death* is its claim that American troops fled to Laos where they defected and formed a separate military unit

to fight against U.S. forces. While there are the documented cases of Bobby Garwood and one other soldier who were charged with having crossed over to the enemy in Vietnam, and it can plausibly be argued that a handful of other GIs must have at least tried to lend their services to the other side, there is simply no good reason to believe that anything resembling the claims made about defectors in *Valley of Death* ever occurred.

11. Speculation and casual talk of a "what if" type involving collaboration with the enemy may, however, have fed the rumor mill about actual defections. In 1969, I was in a unit where passions against officers ran very high. I recall one late-night "what if" conversation about using the Vietnamese kids who worked in the camp as go-betweens to arrange a Viet Cong attack on our officers. The plan would have been for dissidents to control two adjacent guard bunkers and then allow VC sappers to sneak into the camp, make a hit on the officers' "hootches," and then depart the way they came in, between designated bunkers. Pitfalls too numerous (and obvious) to mention were immediately apparent, and the conversation ended quickly, but it is easy to imagine how in the telling and retelling of such a story it could be remembered by someone, perhaps someone who was never in Vietnam, as a kind of defection story that actually happened.

12. See Nelson Demille, *The Charm School* (New York: Warner Books, 1988), foreword.

13. The legend was made into a film, *The Lost Command*. The latest telling of the legend is in the August 2002 issue of *Military History*, although the author, Taylor Beattie, does not touch on the deserter part of the story.

14. See Paul Fussell, *The Great War and Modern Memory* (New York: Oxford University Press, 1975), 123.

15. The principle is if you're going to tell a Tall Tale, have it happen in a place that exists for most people in the imagination only; put it in a place that is so totally divorced from the listeners' experience that, well, maybe anything could happen *there*.

16. When I got beyond Mang Yang Pass it was usually by way of helicopter, not surface travel. Once I hitched a ride on a small civilian aircraft going from Pleiku to Ban Me Thout, with only the American pilot and me on board. We flew straight west into the setting sun for a while before landing at a tiny isolated airstrip in what I thought had to be Cambodia. We were on the ground only long enough to pick up a package; then, in the dark, we reversed course and landed at Ban Me Thout.

17. In the notes of her interview with Gen. John Singlaub, Oliver asks about the defectors. She is trying to get Singlaub to say that the so-called defectors may have really been POWs. She tells him, "[Admiral Thomas] Moorer made it sound as if the Tailwind defectors, in his opinion, might have had an element of coercion to their presence. He makes them sound like deserters who were sick of the war and

wanted to go back home through Laos, but got picked up by the Laotian military and made captive. . . . So would they be POWs or defectors?" Singlaub didn't take the POW bait.

The exchange is interesting as another example of how Oliver used one source, Moorer in this case, to lead Singlaub into saying what she wanted to hear. It also confirms that she had been drawn to the POW assassination theory early in her research. The image of GIs trying to go home by walking into Laos—whether Moorer told it to her or not—is, of course, right out of Tim O'Brien's novel.

18. See Johanna McGeary and Karen Tumulty, "The Fog of War: 32 Years after Leaving Vietnam, Bob Kerrey Admits a Terrible Secret," *Time*, May 7, 2001.

19. Van Buskirk apparently tells different versions of his story. In one of them, recounted by Oliver and Smith in their rebuttal of the Abrams report, he says the following: "There was this one enemy encampment that we found. And I saw a white guy running through it. And he jumped in a foxhole. When I told him to come out he said in perfect English fuck you. And I called for an air strike. It was a Russian adviser. *I got his ring and all his stuff*" [emphasis mine]. There is no indication that Smith and Oliver asked to see the ring; on the next page of the report Van Buskirk is back to insisting that the Caucasians he chased were GIs.

20. In the case of "pepper," even if the "white man" is black, I guess.

21. James "Bo" Gritz led a couple of postwar missions to Southeast Asia to recover POWs he believed were still being held there. See James Gritz, *Called to Serve* (Sandy Valley, Nev.: Lazarus, 1991). As recounted in chapter 5, he attributed his failure to find any prisoners to another betrayal by America. Questions about security also surrounded the 1970 raid on Son Tay in North Vietnam, where, again, the commandos arrived at a camp that had been emptied of its POWs.

22. As is pointed out elsewhere, Van Buskirk's description of the defector he chases is a perfect fit for Steve Shepard in the 1988 film *White Ghost*, about a hunter-killer team pursuing a renegade GI. Shepard appears to be attired in swim trunks—even after fifteen years in the jungle!

23. The image of betrayal by "the female" is developed more fully in Gibson's *Warrior Dreams* and in my book *The Spitting Image*.

24. At this point of Graves's testimony in *Valley of Death*, narrator Peter Arnett says, "[Graves's] recon team spotted several Americans, roundeyes—either POW's or defectors."

25. A letter writer in the May 17, 2001, edition of the *Akron (Ohio) Beacon Journal* claimed firsthand knowledge that sarin had been used to "eradicate American deserters" in 1970 and 1971, calling it "a military and historical disgrace that bordered on treason."

26. Eugene McCarley, one of the Tailwind veterans, said he never heard about nerve gas and defectors until April Oliver asked him about it. To me, he

quipped that such stories grew out of "Jim Beam talking to Bud Weiser" and suspects that Van Buskirk had talked Jim Cathey, another of Oliver's on-camera sources, into believing them.

27. Bill Stroud interview by Waldo Salt, November 5, 1974. The Waldo Salt Papers, Research Library, University of California Los Angeles. Men who did not see combat can also play the "reticent veteran" role. They can invoke the trauma of war experience and ask that those memories be allowed to stay buried. By feigning the fear of reliving the horror and refusing to talk about "what happened over there," they leave the listener to fill in the blanks with his or her imagination.

28. See Fox Butterfield, "A Portrait of the Detective in the 'O. J. Whirlpool,'" *New York Times*, March 2, 1996, A1; Tim Weiner, "Military Combat Insignia Signify Esteem of Officers," *New York Times*, May 18, 1996, A11; and Murray Chass, "Dogged by War Tales, Johnson Is Let Go by Jays," *New York Times*, March 18, 1999.

29. See Allan Young, *The Harmony of Illusion: Inventing Post-Traumatic Stress Disorder* (Princeton, N.J.: Princeton University Press, 1995); Jerry Lembcke, "The 'Right Stuff' Gone Wrong: Vietnam Veterans and the Social Construction of Post-Traumatic Stress Disorder," *Critical Sociology* 24, nos. 1–2 (1999); Elaine Showalter, *Hystories: Hysterical Epidemics and Modern Culture* (New York: Columbia University Press, 1997); Robert Fleming, "Post Vietnam Syndrome: Neurosis or Sociosis?" *Psychiatry* 48 (May 1985): 122–39; and Landy Sparr and Loran D. Pankratz, "Factitious Posttraumatic Stress Disorder," *American Journal of Psychiatry* 140 (1983): 1016–19. The Los Angeles cop, Mark Fuhrman, started telling his "war stories" in 1981, when he applied for a stress-disability pension from the police department.

30. While Burkett may be the best-known sleuth of bogus veteran stories (see his 1998 book *Stolen Valor*), he is not the only one. *New York Times* reporter Pam Belluck wrote about a Skidmore, Missouri, couple, Mary and Chuck Schantag, who also work at unmasking counterfeit warriors.

31. See the research reported in Cynthia Gimbel and Alan Booth, "Why Does Military Combat Experience Adversely Affect Marital Relations?" *Journal of Marriage and the Family* 56 (1994): 691–703.

32. See Carey Goldberg, "His Vietnam Tale Exposed as a Lie, a Killer Is Back in Custody," *New York Times*, August 27, 1998, A21.

33. See Butterfield for the Furman story and Associated Press, "Vietnam Vet Concedes Overstating Role in Napalm Attack," *Worcester (Mass.) Telegram and Gazette*, December 18, 1997, A6, for the Plummer story.

34. Post-traumatic stress disorder had been in Hollywood film for well over a decade before it was a canonized as a diagnostic category by the American Psychiatric Association. The character "Brahmin" in Russ Meyer's *Motor Psycho* displayed the symptoms of PTSD in 1965, as did Jud (1971) and Stanley (1972) in movies by those names, respectively.

Chapter 5

1. Thanks to Craig Jensen, I found lines very similar to those spoken by Van Buskirk in the movie *Usual Suspects*, a film that Van Buskirk is likely to have seen as part of his prison missionary work.

2. The creation of the victim-veteran image in popular culture is not incidental to understanding the origins of *Valley of Death*. Robert Van Buskirk claimed to have suffered from PTSD, as did many of the veterans connected to the hunter-killer stories reported in Monika Jensen-Stevenson's *Spite House*. In many ways, victim-veteran status became the currency that underwrote truth claims about the war.

3. Read another way, some of these films may have been expressions of latent civilian fears of the warriors the society had trained and sent off to war. Biker films featuring Vietnam veterans, like *Motor Psycho* (1965), *Satan's Sadists* (1969), *The Black Six* (1974), and *The Brotherhood of Death* (1976), can be interpreted that way. Jason Katzman, "From Outcast to Cliche: How Film Shaped, Warped and Developed the Image of the Vietnam Veteran, 1969–1990," *Journal of American Culture* 16 (Spring 1993): 7–24, and Alfred Schuetz, "The Homecomer," in *Strangers at Home: Vietnam Veterans since the War*, ed. John W. Figley and Seymour Leventman (New York: Brunner/Mazel, 1990, have written about the way civilian culture marginalizes veterans.

4. The allusions to atomic weaponry as the film moves to its apocalyptic ending suggests that in this film they function artistically as the exotic equivalent of nerve gas.

5. Filming for *Apocalypse Now* began early in 1976. The existence of SOG trickled into public awareness throughout the postwar period. Karnow (1983) mentions SOG's OPLAN 34-A in connection with its role in the Gulf of Tonkin incident. One of the earliest detailed accounts of SOG's origins and mission was a little-known book called *War in the Shadows,* published by Boston Publishing Company in 1988. Although that volume is about SOG, none of the entries in its lengthy bibliography of secondary and published government sources contains "Studies and Observations Group" or "SOG" in its title; only the unpublished government documents cited made explicit reference to SOG.

6. The more common code word is "Company," but in the context of the film, "Corporation" must have been intended to convey the same thing.

7. In a review essay on *Apocalypse Now Redux* ("*Apocalypse Now* Redux: The Politics of Paranoia in America Today," *TomPaine.com,* 2001), I argue that the film's lasting importance lies in its political interpretation of the war in Vietnam more than in its interpretation of Conrad's work.

8. Zoetrope films, Francis Ford Coppola's film company, allows very limited access to its archives. However, Peter Cowie was allowed to see early drafts of the script for his book *The Apocalypse Now Book.* In the scene where

the air cavalry attacks a coastal village, Willard introduces himself to the Cav's Colonel Kilgore (named Kharnage in early scripts). Kilgore says, "Na Trang [home of the Fifth Special Forces] told me to expect you." In words that virtually confirm Coppola's intent to encode the film with a conspiratorial subtext, he penciled in the margin, "There must always be the stink of *conspiracy* [*sic*] in the air." Peter Cowie, *The Apocalypse Now Book* (New York: Da Capo Press, 2000), 39.

9. In the aftermath of the attacks on the World Trade Center and Pentagon of September 11, 2001, the foresight of *Apocalypse Now* seems even clearer. Important leaders of the fundamentalist Christian right, like Jerry Farwell and Pat Robertson, understood the attacks as God's retribution against an American culture degraded by feminism and homosexuality. For them, as for Kurtz, the will of the enemy to make the ultimate sacrifice illuminates America's moral weakness.

10. The religious symbolism in the film's title, *Apocalypse Now*, anticipated another development of the 1980s, the rise of religious fundamentalism and its belief that corruption and duplicity in government were signs that the Apocalypse, the end of time, was near. In an early draft of the final scene, writer John Milius cast Kurtz in an Alamo-type pose, saying, "We are chosen to be the warriors of heaven—in this the Twilight of the Gods—This—the Götterdämmerung—This the Apocalypse—Now!" Cowie, *The Apocalypse Now Book*, 43.

11. The point is debatable, of course, but film buffs will recall that *Saving Private Ryan* (1998) was criticized for its overly realistic portrayals of death and dismemberment at Normandy. And *Apocalypse Now*, for all its emphasis on the savagery of humankind, showed little blood. While Willard assassinates Kurtz, apparently with a knife, we are shown instead an ox being bloodily hacked to death by Cambodians.

12. The use of exotica in a story works in complex ways. Used well by the writer, its presence as, say, the machinery of war, establishes the plausibility of "the unknown" as a factor in the outcome of events. We know that nerve gas is real—it does exist—even though our own senses have never confirmed that existence. Why, then, might not some other unconfirmed element of the story—like, say, defectors in Laos—not be true? Our imagination, by participating in one dimension of the story, in other words, becomes an unwitting accomplice in selling us on the veracity of other hard-to-believe parts of the story.

13. Having written the best-selling novels *Plum Island* and *The General's Daughter*, Demille was a very well known author. Demille's politics are consistent with the ultraconservative subtext of the Tailwind tale. A professed libertarian, Demille wrote an endorsement of Henry Holzer's recent book *Aid & Comfort: Jane Fonda in North Vietnam*, which traffics in the same betrayal mythologies as the purveyors of Tailwind.

14. The power of fiction to influence people's sense of history is undeniable. On a flight into Providence, Rhode Island, in March 2002, I sat next to a woman who was reading Demille's more recent novel, *Up Country,* which is set in Vietnam. I commented that I had read *Charm School,* to which she responded that it was her favorite of the author's works. She went on to say, "What was amazing is that so much of it turned out to be true." "Oh really," I asked, "like what?" "Like all the U.S. POWs who were found buried in the Soviet Union," she said. Saying the story was "in all the newspapers," she expressed surprise that I had not heard about it.

15. When Duane Frederic reviewed Monika Jensen-Stevenson's book *Spite House: The Last Secret of the War in Vietnam* for Amazon.com, he asked if the book shouldn't be subtitled "the last fairy tale" of the war.

16. Monika Jensen-Stevenson and William Stevenson, *Kiss the Boys Goodbye: How the United States Betrayed Its Own POWs in Vietnam* (New York: Dutton, 1990), 307, reports other missions to rescue POWs during the 1980s. See James Bo Gritz, *Called to Serve* (Sandy Valley, Nev.: Lazarus, 1991), for other another account of someone claiming to have been involved in raids to recover POWs in Laos during the 1980s.

17. Jensen-Stevenson and Stevenson, 306.

18. Jensen-Stevenson's use of sources is even more slippery than April Oliver's. She initially reported (with William Stevenson) her so-called research findings in a 1990 book, *Kiss the Boys Goodbye: How the United States Betrayed Its Own POWs in Vietnam. Kiss the Boys* reads like a cheap mystery novel: a parade of cloaked figures, some named, others anonymous, make middle-of-the-night phone calls to arrange secret rendezvouses with the author; and references are made to vaguely identified documents with such questionable provenance and sketchy attributions that it's sometimes hard to tell if a primary or secondary source is being quoted. The reference to Scott Barnes's claim to have targeted POWs for assassination, for example, is dribbled into the text (pp. 84 and 321) in quotes that have little documentation as to when, where, and to whom he made the statements.

In *Spite House*'s 364 pages of small print there are 104 footnotes, most of which are elaborations of the author's own points rather than documentation.

19. Interspersed with the hunter's side of the story is the supposed-defector's side, which is what the author learned from Garwood about what he was doing while he was being hunted. What makes the book so interesting is that Garwood does not know he is being hunted—because in "fact," as the author develops the story, he is a POW, not a defector. Had *Spite House* been marketed as a novel, Jensen-Stevenson may have had a best-seller in it.

20. Monika Jensen-Stevenson, *Spite House: The Last Secret of the War in Vietnam* (New York: Avon, 1997), 10.

21. Jensen-Stevenson, *Spite House,* 188–90.

22. According to Jensen-Stevenson, *Spite House*, 58, "nobody in the CIA except those at the very top had the authority to give any Green Beret any orders," leading McKenney to the "assumption that 'the very top' is where the Garwood directive came from."

This and the following paragraphs about McKenney and his role in hunting Garwood are drawn from Jensen-Stevenson's account. She appears to have relied on McKenney's recall for what she wrote, a method that is problematic, given the importance and controversial nature of the issues.

23. Jensen-Stevenson, *Spite House*, 202.

24. Womack's story is in Wes Keith, *Victories: Stories of Christian Vietnam Veterans* (Mountainlake Terrace, Wash.: WinePress, 1995).

25. Jensen-Stevenson, *Spite House*, 346.

26. Jensen-Stevenson, *Spite House*, 357.

27. If not Russians, McKenney speculates that the assassinated defectors/POWs might have been "low-level assets the CIA wanted eliminated."

28. Peter Arnett's use of the "hunter-killer" combination in his narration of *Valley of Death* is almost certainly indebted to Monika Jensen-Stevensen's coinage of the phrase. In a December 4, 2002, telephone interview, Jensen-Stevenson said she "spoke to April Oliver and others at CNN" during *Valley of Death*'s development.

Chapter 6

1. See Hal Lindsey, *There's a New World Coming: A Prophetic Odyssey* (New York: Bantam, 1973), 123–24, for the quote. Lindsey is a leading author of prophetic Christian books, including *The Late Great Planet Earth*.

2. The best analysis of the middle-class cultural backlash is Barbara Ehrenreich's *Fear of Falling: The Inner Life of the Middle Class* (New York: Pantheon, 1989). David Brock, *Blinded by the Right: The Conscience of an Ex-conservative* (New York: Crown, 2002), and Alan Goldberg, *Enemies Within: The Culture of Conspiracy in Modern America* (New Haven: Yale University Press, 2001) also have interesting reflections on that topic.

3. A June 2001 conversation with a friend in Iowa confirmed for me that these issues come bundled together for some people. Within a few minutes, my friend, a small-business owner who is not particularly religious or conservative, complained that his son had come home from college questioning Creationism: "I guess he got that from his professors, Huh?" He asked me if I thought we were headed for "one-world government," the signs for which he saw in "them" buying up everything (his example was Wal-Mart, which he said drives local stores out of business and invests its profits elsewhere) and in immigrants who, he said, drain money from the local economy ("You can

see 'em lined up at the Post Office on Friday night to send their money home").

Most interesting was his conflation of "one-world government" with economic monopolies and his understanding that immigrants and monopolies like Wal-Mart mean the same thing for the community—they are outsiders who take away more value than they put in. As sociologists see it, his view of the world is classically that of the "middle man" who feels pinched by socio-economic forces from above (big business) and below (poor immigrants), a worldview that is sometimes called "producerism." Chip Berlet and Matthew Lyons, *Right-Wing Populism in America: Too Close for Comfort* (New York: Guilford Press, 2000).

4. The prophetic tradition divides between *pre-* and *post-*millennialists. Premillennialism is associated with fundamentalism and holds that earthly woes will be ended only by God's intervention. Its followers believe that the second coming of Christ begins a thousand-year period of his reign on earth, known as the millennium.

Postmillennialism has a liberal variant, sometimes associated with liberation theology, which argues that humankind can solve social problems and bring about God's kingdom during human history. Its right-wing version is associated with theocratic Christian Reconstructionism and contends that godly men must reign and rule for one thousand years before Christ returns. Berlet and Lyons provide an extended discussion of millennialism in chapters 10 and 16 of *Right-Wing Populism in America.*

5. Paul Boyer, *When Time Shall Be No More* (Cambridge, Mass.: Harvard University Press, 1992), 69.

6. See Boyer, *When Time Shall Be No More*, 73–75, for more details on the Revolutionary War period. The quote is Boyer's of Tom Paine.

7. "The Protocols of the Elders Zion" is the template for conspiracy theories having Jews at the center. For an easy introduction to "The Protocols" see James Ridgeway, *Blood in the Face: The Ku Klux Klan, Aryan Nations, Nazi Skinheads, and the Rise of a New White Culture* (New York: Thunder's Mouth Press, 1995).

8. Paul Boyer's chapter 6, "Antichrist, 666, and the Mark of the Beast," provides a richly documented summary of the application of Bible prophecy to current political conditions.

9. Van Impe is quoted by Boyer, *When Time Shall Be No More*, 264.

10. Lindsey, *There's a New World Coming*, 175; and Boyer, *When Time Shall Be No More*, 265. The interconnections between the Trilateral Commission and the presidency of Jimmy Carter help explain why Carter was a special target for ultraconservatives. There is more on Carter and the right wing's dislike of him in chapter 7.

11. By some interpretations, the U.S. defeat by Asians also seemed to bear out another of John's revelations, that a great army from the East would play a part in the apocalypse.

12. There is more on the Birch Society and Admiral Moorer's relationship to it in the next chapter.

13. See chapter 2 of Osha Gray Davidson, *Broken Heartland: The Rise of America's Rural Ghetto* (New York: Free Press, 1990), for more on the farm crisis.

Posse Comitatus takes its name from the law that effectively ended Reconstruction by banning the use of federal troops in the South after the Civil War. A good introduction to the Posse can be found in Ridgeway, *Blood in the Face*. Like the John Birch Society, the Posse believes that the international conspiracy includes communists.

A Harris poll conducted for the Anti-Defamation League of B'nai B'rith in February 1986 found that 75 percent of farmers blamed "big international bankers" for the farm crisis, 35 percent blamed "an international communist conspiracy," and 13 percent blamed "certain religious groups such as Jews." Respondents could assign blame to more than one group. Louis Harris, *A Study of Anti-Semitism in Rural Iowa and Nebraska* (New York: Louis Harris, 1986).

14. The failure of epidemiological studies to confirm the reality of Gulf War syndrome led Michael Fumento ("Gulf Lore Syndrome," *Reason*, March 22–23, 1997) to refer to the phenomenon as "Gulf *Lore* Syndrome" and Elaine Showalter (*Hystories: Hysterical Epidemics and Modern Culture* [New York: Columbia University Press, 1997]) to call it a form of male hysteria.

My critique of PTSD, the concept, is informed by constructionist traditions. Other insightful approaches are taken by Fred Turner, *Echoes of Combat: The Vietnam War in American Memory* (New York: Anchor, 1996), and Wilbur J. Scott, *The Politics of Readjustment: Vietnam Veterans since the War* (New York: Aldine de Gruyter, 1993).

15. The point of the gas stories was to construct the one comparison that no one would mistake—that Saddam Hussein was like Hitler.

16. The right-wing metanarrative for the Persian Gulf war was provided by the first Bush administration's characterization of the war as the beginning of a "new world order." For the right, that expression signaled the beginning of "one-world government" under the control of bankers and Washington "insiders."

17. This account of Ruby Ridge is largely based on Morris Dees, *Gathering Storm: America's Militia Threat* (New York: HarperCollins, 1996).

18. Gritz begins the preface to *Called to Serve* with the following words: "This is the definitive account of a nation betrayed. A spider web of 'patriots for profit,' operating from the highest positions of special trust and confidence . . . have infused America with drugs in order to fund covert operations while sealing the fate of our servicemen left in Communist prisons. [This book] will produce a crack in the facade of 20th Century American government, through which concerned citizens can view the looming peril

and act in time to reverse our course while God gives us time." James Gritz, *Called to Serve* (Sandy Valley, Nev.: Lazarus, 1991).

19. Besides Gritz's *Called to Serve*, Morris Dees's *Gathering Storm*, and Michael Novick's chapter "Front Man for Fascism: Bo Gritz and the Racist Populist Party" in his collection *White Lies, White Power: The Fight against White Supremacy and Reactionary Violence* (Monroe, Me.: Common Courage Press, 1995) provide valuable background information on Gritz.

20. Gritz also founded SPIKE (Specially Trained Individuals for Key Events), which conducts training sessions in intelligence gathering, weapons use, survivalist tactics, white supremacy, and Christian Identity proselytizing.

21. The BATF action was called a "search and arrest" operation that was based on allegations the Davidians possessed illegal firearms. Speculation that the group engaged in bizarre and possibly illegal sexual and child-rearing practices added to public interest in the raid.

22. See Dees, *Gathering Storm*, for the connection between Waco and the larger paramilitary movement.

23. See *Waco: A New Revelation*, MGA Films, Inc., 1999. Koresh's views are presented in greater depth in James D. Tabor and Eugene V. Gallagher, *Why Waco? Cults and the Battle for Religious Freedom in America* (Berkeley: University of California Press, 1995).

24. David Valdes Greenwood, "Waco: The Fire Next Time," *Boston/Worcester Phoenix*, September 17, 1999.

25. Goldberg, *Enemies Within*, 84–92, gives particular credit to televangelist Pat Robertson for inciting the apocalyptic climate of fear during the last quarter-century.

26. In *The Higher Circles: The Governing Class in America* (New York: Random/Vintage, 1971), sociologist G. William Domhoff uses McBirnie as an example of an ultraconservative conspiricist in order to distinguish conspiracy theory from his own theory of power.

Chapter 7

1. The Abrams report, for example, provided no background information on Moorer and Singlaub.

2. This characterization of the hard right is taken from chart 1 of Chip Berlet and Matthew Lyons, *Right-Wing Populism in America: Too Close for Comfort* (New York: Guilford Press, 2000). Berlet has been following and writing about the American political right for over twenty years.

3. See Seymour M. Hersh, *The Price of Power: Kissinger in the Nixon White House* (New York: Summit Books), 1983, 120–21, for details on Duck Hook. Duck Hook was never executed. A combination of the antiwar movement's successful demonstrations during the October and November Moratorium

Days, and the administration's assessment that the plan would not produce the desired response from the Vietnamese, convinced Nixon that a deeper war in the North was not the way out of Vietnam.

Hersh says (p. 130) that the antiwar movement underestimated the impact of the Moratorium Days on Nixon. Kissinger, on the other hand, was unmoved by the demonstrations, according to Hersh. For details on Kissinger's disdain for Melvin Laird, see pp. 90–91.

4. On Nixon's distrust of Laird, see Hersh, *The Price of Power*, 112.

5. Eight years later, as a civilian, Bull Simons would answer H. Ross Perot's call to rescue two employees of Perot's Electronic Data Systems company who were being held in Tehran following the overthrow of the shah (Richard H. Shultz, Jr., *The Secret War against Hanoi: Kennedy's and Johnson's Use of Spies, Saboteurs, and Covert Warriors in North Vietnam* [New York: Harper-Collins, 1999], 346). More specifics on the logistics of the Son Tay raid can be found in *War in the Shadows* (Boston: Boston Publishing, 1988).

6. See *War in the Shadows*, 182, and H. Bruce Franklin, *M.I.A., or Myth-making in America* (New York: Lawrence Hill Books, 1992), 72, for the after-math of the Son Tay raid.

The government had intended to conceal the raid, and on November 22 Secretary Laird denied Radio Hanoi's claims that it had occurred. A day later he fessed up, claiming the mission had been carried out because POWs were dying in the camps. On November 25 Simons and another commando accompanied Laird at a press conference to discuss the Son Tay attack but revealed few of its embarrassing details.

7. In his memoir (*On Watch: A Memoir* [New York: Quadrangle, 1976], 375) Adm. Elmo R. Zumwalt says that Moorer never met Radford personally. Robinson was replaced by Welander in June 1971.

8. This account of "Yeoman Radford's Spy Ring" is taken from Walter Isaacson, *Kissinger: A Biography* (New York: Simon and Schuster, 1992), 380–85. The details on Radford's pilfering come from Hersh, *The Price of Power*, 467–69.

9. See Hersh, *The Price of Power*, 477–78.

10. McDonald died aboard Korean Air Lines flight 007 in 1983.

11. Other organizations under the ASC umbrella were the America First Committee and the American Vigilante Intelligence Federation, founded in 1927 by Harry Jung who was the first major distributor in the U.S. of the anti-Semitic publication *The Protocols of the Learned Elders of Zion*. Another affiliate was the Coalition for Peace Through Strength which brought together the United States Council for World Freedom and several fascist organizations, including the Bulgarian National Front, the Byelorussian American Committee, and the Slovak World Congress.

For more details on the ASC see Russ Bellant, *Old Nazis, the New Right, and the Republican Party* (Boston: South End Press, 1991), 29–58, and

Scott Anderson and Jon Lee Anderson, *Inside the League: The Shocking Ex- pose of How Terrorists, Nazis, and Latin American Death Squads Have In- filtrated the World Anti-Communist League* (New York: Dodd, Mead, 1986), 157.

12. See Bellant, *Old Nazis, the New Right, and the Republican Party,* 41.

13. NewsMax.com was started by right-wing activist Christopher Ruddy, ac- cording to Chip Berlet. The Associated Press reported on Moorer's speech to the John Birch Society in the fall of 1999. See Chip Berlet, *Clinton, Conspir- acism, and the Continuing Culture War* (Somerville, Mass.: Political Research Associates, 1999), and John LeBoutillier, "The Most Shameful Act of Betrayal in American History," *NewsMax.com,* January 26, 2001.

14. It is even less likely that Walter Isaacson, the editor at *Time* who gave the go-ahead for the magazine's version of *Valley of Death,* would not have known Moorer's background as a schemer because he wrote a very important 1992 biography (cited) of Kissinger.

15. Floyd Abrams and David Kohler, "Report on CNN Broadcast 'Valley of Death,'" July 2, 1998, 3.

16. Bernard Weinraub, "General Returns from South Korea to Face Carter," *New York Times,* May 21, 1977; "Carter Defends Plan to Reduce Forces in Korea," *New York Times,* May 27, 1977, A1; and "The Korea With- drawal: Some Officers Are Nervous and Congress Wants to Have a Say," *New York Times,* May 30, 1977.

17. See Bernard Weinraub, "Defense Chief Backs Korea Plan, Says the Mil- itary Must Support It," *New York Times,* May 23, 1977.

18. As with the Korea dispute, and as he would do in the aftermath of the Tailgate affair twenty years later, Singlaub raised questions about the honesty of the journalists who reported his remarks on the neutron bomb. See "Gen- eral Who Attacked Carter," *New York Times,* April 29, 1978.

19. A useful introduction to the history of U.S. collaboration with Nazis in the post–World War II period can be found in Bill Moyer's documentary *Secret Government,* made for public television in 1989.

20. These details about Throne are drawn from Richard H. Shultz, Jr., *The Secret War against Hanoi,* 219–20 and 229–30; and Shelby Stanton, "Special Military Operations," *War in the Shadows* (Boston: Boston Publishing, 1988), 86–87.

21. Rumors that U.S. POWs were being held in the Soviet Union have been a part of the POW/MIA lore for years. Nelson Demille's novel *The Charm School,* which contains elements of the CNN version of Operation Tailwind and is discussed in an earlier chapter, is based on that premise.

Soviet-held POWs are a vivid image in the minds of Cold Warriors like Singlaub. I did not speak with the general, but his aide, Keith Freeman, was quite willing to talk about POW/MIA issues and promised to get back to me with rare documentation about an MIA sighting in Vietnam. He did not do so, even after a follow-up and reminder. He also praised Slavomir Rawicz's *The Long Walk: The True Story of a Trek to Freedom* (New York: Lyons Press, 1956 [1997]), about a prisoner who walks from Siberia (in the winter), across the Gobi Desert and Himalayan Mountains to India, where he is reunited with friendly westerners. I read it and found the supposedly *true* story to be utterly fantastic, which left me thoroughly puzzled as to why Freeman thought I had to read it.

22. Through his personal relationship with Cline, Singlaub was certainly aware of the league long before he became openly involved in its activities after his resignation from the army. Also, given that his area of operation had been Asia, it is likely that he had some hand in setting up the training academy in Taiwan.

23. According to Anderson and Anderson, *Inside the League,* 271, Singlaub opposed the efforts of Justice Department to prosecute Nazi war criminals in the United States.

24. Anderson and Anderson, *Inside the League,* 109–12.

25. See Anderson and Anderson, *Inside the League,* 177.

26. In their *Inside the League,* 254, on the World Anti-Communist League, Anderson and Anderson called Alarcon "the 'Godfather' of Central American death squads."

27. Berlet and Lyon (p. 187) describe the Liberty Lobby as an "essentially neofascist organization" founded in the late 1950s by the anti-Semite Willis Carto. Anderson and Anderson, *Inside the League,* 150–55, provide many more details on Singlaub's involvement with WACL and USCWF. They also note that while not all members of the USCWF share the more extreme-right sentiments held by their international associates, all overlook the presence of anti-Semites and terrorists as necessary "for the greater good." The role of supporters of the Liberty Lobby in the formation of Singlaub's WACL's U.S. chapter is also noted by Bellant, *Old Nazis, the New Right, and the Republican Party,* 67.

28. The Iran-Contra hearings delved into the efforts of Singlaub, North, and others to raise money from private sources to fund the Contra war against the Sandinista government of Nicaragua which Congress had voted not to fund. The hearings revealed that some members of the National Security Council had illegally sold U.S. missiles to Iran, kept some of the money for themselves, and donated the remainder of the profit to the Contras. Singlaub was involved in a related effort to raise money from wealthy right-wing individuals and businesses like the family of beer magnate Joseph Coors. The hearings resulted in convictions of several participants in the scheme.

Chapter 8

1. See Bruce Jackson, "The Perfect Informant," *Journal of American Folklore* 103 (1990): 400–16. Stefan Maechler makes a similar analysis in his *The*

Wilkomirski Affair: A Study in Biographical Truth (New York: Schocken Books, 2001). Wilkomirski claimed to have spent his childhood years in a Nazi concentration camp. He constructed an elaborate biography about having been adopted after the war and raised as a gentile, only to rediscover in his later life who he really was. Wilkomirski's story was later revealed to have been false. Maechler's study is about how journalists, book editors, academics, and a large segment of the general public came to believe his story.

2. Oliver's response to my inquiries was to refer me to public statements she or Smith had made. Refusing, as she put it, to allow herself to become "the story," she would not, for example, give me a copy of her college transcript (even with the grades obscured), which would have enabled me to see what courses she might have taken related to the war in Vietnam.

3. The name of Rense's website was changed to Rense.com in 2001. At the time of Oliver's appearance on his radio show in 1998, and for more than two years following, however, it was *Sightings*.

4. The idea that "Hitler won the war" appears in literature advertised on right-wing Internet sites. It seems to be a variation—with a 180-degree ideological twist—on the John Birch Society theme that a *Jewish* foreign power already runs America through a secret cabal of Washington "insiders."

5. Chip Berlet, *Right Woos Left: Populist Party, LaRouchian, and Other Neo-Fascist Overtures to Progressives, and Why They Must Be Rejected* (Somerville, Mass.: Political Research Associates, 1994), calls the IHR "the largest distributor of pro-Nazi, anti-Jewish, white supremacist literature in the United States."

6. Minor figures though they are, Ruppert and Rense are not without influence. At a conference in 2001 I overheard a colleague talking about a recent guest speaker on his campus. I recognized the views of the speaker immediately, and my friend confirmed that the guest had been Ruppert. Likewise, when I mentioned the Jeff Rense show to my friend, he already knew about it. I return to Ruppert's post-9/11 influence in the last chapter.

7. At places in the interview, the exchanges between Oliver and Ruppert took an affective form. At one point, Ruppert said, "April has my undying affection," to which Oliver emits a fawning "Michael, oh, well, that is so helpful, you know, at times it's really lonely and I never expected to be in this position. . . ."

Oliver's style is not incidental to an understanding of how *Valley of Death* got produced. One critic who had access to unused portions of the interview tapes told me that at times Oliver seemed to be flirting with Admiral Moorer. The critic wondered if Moorer might have been seduced by Oliver's come-ons to say things he did not really mean. The other possibility, of course, is that Moorer had Oliver in his thrall, leading her to take his conspiratorial teasings more seriously than he intended.

8. It is well known that Prouty was the basis for the secret informant, "Col. X," played by Donald Sutherland in Oliver Stone's 1991 film *JFK*.

9. The nineteenth-century religious movements referred to by Hofstadter are also discussed in chapter 6.

10. W. J. Cash, *The Mind of the South* (New York: Vintage, 1941 [1991]), 295. Richard Hofstadter, *The Paranoid Style in American Politics and Other Essays* (New York: Knopf, 1965), 72–75, also notes that many mid-twentieth-century right-wing movements like the John Birch Society have roots in southern fundamentalist Christian culture. Birch founder Robert H. Welch grew up in a fundamentalist Baptist family in North Carolina.

11. The landscape metaphor is instructive, because just as two people standing at different positions in, say, a forest will be able to look at the same distant point and, because of shadows, obstructed sight lines, etc., see different things, two people in different societal positions will have divergent senses of social reality.

The quote of Ortega y Gasset is taken from Susan Ferguson, *Mapping The Social Landscape: Readings in Sociology* (New York: WCB/McGraw-Hill, 2001). Ferguson was unable to supply me with a primary citation.

12. These details are drawn from Oliver's resumé.

13. Sociologist Herbert Gans, *Deciding What's News: A Study of* CBS Evening News, NBC Nightly News, Newsweek, *and* Time (New York: Vintage, 1980), 208, reported that journalists' reality judgments and values come from "personal experience and background; and from the lifestyles journalists experienced as children, and now as adults, in their own families and communities."

14. These details on the pre–Civil War Hampton empire are drawn from Manly Wade Wellman, *Giant in Gray: A Biography of Wade Hampton of South Carolina* (New York: Charles Scribner, 1949), chap. 4.

15. Although several states did restore the slave trade at that time, South Carolina did not. See Wellman, *Giant in Gray*, 34–36.

16. See Wellman, *Giant in Gray*, 47.

17. Wellman, *Giant in Gray*, 195.

18. See Wellman, *Giant in Gray*, 206–7, 235–36.

19. President Grant set up a congressional committee to investigate Klan activities. Wellman, *Giant in Gray*, 231–32, reports that when the committee came to South Carolina, "Hampton was among the Southern leaders who testified." He adds the curious note that "no evidence has ever shown that [Hampton] belonged to the order."

20. In an autumn 1866 speech Hampton criticized the North for having forced abolition upon the South but advised his followers to accept the reality of a new order; he spoke in favor of black suffrage—but only if there were property and educational qualifications on all voters, black and white. Against Hampton's wishes, free blacks got full voting rights, and in the November 1868

elections, the state voted for former Union general Ulysses S. Grant for president and put ninety-nine Negroes, a 66 percent majority, in its legislature. Hampton was forced into bankruptcy, with personal debts of more than a million dollars. The Millwood homestead and the Mississippi plantation were lost in the proceedings.

21. Wellman, *Giant in Gray*, 265.

22. In a 1927 tribute to Hampton, *Hampton and His Red Shirts: South Carolina's Deliverance in 1876* (Freeport, N.Y.: Books for Libraries Press, 1927), journalist Alfred Williams wrote (p. 365) of the election: "Hundreds of men from Georgia and North Carolina came over the lines to 'help Hampton' by voting time and time again at South Carolina polls. . . . United States soldiers as they were relieved from duty put themselves in citizens' clothes and voted for Hampton as many times as they could be taken from one poll to another."

23. Wellman's description of the post-vote maneuverings in South Carolina could have been recycled for the aftermath of the 2000 election in Florida.

24. Daisy Hampton's endorsement was published as the foreword to Williams's book; for the Associated Press story, see Jim Davenport, "Flag at Statue Concerns Hampton Family," *State*, April 22, 2000. Other Hampton relatives were not so pleased to have the flag flown over the family statue.

25. The details on Atwater come from John Brady, *Bad Boy: The Life and Politics of Lee Atwater* (New York: Addison-Wesley, 1997). It was Atwater who crafted the racist Willy Horton strategy for George Bush's 1988 presidential run against Michael Dukakis. Horton, imprisoned for murder in Massachusetts, had received a weekend pass in April 1987. During his few hours of freedom he raped a woman and severely stabbed her husband. Atwater's staff produced campaign advertisements that played on the idea that the liberalism of Massachusetts's Governor Dukakis had been responsible for Horton's crime spree.

26. Westmoreland lost in the Republican primary. Brady, *Bad Boy*, writes (pp. 46–48) that Atwater hated losing so badly that he "had the dry heaves for two days" after the election.

27. April Oliver, "The Great Migration: Political Transformation Caused by Afghan Refugees in Pakistan," senior thesis, Princeton, N.J., Woodrow Wilson School of International Affairs, 1983, 77. While in Pakistan, Oliver stayed briefly with "personal friends of the Bhuttos," one of Pakistan's leading political families (p. 69).

28. Two years after his interview with Oliver, Fisher's impression was that her infatuation with covert operations and the men who do them had been spawned in the Afghan refugee camps. He was unable to provide further information, however.

29. See "According to Official Sources . . ." *NACLA: Report on the Americas*, July/August 1983, 18–19.

30. See H. Bruce Franklin, *M.I.A., or Mythmaking in America* (New York: Lawrence Hill Books, 1992), 151, for more on Rambo and the Reagan administration.

31. Herr subsequently wrote *Dispatches*, one of the most widely read books on the war, and consulted on the production of *Apocalypse Now*. A recent rereading of *Dispatches* underscored for me just how implicated journalists have been in the mythologizing of the war from the outset.

32. In my *The Spitting Image: Myth, Memory, and the Legacy of Vietnam* (New York: New York University Press, 1998), I explore at greater length the politics of PTSD and filmic images of veterans.

33. Parrying critics, Oliver very cleverly makes an analogy between Moorer's age and Van Buskirk's PTSD: just as Moorer's eighty-six years should not be used to discount his veracity, neither should Van Buskirk's condition detract from the merit of his testimony. See April Oliver and Jack Smith, "'Tailwind,' rebuttal to the Abrams/Kohler Report," 1998.

34. Transcript from National Press Club speech, June 15, 1999.

Chapter 9

1. All the quotes in the epigraph are taken from the September/October 1998 issue of *Columbia Journalism Review*.

2. In a July 8, 1998, interview on Fox News Network, Oliver told Brit Hume that she had asked management for an hour of broadcast time and was given only eighteen minutes.

3. Hickey wrote, "The CNN/Time combination was, said Henry Muller, editorial director of Time, Inc., 'not synergy of the kind imagined by our corporate chieftains. This was marketing synergy, not journalistic synergy.'"

4. A good source on the history of government regulation of media and the recent wave of takeovers is Patricia Aufderheide, *Communications Policy and the Public Interest: The Telecommunications Act of 1996* (New York: Guilford Press, 1999). I'm grateful to Josh Porter for help in understanding the issues on regulation.

5. See Ben H. Bagdikian, *The Media Monopoly* (Boston: Beacon Press, 1997), for more on media monopolies. Mark Crispin Miller's work in *The Nation* ("Free the Media," January 3, 1996, and "What's Wrong with This Picture?" January 7, 2002) and the visuals produced for his articles are collectively probably the best single source on the concentration of media power. For NBC's suppression of news unfavorable to GE, see Todd Putnam, "The GE Boycott: A Story NBC Wouldn't Buy," *Extra!* (January/February 1991), Megan Rosenfeld, "Bringing Bad Things to Light: GE Exposé Gets Debra Chasnoff an Oscar . . . and Maybe Even a Second Phone," *Washington Post*, April 23, 1992, and Robert Feder, "Channel 5 Rips NBC over 'Today' Editing," *Chicago Sun-Times*, December 5, 1998.

6. "Controversy" is a relative term. By deciding that this story was *not* controversial, he was making the assumption, perhaps unconsciously, that *Time*'s readership had the same sense of plausibility about wartime events as he did.

7. Pearlstein went on to quote David Halberstam as saying, "Vietnam is never ancient history. It is here today, alive." See Mary Murphy and Dennis McDougal, "Tailwind: Behind the TV Story of the Year," *TV Guide*, January 16–22, 1999, part 4, 58.

8. There are two broad sets of literature in the studies of journalism. One is the constructionist literature, which emphasizes how the news business constructs the reality that the rest of us live within. It also points out that the news reported is a construct of the journalists themselves rather than an objective set of "facts" they find, assemble, and relay to readers and viewers. Another body of literature (e.g., Herbert Gans, *Deciding What's News: A Study of* CBS Evening News, NBC Nightly News, Newsweek, *and* Time [New York: Vintage, 1980]) focuses on the internal dynamics of news organizations. While there is some overlap in those approaches, they lead in two quite different directions with respect to an understanding of the CNN-Tailwind affair. The organizational literature would highlight "bottom line" issues like *CJR*'s contention that CNN smelled a profitable story in Tailwind and set aside journalistic integrity to pursue it. The constructionist tradition prompts questions about the origins and authenticity of the story itself, in the manner I've done for this book. This chapter (and the last) broadens that approach to inquire into the construction of the journalists' worldviews—asking, in a sense, how the worldview of the constructors of the news is constructed.

9. Gans, *Deciding What's News*, 213.

10. Gans, *Deciding What's News*, xv.

11. It has long been the practice of the fascist right to co-opt the symbolism of the left. The Nazi use of "socialism" in that way is the strongest case in point.

12. I grew up in Hinton, Iowa. In the 1950s it had a stable population of 350 and a thriving town center with two grocery stores, a car dealership, two train depots, two implement dealers, a lawyer, a telephone exchange, three gas stations, a large commercial feed lot, a plumbing shop, a blacksmith, two restaurants, three bars, a grain exchange with a lumber-yard, a hardware store, two barber shops, a bank, a post office, and a K–12 school. Every bit of it was locally owned—even the postmaster lived in town.

Fifty years later, almost all of it was gone, and what remained or had come in (like the multipump gas emporium occupying the space where the lumber-yard used to be) was owned by nonresidents. In 2002, the town numbered about eight hundred with the growth coming from residents of a new housing development, most of whom work in Sioux City, ten miles south. Many area families, formerly sustained by the farm economy, worked for Gateway computer company or Iowa Beef Producers, the largest producer of beef products in the country. As the earlier stability disappeared, Rush Limbaugh found eager listeners in the remaining barns, shops, and family kitchens.

13. It would be hard to overstate the effect on the country's political culture of the proliferation of conspiracy films in the 1990s; it's a subject almost deserving of another chapter. In *Dangerous Knowledge* (p. 168) Art Simon identifies Oliver Stone's 1991 *JFK* as the grandparent of the decade's paranoid Hollywood products. The event itself, Kennedy's assassination in 1963, is, of course, the generator of stories, but by the 1990s half of the American population was too young to know much about it, and many people in the older half had "put it behind them." Stone returned the story to American living rooms with all the conspiratorial trappings he could assemble. Besides *JFK*, the film *Conspiracy* gave a major boost to the nation's collective paranoia.

14. See Seymour M. Hersh, "Overwhelming Force: What Happened in the Final Days of the Gulf War?" *New Yorker*, May 22, 2000. Tension between the press establishment and the government reached a peak when the latter ordered all reporters out of Baghdad just before the bombing began in 1991. Most news organizations complied, but CNN didn't, keeping Peter Arnett on the ground to provide blow-by-blow accounts of the bombing. Government and pro-military civilians were furious at CNN's defiance of the ban, some accusing the CNN of treason.

15. See Chip Berlet, *Right Woos Left: Populist Party, LaRouchian, and Other Neo-Fascist Overtures to Progressives, and Why They Must Be Rejected* (Somerville, Mass.: Political Research Associates, 1994).

16. Ruppert seems to be cleverly maintaining that he says *only* that the CIA *knew* about the attacks, but did not necessarily plan them. At the same time, he clearly leads his readers to believe the worst. The subtext of the AWACS story is that someone (who?) within the U.S. government approved the sale of those planes to communist and Jewish states.

On Rense.com, Rense was running stories like "Enemy Is Inside the Gates" and "Apocalypse? For Some Christians It Is Now, After WTC & Anthrax." Ruppert's website listed his appearances on Rense's radio show on March 1 and April 17, 2002.

17. Having heard I was working on a book about the story, Weinberg contacted me to see what my angle was. We traded comments until it was clear we were headed in opposite directions. Just before September 11, 2001, I inquired of Weinberg about the state of his report. He said it was finished and due out in *The Nation* shortly. I asked about his findings and he brusquely replied that I would have to read it in *The Nation* like everyone else, adding that his conclusions were "about as far from yours as possible."

18. Corn's article appeared before I heard any more about Weinberg's piece, so I wondered if Corn might have made the Ruppert connection and, even though he never wrote about it, used the finding to have *The Nation* dump the freelancer's work. I learned from Weinberg that *The Nation* had paid him for

his effort and canceled the project. When I asked Corn if he, or someone at the magazine, had put two and two together and figured out that Oliver had been riding the same paranoia wave as Ruppert—and that Weinberg's effort to rescue her reputation was, therefore, ill advised—he replied that he knew nothing about an Oliver-Ruppert link. How he could *not* know baffled me because Ruppert's website, which Corn acknowledged visiting, tells us he began publishing *From The Wilderness* in 1998, and that the CNN Tailwind tale was, if not his inaugural story, his first big "scoop."

19. Some observers have suggested that the appeal of rightists like Ruppert to the political left has to do with how little difference there is between the two. Writing for *National Review Online*, for example, Jonah Goldberg characterized belief in 9/11 conspiracies as "paranoid, America-hating, crypto-Marxist conspiratorial delusions."

20. There are many instances of the press playing coyly with conspiracist stories. The February 23, 2002, *Vancouver Sun* carried a column by Ian Mulgrew that, read carefully, was a critical commentary on the conspiracists, but it walked a fine enough line in its references to Mike Ruppert to be reposted on right-wing websites.

21. See Katherine Q. Seelye, "When Hollywood's Big Guns Come Right from the Source," *New York Times*, June 10, 2002, A1.

22. That preconditioning could work cognitively to make the threat of a dirty bomb seem more realistic than it might otherwise be perceived as well as to emotionally raise fears that need to be assuaged by the perception of a legitimate arrest.

In other cases, the braiding of hard news with entertainment news seems to use the former to sell the latter. Boston news channels carried a supposedly major story about a smallpox threat during the spring of 2002. The story "broke" on the very day that an episode of the popular show *ER* aired about a little girl with smallpox. During the day, before *ER* aired, and throughout the post-broadcast evening, news reporters wove the "smallpox news" together with the "smallpox show" to create a "story of the day" that was fit for both the "hard" and entertainment segments of "the news."

BIBLIOGRAPHY

Abrams, Floyd, and David Kohler. "Report on CNN Broadcast 'Valley of Death.'" July 2, 1998.

"According to Official Sources . . ." *NACLA: Report on the Americas*, July/August 1983, 7–21.

Allen, Arthur. "April Oliver's War: How a Single-Minded Journalist Tripped over the Ghosts of Vietnam." *Washington Post Magazine,* November 29, 1998.

Altschull, J. Herbert. *Agents of Power: The Role of the News Media in Human Affairs.* New York: Addison Wesley, 1984.

Anderson, Scott, and Jon Lee Anderson. *Inside the League: The Shocking Expose of How Terrorists, Nazis, and Latin American Death Squads Have Infiltrated the World Anti-Communist League.* New York: Dodd, Mead, 1986.

"Arnaud de Borchgrave Joins NewsMax.com Board." *NewsMax.com,* July 5, 1999.

Associated Press. "Vietnam Vet Concedes Overstating Role in Napalm Attack." *Worcester (Mass.) Telegram and Gazette,* December 18, 1997, A6.

———. "De Borchgrave Named UPI President and CEO." December 19, 1998.

Aufderheide, Patricia. *Communications Policy and the Public Interest: The Telecommunications Act of 1996.* New York: Guilford Press, 1999.

Bagdikian, Ben H. *The Media Monopoly.* Boston: Beacon Press, 1997.

Beattie, Taylor V. "Ghosts of The Lost Battalion." *Military History*, August 2002, 26–32.

Bellant, Russ. *Old Nazis, the New Right, and the Republican Party*. Boston: South End Press, 1991.

Belluck, Pam. "A Sworn Mission to Unmask Pretenders to Military Glory." *New York Times*, August 10, 2001, A1.

Berlet, Chip. *Clinton, Conspiracism, and the Continuing Culture War*. Somerville, Mass.: Political Research Associates, 1999.

———. *Right Woos Left: Populist Party, LaRouchian, and Other Neo-Fascist Overtures to Progressives, and Why They Must Be Rejected*. Somerville, Mass.: Political Research Associates, 1994.

Berlet, Chip, and Matthew Lyons. *Right-Wing Populism in America: Too Close for Comfort*. New York: Guilford Press, 2000.

Boyer, Paul. *When Time Shall Be No More*. Cambridge, Mass.: Harvard University Press, 1992.

Brady, John. *Bad Boy: The Life and Politics of Lee Atwater*. New York: Addison-Wesley, 1997.

Branfman, Fred. *Voices from the Plain of Jars: Life under an Air War*. New York: Harper and Row, 1972.

Brock, David. *Blinded By The Right: The Conscience of an Ex-conservative*. New York: Crown, 2002.

Brunvand, Jan Harold. *The Truth Never Stands in the Way of a Good Story*. Chicago: University of Illinois Press, 2000.

Burkett, B. G., and Glenna Whitley. *Stolen Valor: How the Vietnam Generation Was Robbed of Its Heroes and Its History*. Dallas: Verity, 1998.

Butterfield, Fox. "A Portrait of the Detective in the 'O. J. Whirlpool.'" *New York Times*, March 2, 1996, A1.

Cash, W. J. *The Mind of the South*. New York: Vintage, 1941 [1991].

Chass, Murray. "Dogged by War Tales, Johnson Is Let Go by Jays." *New York Times*, March 18, 1999.

Cheshire, William P. "Letter to the Editor: The Independence of the Times." *Washington Times*, June 4, 1991.

Cockburn, Alexander. "The Press Devours Its Own." *Nation*, August 24/31, 1998.

Conrad, Joseph. *Heart of Darkness*. New York: Signet Classic, 1997.

Cowie, Peter. *The Apocalypse Now Book*. New York: Da Capo Press, 2000.

Curry, David. *Sunshine Patriots: Punishment and the Vietnam Offender*. Notre Dame, Ind.: University of Notre Dame Press, 1985.

Davenport, Jim. "Flag at Statue Concerns Hampton Family." *State*, April 22, 2000.

Davidson, Osha Gray. *Broken Heartland: The Rise of America's Rural Ghetto*. New York: Free Press, 1990.

de Borchgrave, Arnaud. *The Spike*. New York: Avon Books, 1981.

Dees, Morris. *Gathering Storm: America's Militia Threat*. New York: Harper-Collins, 1996.

Dellinger, David. *From Yale to Jail: The Life Story of a Moral Dissenter*. New York: Pantheon, 1993.

Demille, Nelson. *The Charm School*. New York: Warner Books, 1988.

Denton, Jeremiah. *When Hell Was in Session*. Clover, S.C.: River Hills Plantation, 1976.

Domhoff, G. William. *The Higher Circles: The Governing Class in America*. New York: Random/Vintage, 1971.

Ehrenreich, Barbara. *Fear of Falling: The Inner Life of the Middle Class*. New York: Pantheon, 1989.

"Experiment That Failed." *Newsweek*, April 5, 1965.

Feder, Robert. "Channel 5 Rips NBC over 'Today' Editing." *Chicago Sun-Times*, December 5, 1998.

Feola, Christopher J. "The Americans Who Fought on the Other Side." *New York Folklore* 15, nos. 1–2 (1989).

Ferguson, Susan. *Mapping the Social Landscape: Readings in Sociology*. New York: WCB/McGraw-Hill, 2001.

Fisher, Marc. "April Oliver '83 Continues Work on Operation Tailwind." *Princeton Alumni Weekly*, September 9, 1998, 54.

Fleming, Robert. "Post Vietnam Syndrome: Neurosis or Sociosis?" *Psychiatry* 48 (May 1985): 122–39.

"Foreign Relations: The Great Gas Flap." *Time*, April 2, 1965.

Franklin, H. Bruce. *M.I.A., or Mythmaking in America*. New York: Lawrence Hill Books, 1992.

Fumento, Michael. "Gulf Lore Syndrome." *Reason*, March 22–23, 1997.

Fussell, Paul. *The Great War and Modern Memory*. New York: Oxford University Press, 1975.

———. *Wartime: Understanding and Behavior in the Second World War*. New York: Oxford University Press, 1989.

Gans, Herbert. *Deciding What's News: A Study of* CBS Evening News, NBC Nightly News, Newsweek, *and* Time. New York: Vintage, 1980.

"General Who Attacked Carter." *New York Times*, April 29, 1978.

Gibson, James William. *Warrior Dreams: Violence and Manhood in Post-Vietnam America*. New York: Hill and Wang, 1994.

Gilbert, Martin. *The First World War: A Complete History*. New York: Henry Holt, 1994.

Gimbel, Cynthia, and Alan Booth. "Why Does Military Combat Experience Adversely Affect Marital Relations?" *Journal of Marriage and the Family* 56 (1994): 691–703.

Goldberg, Alan. *Enemies Within: The Culture of Conspiracy in Modern America*. New Haven: Yale University Press, 2001.

Goldberg, Carey. "His Vietnam Tale Exposed as a Lie, a Killer Is Back in Custody." *New York Times*, August 27, 1998, A21.

Greenwood, David Valdes. "Waco: The Fire Next Time." *Boston/Worcester Phoenix*, September 17, 1999.

Gritz, James. *Called to Serve*. Sandy Valley, Nev.: Lazarus, 1991.

Harris, Louis. *A Study of Anti-Semitism in Rural Iowa and Nebraska*. New York: Louis Harris, 1986.

Harris, Robert, and Jeremy Paxman. *A Higher Form of Killing: The Secret Story of Chemical and Biological Warfare*. New York: Hill and Wang, 1982.

Hausman, Carl. *Crisis of Conscience: Perspectives on Journalism Ethics*. HarperCollins, 1992.

Helmer, John. *Bringing the War Home: The American Soldier in Vietnam and After*. New York: Free Press, 1974.

Herr, Michael. *Dispatches*. New York: Vintage, 1991.

Hersh, Seymour M. "Overwhelming Force: What Happened in the Final Days of the Gulf War?" *New Yorker*, May 22, 2000.

———. *The Price of Power: Kissinger in the Nixon White House*. New York: Summit Books, 1983.

Hershberger, Mary. *Traveling to Vietnam: American Peace Activists and the War*. Syracuse, N.Y.: Syracuse University Press, 1999.

Hickey, Neil. "Ten Mistakes That Led to the Great Fiasco." *Columbia Journalism Review* (September/October 1998).

Hofstadter, Richard. *The Paranoid Style in American Politics and Other Essays*. New York: Knopf, 1965.

Isaacson, Walter. *Kissinger: A Biography*. New York: Simon and Schuster, 1992.

Jackson, Bruce. "The Perfect Informant." *Journal of American Folklore* 103 (1990): 400–16.

Jensen-Stevenson, Monika. *Spite House: The Last Secret of the War in Vietnam*. New York: Avon, 1997.

Jensen-Stevenson, Monika, and William Stevenson. *Kiss the Boys Goodbye: How the United States Betrayed Its Own POWs in Vietnam*. New York: Dutton, 1990.

Karnow, Stanley. *Vietnam: A History*. New York: Viking Press, 1983.

Katzman, Jason. "From Outcast to Cliche: How Film Shaped, Warped and Developed the Image of the Vietnam Veteran, 1969–1990." *Journal of American Culture* 16 (Spring 1993): 7–24.

Keith, Wes. *Victories: Stories of Christian Vietnam Veterans*. Mountainlake Terrace, Wash.: WinePress, 1995.

Kelley, Matt. "Military Used Nerve Gas in '60s." Associated Press, May 24, 2002.

Kelly, Michael. "The Road to Paranoia." *New Yorker*, June 9, 1995.

LeBoutillier, John. "The Most Shameful Act of Betrayal in American History." *NewsMax.com*, January 26, 2001.

Leed, Eric J. *No Man's Land: Combat & Identity in World War I*. New York: Cambridge University Press, 1979.

Lembcke, Jerry. "*Apocalypse Now* Redux: The Politics of Paranoia in America Today." *Tompaine.com,* 2001.

——. "Media Myth: Vietnam Vets and Spit." *Tompaine.com,* June 21, 2000.

——. "The 'Right Stuff' Gone Wrong: Vietnam Veterans and the Social Construction of Post-Traumatic Stress Disorder." *Critical Sociology* 24, nos. (1999): 1–2.

——. *The Spitting Image: Myth, Memory, and the Legacy of Vietnam.* New York: New York University Press, 1998.

Lindsey, Hal. *There's a New World Coming: A Prophetic Odyssey.* New York: Bantam, 1973.

Maechler, Stefan. *The Wilkomirski Affair: A Study in Biographical Truth.* New York: Schocken Books, 2001.

Manoff, Robert Karl, and M. Schudson. *Reading the News: A Pantheon Guide to Popular Culture.* Pantheon Books, 1986.

McBirnie, W. S. *World War II and the United States.* Dallas: American Evangelistic Association, n.d.

McCollum, L. C. *History and Rhymes of the Lost Battalion.* N.p.: n.p., 1919.

McCoy, Alfred W. *The Politics of Heroin in Southeast Asia.* New York: Lawrence Hill, 1972.

McDowell, Edwin. "Behind the Best Sellers Arnaud de Borchgrave and Robert Moss." *New York Times,* June 22, 1980.

McGeary, Johanna, and Karen Tumulty. "The Fog of War: 32 Years after Leaving Vietnam, Bob Kerrey Admits a Terrible Secret." *Time,* May 7, 2001.

Merritt, Davis "Buzz." *Public Journalism and Public Life.* Lawrence Erlbaum Associates, 1998.

Michel, Lou, and Dan Herbeck. *American Terrorist: Timothy McVeigh and the Oklahoma City Bombing.* New York: Regan Books, 2001.

Miller, Mark Crispin. "Free the Media." *Nation,* January 3, 1996.

——. "What's Wrong with This Picture?" *Nation,* January 7, 2002.

Moser, Richard. *The New Winter Soldiers: GI and Veteran Dissent during the Vietnam Era.* New Brunswick, N.J.: Rutgers University Press, 1996.

Murphy, Mary, and Dennis McDougal. "Tailwind: Behind the TV Story of the Year," parts 1–4. *TV Guide,* December 26, 1998–January 16, 1999.

Novick, Michael. *White Lies, White Power: The Fight against White Supremacy and Reactionary Violence.* Monroe, Me.: Common Courage Press, 1995.

O'Brien, Tim. *Going after Cacciato.* New York: Dell, 1975.

Oliver, April. "The Great Migration: Political Transformation Caused by Afghan Refugees in Pakistan." Senior thesis. Princeton, N.J.: Woodrow Wilson School of International Affairs, 1983.

Oliver, April, and Jack Smith. "'Tailwind.' Rebuttal to the Abrams/Kohler Report," 1998.

Pearlstine, Norman. "The Trouble with Ground Rules." *Columbia Journalism Review* (September/October 1998).

Pedelty, Mark. *War Stories: The Culture of Foreign Correspondents*. New York: Routledge, 1995.

Plaster, John L. *SOG: The Secret Wars of America's Commandos in Vietnam*. New York: Onyx/Simon and Schuster, 1997.

———. "Vietnam the Way It Wasn't." *New York Times,* June 18, 1998, A35.

Postman, Neil. *Amusing Ourselves to Death: Public Discourse in the Age of Show Business*. New York: Penguin Books, 1986.

Powers, Richard Gid. "The Evil That Lurks in the Enemy Within." *New York Times*, June 16, 2002.

Prouty, Fletcher. *The Secret Team*. Englewood Cliffs, N.J.: Prentice Hall, 1973.

Putnam, Todd. "The GE Boycott: A Story NBC Wouldn't Buy." *Extra!* (January/February 1991).

Randolph, Eleanor. "*Washington Times* Editor's NPC Bid Draws Opposition." *Washington Post*, November 22, 1988, E3.

Randolph, Eleanor, and Michael Isikoff. "*Washington Times* Gets New Editor." *Washington Post*, March 20, 1985, D1.

Rawicz, Slavomir. *The Long Walk: The True Story of a Trek to Freedom*. New York: Lyons Press, 1956 [1997].

Raymond, Jack. "Gas as Weapon: Pro and Con." *New York Times*, March 28, 1965.

Reid, Charles J. "Broken Winds of Accountability: The Tailwind Cover-Up," at www.wmin.ac.uk/media/tailwind/reid.html.

Reston, James. "Washington: Just a Little Old 'Benevolent Incapacitator.'" *New York Times*, March 24, 1965.

Ridgeway, James. *Blood in the Face: The Ku Klux Klan, Aryan Nations, Nazi Skinheads, and the Rise of a New White Culture*. New York: Thunder's Mouth Press, 1995.

Rosenfeld, Megan. "Bringing Bad Things to Light: GE Exposé Gets Debra Chasnoff an Oscar . . . and Maybe Even a Second Phone." *Washington Post*, April 23, 1992.

Ruppert, Michael. "The POWs, CIA, and Drugs: Uglier Truths behind the Sarin Gas Stories." *From the Wilderness*, July 1998.

Schaap, William. "Interview with H. Bruce Franklin." *Lies of Our Times*, December 1993, 10–13.

Schuetz, Alfred. "The Homecomer." In *Strangers at Home: Vietnam Veterans since the War.* Edited by John W. Figley and Seymour Leventman. New York: Brunner/Mazel, 1990.

Scott, Wilbur J. *The Politics of Readjustment: Vietnam Veterans since the War*. New York: Aldine de Gruyter, 1993.

Seelye, Katherine Q. "When Hollywood's Big Guns Come Right from the Source." *New York Times*, June 10, 2002, A1.

Shanker, Thom, and William J. Broad. "Sailors Sprayed with Nerve Gas in Cold War Test, Pentagon Says." *New York Times*, May 24, 2002, A1.

Sharkey, Joe. "Memories of Wars Never Fought." *New York Times*, June 28, 1998, WK 6.

Showalter, Elaine. *Hystories: Hysterical Epidemics and Modern Culture*. New York: Columbia University Press, 1997.

Shultz, Richard H., Jr. *The Secret War against Hanoi: Kennedy's and Johnson's Use of Spies, Saboteurs, and Covert Warriors in North Vietnam*. New York: HarperCollins, 1999.

Simon, Art. *Dangerous Knowledge: The JFK Assassination in Art and Film*. Philadelphia: Temple University Press, 1996.

Singlaub, John K. *Hazardous Duty: An American Soldier in the Twentieth Century*. New York: Summit Books, 1991.

Sokal, Alan D. Transgressing the Boundaries: Toward a Transformative Hermeneutics of Quantum Gravity." *Social Text* (Spring/Summer 1996), 217–52.

Sparr, Landy, and Loran D. Pankratz. "Factitious Posttraumatic Stress Disorder." *American Journal of Psychiatry* 140 (1983):1016–19.

Stanton, Shelby. "Special Military Operations." In *War in the Shadows*. Boston: Boston Publishing, 1988.

Starr, Paul. *The Discarded Army: Veterans after Vietnam*. New York: Charterhouse, 1973.

———. "Home from the War: Vietnam Veterans—Neither Victims nor Executioners." *Worldview* (October 1973): 53–55.

Sturken, Marita. *Tangled Memories: The Vietnam War, the Aids Epidemic, and the Politics of Remembering*. Berkeley: University of California Press, 1997.

Tabor, James D., and Eugene V. Gallagher. *Why Waco? Cults and the Battle for Religious Freedom in America*. Berkeley: University of California Press, 1995.

Thomas, Evan. "What's the Truth about Tailwind?" *Newsweek*, June 22, 1998, 32.

"The Truth about 'Gas Warfare' in Vietnam." *U.S. News and World Report*, April 5, 1965.

Turner, Fred. *Echoes of Combat: The Vietnam War in American Memory*. New York: Anchor, 1996.

Van Buskirk, Robert. *Tailwind*. Dallas: International Prison Ministry, 1983.

Van Impe, Jack. *11:59 and Counting*. Royal Oak, Mich.: Jack Van Impe Ministries, 1983.

Wald, Matthew L. "For Air Crash Detectives, Seeing Isn't Believing." *New York Times*, June 23, 2002, WK5.

War in the Shadows. Boston: Boston Publishing, 1988.

Weiner, Tim. "Military Combat Insignia Signify Esteem of Officers." *New York Times*, May 18, 1996, A11.

Weinraub, Bernard. "Carter Defends Plan to Reduce Forces in Korea." *New York Times*. May 27, 1977, A1.

———. "Defense Chief Backs Korea Plan, Says the Military Must Support It." *New York Times*, May 23, 1977, A1.

———. "General Returns from South Korea to Face Carter." *New York Times*, May 21, 1977, A5.

———. "The Korea Withdrawal: Some Officers Are Nervous and Congress Wants to Have a Say," *New York Times*, May 30, 1977, A2.

———. "Ousted General Says Most U.S. Officials in Korea Fear Removal of Ground Troops Will Lead to War." *New York Times*, May 26, 1977, A3.

Wellman, Manly Wade. *Giant in Gray: A Biography of Wade Hampton of South Carolina*. New York: Charles Scribner, 1949.

Whitehouse, Arch. *Heroes and Legends of World War I*. New York: Doubleday, 1964.

Williams, Alfred B. *Hampton and His Red Shirts: South Carolina's Deliverance in 1876*. Freeport, N.Y.: Books for Libraries Press, 1927.

Wolf, Jim. "Vietnam-Era Nerve Gas Report to Be Checked." *Boston Globe*, June 9, 1998, A2.

Young, Allan. *The Harmony of Illusion: Inventing Post-Traumatic Stress Disorder*. Princeton, N.J.: Princeton University Press, 1995.

Zumwalt, Elmo R., Jr. *On Watch: A Memoir*. New York: Quadrangle, 1976.

INDEX

Abrams, Floyd: Investigates *Valley of Death*, 8–13

Absence Without Leave (AWOL). *See* deserters

Alarcon, Mario Sandoval: Guatemalan rightist, 123–24

American Security Council (ASC), 116–17

anti-Semitism, 97–99, 103–4, 117; "hard right" expresses, 112; Jeff Rense Show has themes of, 130–33; Lee Atwater and, 138; Posse Comitatus holds views of, 100; Zionist Occupation Government (ZOG) and, 130, 132

Apocalypse Now, 57, 72–75, 79

apocalyptic prophecy: Branch Davidians taught, 105–7; "Old Testament" versions of, 94; political stories in, 95–97; pre- vs. postmillennialism in, 187n4; "Revelation" and, 94–95; Robert Van Buskirk and, 93; Tailwind tale's subtext, 108

Arnett, Peter: gas use in Vietnam reported by, 50; *Impact* show read by, 39, 41; intonation on POWs, 33, 41; leaves CNN, 14; reprimanded by CNN, 10; *Valley of Death* read by, 1–6

assassination: Diem, Ngo Dinh, 19; George Wallace attempted, 116; Kennedy, John F., 19; U.S. POWs alleged, 32–43, 53; U.S. POWs, believed by April Oliver, 180n17

Atwater, Lee: April Oliver works for, 138–39; Ronald Reagan campaign manager, 138–39

betrayal, 15, 18, 71, 130; narrative for loss of war, 40, 138, 140, 143, 165; of POWs, 32–36, 104–5; veterans, 101

"Black Operations," 21, 25. *See also* Studies and Observations Group (SOG)

Buffalo Springfield, 2, 63

Cable News Network (CNN):
 investigates *Valley of Death*, 8–11;
 launches *Valley of Death*, 6–7;
 motive for *Valley of Death*, 147;
 retracts *Valley of Death*, 11. *See also*
 Hill, Pam; Johnson, Tom; Kaplan,
 Richard; Oliver, April; *Valley of
 Death*
Cacciato: Tim O'Brien character in
 novel, 58–59
Cameron, William, 97
Captains and Kings, 42–43
Carter, President Jimmy, 117; John
 Singlaub fired by, 119–20; rightists
 attack, 123
Cathey, Jim, 2; not in Laos, 8; preacher,
 107
Central Intelligence Agency (CIA), 8,
 17, 37, 61; *Apocalypse Now* and, 73;
 April Oliver and, 138–39; *Charm
 School* and, 80–81; covert operations
 run by, 19–24, 26; drug running
 allegations and, 32–33, 83, 131;
 Fletcher Prouty works with, 132;
 John Singlaub works with, 119, 122;
 POWs betrayed by, 83–86, 88;
 September 11, 2001 and, 157,
 160–62; site 85, operational site for,
 176n1. *See also* Studies and
 Observation Group (SOG)
Charm School, 79–82, 87
Christian "Identity," 97–99; British-
 Israelism and, 97. *See also* religion
Cline, Ray, 38, 122
Cockburn, Alex: April Oliver defended
 by, 149
Cohen, William S.: findings of
 investigation reported by, 10; *Valley
 of Death* investigated by defense
 secretary, 7–8
Columbia Journalism Review: *Valley of
 Death* analyzed by, 145, 147, 149

Colby, William, 19, 21, 23
Confederation of Associations for the
 Unity of the Societies of America
 (CAUSA), 37 conspiracism, 42–43:
 Apocalypse Now conveys, 73–74,
 183n8; problem with, 160–62;
 "unknown" in, 161; the war in
 Vietnam and, 165–66. *See also*
 conspiracy; Jeff Rense Show;
 Moorer, Adm. Thomas; Oliver, April;
 Singlaub, Gen. John; Ruppert,
 Michael
conspiracy, 21, 37, 42–43, 97, 99, 100,
 115, 124, 184n8; April Oliver and,
 133, 143; Gulf War and, 101–2; Jeff
 Rense Show and, 130–33; problems
 with theories of, 158, 160–62;
 themes in American culture, 18, 154,
 156, 158–59, 165, 198n13. *See also*
 conspiracism

Daley, Edward: No Gun Ri story told
 by, 66
Darby, John, 96
D'Aubuisson, Roberto: Salvadoran
 rightist, 124
de Borchgrave, Arnaud, 37–38
defectors, 1–4, 6, 8–9, 12–13, 18, 29,
 92; Chris Matthews and, 34–38;
 Laos and, 180n17; as liminal figures,
 59–61; POWs or, 32–34. *See also*
 Apocalypse Now; deserters;
 Garwood, Robert
deserters, 46, 51–53, 179n9;
 assassination alleged, 181n25; *The
 Deer Hunter* has, 53; liminal
 figures as, 56; "salt and pepper" in
 legends of, 60; World War I
 legends and, 53–56. *See also*
 defectors
Diem, Ngo Dinh, 18–19
Duke, David, 104

Dutton, Susan: Lao PDR, U.S.
    embassy, 61

"Emperor's New Clothes," 128–29
"enduring values": Herbert Gans
    names, 152; 1990s and, 153. *See also*
    journalism

film themes: anti-Vietnam War, 71;
    conspiracy, 73–74, 154, 160, 198n13;
    deserters, 57–59, 71; gas warfare,
    76–79; hunter-killer, 72–73, 75; post-
    World War II, 70; POW/MIA, 67,
    71–73, 75, 87, 140; SOG, 72. *See
    also Apocalypse Now*
Forest, Kathy, xii
"fusion paranoia," 155–56

Galloway, Joseph: reports battle of Ia
    Drang Valley, writes screenplay, 168
Garwood, Robert, 179n10: *Spite House*,
    subject in, 82–87, 89
gas warfare: BZ, 178n5; CS (tear), 4–5,
    7, 17, 28, 51; GB, 2, 5; grist for
    myth, 49–51; Gulf War, rumored use
    of, 102; in Hollywood films, 75–78,
    184n12; nerve, 2–3, 5–6, 8, 11, 29,
    34–39, 45–46, 92; sleeping, 2–3,
    4–5; types described, 51, 178n6;
    used in Waco, 102, 106; Vietnam,
    early reports of use, 49–51; VX,
    178n3; and World War I, 54. *See
    also* sarin
Graves, Jay, 2, 4–5, 9–10, 14; alleges
    mistreatment by April Oliver,
    174n9; reported not in Laos, 7–8,
    174n14
Gresham, Rudi, 8
Gritz, James "Bo," 103–5
Gulf War: conspiracism in history of,
    155; gas warfare during, 78; nerve
    gas maybe used, 102; PTSD and

veterans, 102; Tailwind tale and
    climate of, 102

Hagan, Michael: Operation Tailwind
    veteran, 5

Hampton, Wade: April Oliver's
    ancestor, 134–35; confederate
    general, 136–37; paramilitary Red
    Shirts formed by, 137–38; plantation
    owner, 135–37; South Carolina
    governor, 137
Hill, Pam: CNN staffer, 7; resigns, 10
Hinton, Iowa, 197n12
Ho Chi Minh Trail: Operation Tailwind
    and, 27–28; SOG operations along,
    25–28
hunter-killer stories, 58, 108, 140. *See
    also Apocalypse Now*; film themes

Increase, Mather, 96
Isaacson, Walter: managing editor of
    Time, 6

Jackson, Bruce, 127–29, 143
Jeff Rense Show, 130–33
John Birch Society, 116, 118–19, 155;
    ambivalence on Vietnam War,
    36–37; secular prophecy and,
    99–100
Johnson, Tom: apologizes for *Valley of
    Death*, 11; CNN chairman, 6
journalism: conspiracy stories attractive
    to, 109, 155–62; Herbert Gans
    studies, 151–56; history needs to be
    known by, 167–69; lessons from
    Valley of Death, 166–69; media
    mergers and, 149–50, 167–68;
    methods of, 141–42; objectivity as a
    standard, 145, 166–67; Orwell vs.
    Huxley and, 147–51; phony
    veterans' stories and, 151; post-9/11

paranoia and, 156–60; the study of, 197n8; as window on American culture. *See also Valley of Death*

Kahl, Gordon: anti-tax activist, 101
Kaplan, Richard: accusations surrounding *Valley of Death*, 145–47; CNN/USA headed by, 6–7; failure to understand Operation Tailwind, 151
Kerrey, Bob: former senator and Vietnam veteran, 59
Koresh, David, 105–7. *See also* religion

Laird, Melvin: President Richard Nixon's secretary of defense, 113
Lane, John: CNN staffer, 10
Laos: Ho Chi Minh Trail and, 25–29; inquiries to embassy about Operation Tailwind, 61; as no-man's-land, 56–59; in *Valley of Death*, 1, 7–9
Le Boutillier, John: former Congressman believes POWs still held, 117–18
Legend of the Lost Command, 53–56
Le Loi, 22–23
Liberty Lobby, 124

MacArthur, Gen. Douglas: President Harry Truman fires, 122
maritime operations (MAROPS), 24–25
Matthews, Chris: April Oliver and Jack Smith as guests of, 34–38, 130; CNBC *Hardball* host, 34; conspiracy-baiting, 130, 82
McCarley, Capt. Eugene: denounces treatment by April Oliver, 9, 174n8, 181n26; Operation Tailwind and, 28
McKenney, Tom: *Spite House*, subject in, 83–87; suspects Russians in Vietnam, 87

McVeigh, Timothy, 74, 155
media mergers: *Valley of Death* fiasco attributed to, 149–51, 167–68
memory: Adm. Jeremy Boorda and, 64; Bill Stroud and, 64, 182n27; Edward Daly and, 66; John Plummer and, 65; male fantasies of war and, 63–67; Mark Fuhrman and, 64, 182n29; memory and how it works, 62–63
Montagnard mercenaries, 3–4, 17, 27–28
Moody, Dwight, 96
Moorer, Adm. Thomas, 109, 128; as chairman of the Joint Chiefs of Staff, 113–16; defended by April Oliver, 11–13; disassociates from *Valley of Death*, 7, 32; John Birch Society and, 99, 116–19; NewsMax.com, joins board of, 117; source for *Valley of Death*, 2–3, 5; supports George Wallace, 116; testimony questioned, 7–13; Western Goals, joins board of, 116
movies. *See* film themes

No Gun Ri, 66. *See also* memory
no-man's-land: Laos as, 56–59; in World War I legends, 55–56

O'Hara, Jerry: leads search for MIA remains, 61
Oliver, April: Alfred Paddock warns in letters to, 40–41; CNN fires, 10–11; commitment to her story, 145–46; conspiracism and, 143; covert operations, "hooked on," 139–40, 142–43; family background, 135–38; gas mask, given to as gift, 7; guest on Chris Matthews's show, 34–38; history of war in Vietnam not well-known by, 140–43; 166–67; *Impact*, produced by, 38–41;

interview style of, 193n7;
investigated for *Valley of Death*,
6–13; Jeff Rense Show has as
guest, 130–33; Operation Tailwind
and, 28–29; oral history method
used by, 141–42; Pakistan toured
by for college research, 139;
positivism and the methodological
assumptions of, 167; as
propagandist, 41; Reagan campaign
worker, 138–39; rebuttal to
Abrams, 11–14, 145–46; resumé, 7,
135; *Valley of Death and*, 3,
145–49
OP, 35, 26
Operation Tailwind: American culture,
a window on, 164–66; broadcast as
Valley of Death by CNN, 1–6; in
criticism of *Valley of Death*, 7–10,
12, 14; history, importance to,
163–64; journalism and importance
of, 166–69; real history of, 17–18,
31–32; site of and inquires about
excavation, 61; subtext of, 31–32,
35, 38–43, 156. *See also Valley of
Death*
OPLAN 34–A: agent teams: Ares,
175n6; Borden, 21; Red Dragon, 20.
See also SOG

Paddock, Alfred H., Jr: letters to April
Oliver, 40–41
Padilla, Jose: alleged "dirty bomber,"
159
paranoia: American political style,
133–34; post-Civil War South and,
134–38; Tailwind's subtext and, 18;
U.S. assumptions about North
Vietnam and, 20. *See also* "fusion
paranoia"
Pearlstine, Norman, 6; explains *Valley
of Death*, 150–51

Pellem, William Dudley, 97
Pentagon, 46, 141, 148–49, 156, 165;
Adm. Thomas Moorer and, 113,
115, 118; Gen. John Singlaub and,
120
Pentagon Papers, 48, 100, 107, 148
Peters, Pete, 104–5
phenomenology, xiv–xv, 129; social
constructionism and, 167
Plaster, John, 128; April Oliver, source,
28–29; *Impact* source, 39–41; *SOG*
author, 129–30; *Valley of Death*
critic, 8
Plummer, John, 65, 151
Posse Comitatus, 100–101; origin of
name, 188n13
post–traumatic stress disorder (PTSD),
10, 64–65, 111, 142, 182n29, 183n2;
Gulf War syndrome and, 101–2,
188n14; journalists and veterans'
stories with, 142
Prisoners of War (POWs), 32–34,
39–40, 42; *Charm School's* story
about, 80–82; films with, 74–75;
identity of vs. defectors, 53, 61,
180n17; John LeBoutillier hopes to
rescue, 117–18; Soviet Union
rumored to have held, 53, 191n21;
Spite House's stories about, 82–87;
U.S. government lies about, 48
Prouty, Fletcher, 131–33. *See also*
Central Intelligence Agency (CIA)
psywar: North Vietnam the target of,
21–25. *See also* SOG
PTSD. *See* post–traumatic stress
disorder

religion: biblical prophecy in, 94–95;
Branch Davidians as, 103, 105–7;
British-Israelism as, 97; Christian
"Identity," and, 97–99; politics and
prophecy in, 95–97; religious right

and, 100–101; Tailwind tale and, 108–9

Reuters News Service: Questions *Valley of Death*, 7, 32

Ruby Ridge, Idaho, 103–5, 154

Ruppert, Michael: "CIA, drugs, and POWs" authored by, 32–35; Jeff Rense Show has as guest, 130–33; September 11, 2001 analysis by, 156–58; *Spite House* and, 83

Russians: *Charm School's* story about, 79–82; rumored holding U.S. POWs, 191n21; rumored in Vietnam, 87, 174n13

Sacred Sword of the Patriot League (SSPL), 21–25

"Salt and Pepper," 60. *See also* deserters

sarin, 2–3, 5–9, 11, 72n25; Aum Shin Rikyo used, 78; metaphorical use of, 74–79

September 11, 2001: conspiricism in aftermath, 156–60. *See also* apocalyptic prophecy

Singlaub, John, 109; called "professional liar," 14; defector stories and, 180n17; *Impact* uses as a source, 39; President Jimmy Carter vs., 119–20; SOG tactics and, 22; *Valley of Death* uses as a source, 3, 12–14; World Anti-Communist League leader, 122–24

Smith, Jack: fired by CNN, 11; Richard Kaplan accused by, 145, 149; *Valley of Death* coproduced by, 7–9

Smith, Perry: military consultant for CNN, 8

Smithson, Amy: Henry L. Stimson Center expert on nerve gas, 5

Son Tay raid, 114–15

Spite House, 82–87

Studies and Observations Group (SOG): CIA and, 19–20, 175n9; film and, 72–73, 183n5; Laos and Cambodia and, 25–28; Nazis recruited by, 120–21; origins of, 18–19; Paradise Island and, 23–25; psywar, 21–23; *Valley of Death* and, 1–5, 8–9, 12–13, 18–19; war on North Vietnam and, 19–21

Thorne, Larry: SOG commando, 121

Thurmond, Sen. Strom: John Singlaub defended by, 120; Lee Atwater supported by, 138

Time magazine, 6–7

Tonkin Gulf incident, 24, 47

Trilateral Commission, 99

Turner, Ed, 6

Turner, Ted, 6, 10

Unification Church ("Moonies"), 122; Arnaud de Borchgrave and, 37–38

U.S. Global Strategy Council, 37

Valley of Death: blame for, 145–47; CNN broadcast of, 1–5; CNN retracts, 11; defense of, 10–13; investigation of, 6–9; management approved, 146; mistakes analyzed, 145–56; press conference for, 5

Van Buskirk, Robert, 128; Abrams's report and, 9–10; born-again Christian, 2, 88–89, 107–8; defectors described by, 61, 93; F— — you story told by, 4, 71–72; memoir written by, 10, 61–62; PTSD claimed by, 10, 111, 142; *Valley of Death* uses as a source, 2–5, 8

Vietnam: CIA in, 19; post–World War II history of, 18–19, 25–26, 46–47; war and betrayal narrative about, 33,

165; war and U.S. government lies
    about, 46–49

Waco, Texas, 103, 105–7, 154
Weaver, Randy, 103–5
Weisshart, Herb: SOG strategist, 23
Wolcoff, Ed, 99
Womack, Bruce: hunter-killer stories
    told by, 85–87

World Anti-Communist League
    (WACL), 37, 122–25; John Singlaub
    linked to Central America by,
    123–24

Yandle, Joseph, 65

Zionist Occupation Government
    (ZOG), 130

ABOUT THE AUTHOR

Jerry Lembcke is associate professor of sociology at the College of the Holy Cross. He is the author of *The Spitting Image: Myth, Memory, and the Legacy of Vietnam,* and several articles on the news media, popular culture, and public memory about the war in Vietnam. He lives in Worcester, Massachusetts.